CW00496696

Tess Whitehurst is an intuitive counselor, energy worker, feng shui consultant, speaker, and author of *Magical Housekeeping, The Good Energy Book,* and *The Magic of Flowers*. She has appeared on the Bravo TV show *Flipping Out,* and her writing has been featured in *Writer's Digest*, *Whole Life Times Magazine*, and online at the Huffington Post and Lemondrop.com. She lives in Colorado. Visit her online at www.tesswhitehurst.com.

The Magic of Trees

A Guide to Their Sacred Wisdom & Metaphysical Properties

Tess Whitehurst

• pear •

Llewellyn Publications
WOODBURY, MINNESOTA

FIRST EDITION
First Printing, 2017

Book design: Rebecca Zins
Cover design: Lisa Novak
Cover illustration: Cheryl Chalmers
Botanical illustrations © Christina Hart-Davies and Dover Publications
For a complete listing of illustration credits, see page v

Llewellyn Publications is a registered trademark of Llewellyn Worldwide Ltd.

Library of Congress Cataloging-in-Publication Data
Names: Whitehurst, Tess, author.
Title: The magic of trees: a guide to their sacred wisdom and metaphysical
   properties / Tess Whitehurst.
Description: FIRST EDITION. | Woodbury : Llewellyn Publications, Ltd, 2017. |
   Includes bibliographical references.
Identifiers: LCCN 2016038891 (print) | LCCN 2016039479 (ebook) | ISBN
   9780738748030 | ISBN 9780738750972 (ebook)
Subjects: LCSH: Magic. | Trees—Miscellanea.
Classification: LCC BF1623.P5 W45 2017 (print) | LCC BF1623.P5 (ebook) | DDC
   133.4/3—dc23
LC record available at https://lccn.loc.gov/2016038891

Llewellyn Publications
A Division of Llewellyn Worldwide Ltd.
2143 Wooddale Drive
Woodbury, MN 55125-2989
www.llewellyn.com
Printed in the United States of America

• *maple* •

mangrove

···

We each became a tree, and the circle became a sacred
grove, a forest glade where arboreal spirits were sprung
from that ancient wedlock of heaven and earth.

PHYLLIS CUROTT, *BOOK OF SHADOWS*

Contents

palm

· *yew* ·

Introduction

I like to write books that I would like to read; it's kind of my thing. And after repeatedly wishing for a comprehensive book about the magical properties of trees, there came a day when I decided I would be the one to write it.

There's one truth I was reminded of again and again over the course of writing this book: since time immemorial and on every possible level, human culture has been inextricably interwoven with the presence of trees. Indeed, the spiritual connection between humans and trees is sacred, primordial, intimate, and enduring. Beyond the simple fact that we can't survive without them, we turn to them to restore our harmonizing connection to the earth, we look to them to fuel our inspiration, and we rely on them to keep us sane.

I will admit that I didn't exactly know what I was getting myself into when I started. I didn't realize just how much tree lore there was to study and dig up, or just how integral it was to so many cultures. In much the same way that their roots knit themselves into the ground to keep the soil from eroding, and their multitiered offerings benefit many facets of their surrounding ecosystems, trees are anchors and unifiers of our ancient, diverse, and yet similarly sacred human heritage.

Something else I learned during the writing of this book: identifying trees is not always easy and is very often difficult. In so many cases, tiny variations indicate the differences between species. In case you run into a similar challenge, check out a field guide with pictures, such as *Field Guide to Trees of North America*, or a field guide more specific to your area (often available at local bookstores). Tree identification does seem to be a knack that gets easier with time, although I certainly wouldn't call myself an expert.

And there are so many trees! I really wanted to include every single one, although that was, of course, impossible. So I brainstormed and scoured gardening and tree reference books and websites, compiling as comprehensive a list as I possibly could before beginning. Still, at the end of the day, some popular trees have not been included, and some more obscure trees have. As much as I would like to say there is some rhyme or reason to this, it's really just the way it worked out. (Although I do believe there's a divine design at work with all my books, and, consequently, what's supposed to be included is included.) If you don't find one of your favorites, however, don't despair! Just go out and communicate with the tree yourself, tuning in to your intuition and taking notes. The wisdom is always there for those who listen.

I sincerely hope that this book becomes a treasured part of your library for many decades to come: something that you can come back to again and again, and that yields different and ever-deepening impressions every time, depending on what your soul needs and your intellect craves.

To all my readers, old and new, thank you for going with me on this journey. Thank you for being as interested as I am in all things natural and magical and sacred. I am so grateful to have discovered my spiritual family, and to be able to share my joy with you in this way. Thank you, thank you, thank you.

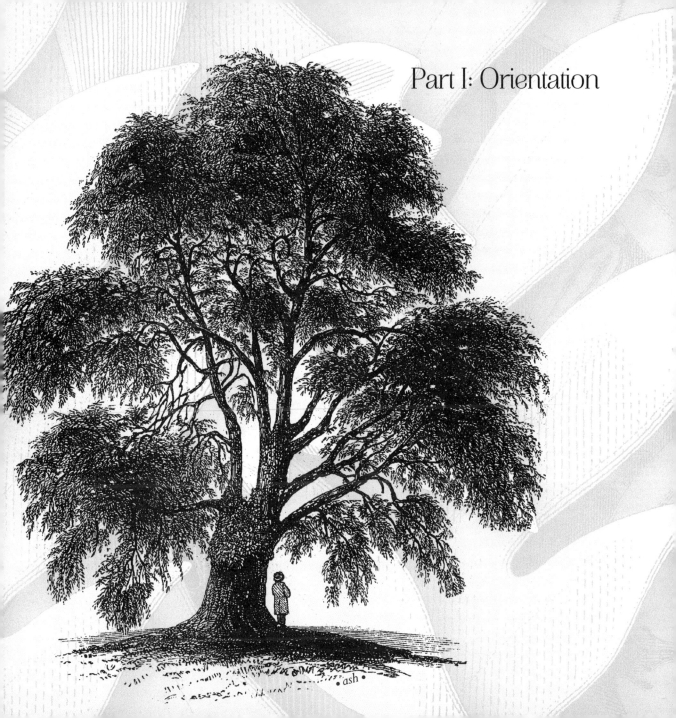

Part I: Orientation

ash

*T*ruly, if any single thing should be sacred to humans it's trees. Even today trees form the framework of our very lives. Just as our fellow primates often literally dwell in and nutritionally rely on trees, we live in homes built and furnished with wood, and many of the tools that we use every day are made from wood. Wood furnishes us from birth to death: our cradles are wood and our caskets are wood. We read and write our ideas on paper. We nourish ourselves with tree fruits and nuts (and many of us could actually live on them if we needed to). Much of our medicine, both holistic and mainstream, is made or derived from trees. Not to mention that the warmth and energy that we so rely on to keep our homes habitable and our food palatable was once (and for many is still) solely reliant on wood-burning fires.

Modern studies demonstrate that simply spending time near or gazing at trees can relieve stress, lower our heart rate, help us heal faster, and improve our mental and emotional health. As if all that weren't more than enough, the delicate atmosphere of our precious planet—which includes *the very air we breathe*—heavily relies on the abundant presence of living trees.

Clearly, we as a species would never have evolved and the planet as we know it could not survive, without trees.

What's more, humans are a philosophical and spiritual species. Dwelling between the realms of earth and sky, we are beings of both worlds, and our very life is a balance and synthesis of form and spirit, below and above. What more appropriate symbol for this could there be than a tree rooted in the earth and stretching its branches and leaves upward into the light?

Indeed, ancient cultures across the globe employ this symbolism. In countless cosmologies some variation of the Tree of Life or the World Tree appears as a central spiritual image. In fact, a tree with spreading branches mirrored below by spreading roots is one of the most apt visual representations of Hermes Trismegistus's classic spiritual and magical precept "As above, so below." The world of form (below) mirrors the world of spirit (above), just as the stars and planets can be read to discern messages about what takes place on earth.

Speaking of which (as implied by the title), this book focuses primarily on the *magic* of trees: their deep wisdom and power, as well as how we can work with them—both physically and spiritually—in order to create positive change in our bodies, minds, spirits, and lives. Trees, after all, are symbols and actual representations of the interconnectedness of all life: the interwoven web of everything from which magic itself draws its power.

As poets, shamans, and other wise people have seen clearly for millennia, trees are not just pretty backdrops or landscape additions. They are wise, conscious beings, and they have been here on earth for an unthinkably longer time than we have. As we as a species have come to value frenetic movement and activity (a primary reason that stress has become such a challenge for so many of us), simply tuning in to the calm presence of a deeply rooted tree is a precious medicine. So is the practice of incorporating trees into your ritual work and other spiritual/magical practices. These are things that everyone can do! With just a bit of focused intention, you'll find that the trees in your yard and neighborhood parks and nature areas can be beloved friends, teachers, and magical partners.

Methods of Tree Magic

Before we get into the specific magic of individual trees, which composes the vast majority of the text, let me introduce the main ways this book will guide you to spiritually and magically work with trees.

Quiet Contemplation

Quite possibly the best way to receive wisdom, guidance, and healing from a tree is to sit or stand in quiet contemplation with it. Think of quiet contemplation as spending time with a wise friend or guru from whom you receive guidance that is so profound that it transcends human language. Just as avatars in India (humans who are believed to be incarnations of a particular divinity or who are simply aware of their true infinite nature) are said to confer spiritual wisdom or even enlightenment by their very presence, consciously tuning in to and being present with a tree can bring similar benefits.

Here's how you might begin: go outside to an area with one or more trees. Slow your breath and consciously relax your body. Notice the feeling of your feet on the earth. Notice your breath as it goes in and out. (Slowing your inner tempo is especially important in order to become receptive to the wisdom of trees.) Continue to relax as you set the intention to receive spiritual wisdom and healing energy from a tree. If you have a specific need, question, or request, gently bring this to mind with the confident inner knowing that you will receive precisely what you desire.

When you feel sufficiently relaxed, gaze at the trees and see which one you feel most drawn to. You might be drawn because one tree looks more beautiful or illuminated to you than the others at this time, or the wind may catch a particular tree more than the others. Or one may just "feel right." Or maybe there's a certain tree in your yard that you'd like to spend some quality time with. Don't worry, you can't make a wrong choice. The tree you choose can't possibly be anything other than precisely the right one for you at this time. When you've chosen, slowly and reverently approach.

Begin by gazing at the tree and just being present with the majestic being before you. Just as you would a beloved friend or partner, appreciate the tree's beauty. Inhale the fresh air and listen to the wind in the leaves. Synchronize your breath and thought with the slow, steady, patient pace of the tree. Continue this tuning-in process until you naturally begin to receive healing and wisdom from the tree.

Because everyone has a different way of metaphysically receiving information and energy, you might hear actual words in your mind, you might see pictures, or you might get feelings. Perhaps you'll have a cathartic release as you let emotions out that have been bottled up, and this will heal you and bring you into greater harmony with yourself and the natural world. Or you might just feel a deep sense of calm that goes beyond words. Later, as you go back to your everyday life, you may find that the answers or shifts that you were seeking just sort of naturally arise.

The main thing to keep in mind is that you are simply making friends with the tree, and simply spending time with and appreciating that tree as you would a friend.

Proximity

Similarly, merely being in the same area as a tree—or even branches, leaves, flowers, or other offerings from the tree (such as an indoor bouquet or artful altar arrangement)—brings healing benefits. Not just in the obvious ways of providing physical beauty, healing scent, oxygen, humidity, and/or shade but also by emanating a conscious, grounding presence and unique spiritual wisdom. That's why you can use the guidance in this book to choose what trees to plant or what trimmings to bring into your home at various times of the year.

Offerings (and Hugs)

Just as putting time and attention into a healthy relationship with a human causes that human to naturally want to put time and attention into the relationship with you, it helps us receive positive energy from a tree when we first offer positive energy *to* the tree. We can do this by placing our hand on the trunk and visualizing sending bright white light from our heart into the tree, by pouring some water or ale around the roots, or even by lovingly placing a small crystal or shiny coin at the base of the tree.

You can also just go ahead and hug that tree, and send love and light straight from your heart to the heart of the tree. You will receive it right back in a cycle of positive, nourishing, instant karma. (It might be a cliché, but it has caught on for a reason!)

Ritual

In addition to honoring their profoundly sacred relationships with trees, ancient cultures of all varieties believed that they could effect positive change with ritual. This was not because they were primitive or misguided or crazy, but rather because they were *observant*. Indeed, as quantum physics is now conclusively demonstrating, our thoughts, feelings, and expectations literally change outcomes and encourage probabilities. That's why you'll also find a variety of tree-related rituals throughout the book that you can employ to help bring about various types of positive change.

Aromatherapy and Incense

It's no secret that some of the most treasured aromatherapeutic oils and incenses—such as cedar, eucalyptus, frankincense, sandalwood, and myrrh—come from trees. In this book, you'll learn about how you can effectively employ many of these natural scents for healing on all levels.

Medicine and Food

Aspirin comes from willow bark. Eucalyptus helps clear congestion and respiratory infections. Cedar oil is an antifungal. These and many other remedies will be mentioned in this book, for both historical and practical purposes as well as to provide insight into a tree's holistic wisdom and energetic dynamic.

Additionally, plenty of trees provide delicious and nutritious sustenance in the form of fruit and nuts. Consuming these foods with reverence and an awareness of the tree's metaphysical wisdom has the added benefit of filling us with magic.

Visualization and Invocation

Whether or not a particular tree resides near your hometown, you can magically commune with any species you choose by familiarizing yourself with the tree's appearance and magical qualities, and then incorporating the tree into invocations and visualizations. For instance, many of us in the United States may not have access to an actual baobab tree, but if you read the section on baobabs and you feel so inspired, you can seek out images of the tree and then bring the tree to mind during a meditation, asking the tree for guidance and support. Additionally, you can adapt the rituals in this book to be done on an energetic level rather than a physical one (i.e., by visualizing and calling on the tree's spiritual presence, rather than actually being close to it in the concrete world). Indeed, if you feel comfortable with visualization, any ritual or ingredient can be conjured through visualization and therefore adapted to be performed or utilized on an energetic level. (And if you *don't* feel comfortable with visualization, practice makes perfect!)

Homeopathic Essences

Finally, trees (and their respective blossoms) possess a vibrational wisdom that can be employed for physical, spiritual, and emotional healing, as well as for various magical intentions. As those familiar with homeopathic remedies know, this vibration can be preserved in water with the help of an ingredient such as glycerin or alcohol, put in a dropper bottle, and then taken under the tongue or in water (or used in other ways such as by adding to bathwater or food). These can be created responsibly or purchased from reputable sources. Many health food stores, for example, offer the Bach Flower Remedies oak, elm, or white chestnut. Additionally, some essence makers (such as Planetary Essences) offer medicines that employ tree vibrations such as apple, ginkgo, or willow.

A Note on Gathering

Only a fraction of the rituals in this book actually require gathering materials from a living tree. And when they do, they usually only recommend gathering a tiny portion. In certain cases, such as for dowsing, removing branches is recommended. In these cases, it's gravely important to be careful not to harm the tree. Only remove a single branch, only do so if the tree's in robust health, and *make absolutely sure it's an ideal time of year for trimming that particular type of tree in your region*. (If you're not sure, consult a local gardening guide, expert, or website.)

Of course, anytime you're gathering magical materials from living beings such as trees, it's important to honor your connection with them and to gather gently and mindfully, with great love and respect. For example, you might gather a pair of scissors or shears (thinking ahead and having the proper tools with you is important), and then take a few moments with a tree before snipping. Place your hands on the trunk and greet her, sending her your love and letting her know that you respect her. Let her know that you'd like a leaf (or whatever you're gathering), and then notice when you feel an inner nudge to go ahead and snip. This might just be a positive feeling or, at the very least, a neutral feeling. (If for some reason you receive a message not to snip—which might manifest as a feeling of reticence on your part to do so—it will be wise for you to thank the tree anyway and move on.) Follow your intuition about which part of the tree to snip, and then thank the tree heartily. It's also a really good idea to offer the tree a token of your gratitude, such as a bit of water or ale, a shiny coin, or a small crystal. This shows—to yourself and the tree—that you are aware of, and honor, the interconnection of all life.

A Note on Correspondences

At the end of each entry, you'll notice an element, gender, and planet that correspond with each tree. Universally, I have gathered this information through dowsing with a pendulum. This method provided me with a number of surprises, most of which fell under two main categories.

My first overarching surprise was this: I expected each element to be one of four, as usually appears in magical botanical literature—earth, air, fire, or water. However, I quickly learned that many trees preferred to be classified under the fifth element: spirit. Upon reflection, this makes sense, as trees are featured so prominently in spiritual traditions of all cultures and are collectively seen as direct links between earth and sky, form and spirit, the everyday and the sacred.

Secondly, I expected each tree's corresponding planet to be one of the main astrological planets (i.e., the planets in our solar system as well as the sun and moon). But when some trees did not seem to align with any of these traditional planetary correspondences, I got creative and looked further. I looked to moons of Saturn, for example, as well as large asteroids and even planets in our neighboring solar system of Alpha Centauri. Indeed, I discovered many of the formerly elusive correspondences once I did. Naturally, these unexpected alignments shed a lot of light on the vibrational wisdom and metaphysical properties of the corresponding trees.

As magical literature is traditionally grounded in history and folklore, this is admittedly unconventional. But when you think about it, it's also rational for a modern metaphysician to take into account all of the scientific information to which we now have access. For readers of an astrological bent, it's my hope that these findings will help spark further insights into these more recently discovered planets, moons, asteroids, and solar systems, as well as their roles in our destiny and the destiny of our world.

Part 2: The Trees

ash

Acacia

Conjuring up images of sacred fires, divine visions, regal elephants, and gentle giraffes at sunset, the acacia tree and magic go way back. This mystical tree (of the legume family Fabaceae) has been famously aligned with the realm of spirit since ancient times.

(For the tree often called *acacia* in Europe, see the "Locust" entry.)

Magical Uses

Divine Authority and Spiritual Leadership

Moses, who is believed by many to have learned magical and alchemical arts during his time in the house of the Pharaoh, directed builders to create the Ark of the Covenant from acacia wood. As you may know, the Ark of the Covenant was a spiritual tool that was likely an actual battery, which symbolically (and possibly energetically) anchored Moses's authority as well as the Israelites' solidarity as a nation. As if that weren't impressive enough, it's been postulated that the burning bush—in which God was believed to have appeared to Moses—was actually an acacia tree.

As such, if it's your intention to step into a role as a spiritual leader of some sort, you might fashion a wand or a staff out of acacia. Consecrate it by holding it in bright sunlight while the moon is waxing. As you do so, ask the Divine to fill it and charge it energetically with the confidence, authority, and integrity you need in order to embody your desired role in the most ideal of ways.

Divine Petitions

Charles Darwin came upon an acacia in Patagonia that was revered by natives as an altar to the Divine. People of all walks of life in the neighboring areas would visit the tree and place offerings in and around it. If you'd like to designate your own acacia altar and request help with manifesting an intention or desire, try the following:

....

ACACIA ALTAR PETITION

Visit an acacia tree while bearing a gift, such as ale, wine, incense, a pinch of organic tobacco, or a piece of cotton yarn. Spend time in quiet contemplation with the acacia for a bit, honoring the moment and the sacred energy of the tree. Then bring your intention to mind. Respectfully introduce yourself and state your desire as you would to a beloved elder. Ask for help with manifesting this desire. Offer your gift as a gesture of thanks—pour out the libation, burn the incense (safely!), place the tobacco on the earth, or tie the cotton yarn around a branch—and then commune with the tree for a bit longer, allowing yourself to receive an infusion of wordless guidance and loving energetic support.

Similarly, burning acacia incense or making a fire with acacia wood and then speaking your intention aloud (as if it's already true) can assist you in manifesting any goal, dream, or desire.

Fidelity

Acacia's vibration is stalwart and true, and acacia honey magically helps ensure fidelity. As an alternative to wine, you might employ a mead made with acacia honey for the ritual drink during a wedding or a handfasting. If you desire to be in a monogamous relationship and you're not entirely sure that your partner shares this desire, empower some acacia honey with the intention to *only be in a relationship with a partner who is true*. Affirm that you are in a relationship that is authentic, honest, and ideal for you in any way, and set the intention that any other type of relationship will quickly fall away. Then serve this honey to your partner—in tea or oatmeal will do just fine.

Immortality

In ancient Egypt acacia wood was used to build a number of things, including coffins and boats. This is significant because boats were symbols of the physical vessel through which our spirits experience this earthly life, and they were also associated with the god Osiris, who was associated with death and rebirth. In a later age the Freemasons adopted this symbolism for the acacia, associating it with the eternity of the soul.

Psychic Abilities

You'll notice that the thread between all of acacia's magical properties is aligning humans with the spiritual/Divine realm. As such, our psychic abilities can be enhanced by an alliance with acacia. For this purpose, you might create an incense blend out of sandalwood and acacia. Burn this incense while reading tarot, casting an I Ching reading, or working with your intuitive abilities in any way. If you're doing readings by a fire of any kind (lucky you!), place some acacia twigs in the flames.

Protection

Acacia is an extremely potent spiritual protector. Sprigs of acacia have been worn or placed above doorways or beds to keep unhappy ghosts and malignant spirits away. Smudging with acacia incense powerfully aligns a space with the realm of the Divine, dissolving and protecting against negative energies. In fact, particularly thorny varieties of acacia have even been employed as powerful protectors in the physical realm, creating a sort of natural barbed-wire fence around homes or other buildings.

Magical Correspondences

Element: Spirit

Gender: Masculine

Planet: Sun

The mysterious, majestic alder (*Alnus*) has been sacred to the Irish, Welsh, and Greeks, and he inhabits the Celtic tree calendar between March 18 and April 14. Alder's relationship with the elements is notably dynamic and multifaceted: his roots actively nourish the earth with nitrogen, his wood doesn't burn well in fires but flourishes as charcoal, and his timber appears weak on land but becomes almost indestructible in water.

Magical Uses

The Air Element

While many trees are in some way aligned with the air element—the element associated with ideas, words, healing, breath, the sunrise, the east, and new beginnings—the alder is *particularly* so. The branches can be fashioned into wind instruments, such as panpipes and flutes, and whistles made from alder have been employed to call on the magical energies associated with wind. Alder wood charcoal is used to burn incense (which is traditionally aligned with the air element) for ceremonial magic, and its smoke is employed to lend flavor to "smoked" foods.

Connection with the Otherworld

The alder tree is associated with the Welsh deity known as Bran, who employs his giant cauldron to resurrect the dead. (Although once he resurrects them, it is said that they are no longer able to speak, though they can gesture and otherwise communicate.)

Although resurrecting the dead is just a bit beyond the magical aptitude of most practitioners, if you're a historian or a medium, or are otherwise concerned with connecting with humans who are not longer in physical form, alder can help. For this purpose, try sitting in quiet contemplation with an alder or taking the flower essence. If you happen to have an alder in your yard or would like to plant one, try this:

CROW ALLIANCE FOR OTHERWORLD COMMUNICATION

Do your best to attract crows (also sacred to Bran) to your alder tree with food and water. Once you strike up a relationship with them and they begin to trust you, ask them for help with connecting with the spirits of the dead.

Environmental and Land Healing

The alder—or more specifically a bacterium with which the alder has a symbiotic relationship—has an amazing ability to heal depleted land by replenishing nitrogen in the soil. This goes right along with the tree's Greek name, *klethra*, which is derived from a word that means "I embrace, I surround." If you're stewarding land that could use some enriching and healing, consider planting alders and consciously enlisting them for the purpose.

Invisibility and Concealment

Robin Hood and other outlaws reportedly dyed their clothes green with a dye made from the alder in order to become less conspicuous in the forest. If you'd like to conceal yourself or your actions (for a noble purpose, of course), try this:

ALDER CONCEALMENT CHARM

Visit an alder the day before you need concealment and explain your mission and why you could use help. When and if you feel that the tree is in sympathy with your cause, respectfully gather two fresh alder leaves, wrapping them in clean green cloth. As a gesture of gratitude, leave two shiny dimes near the tree's base. Take the leaves home and place them on your altar (or an empty surface). Before leaving the house the next day, place one leaf in each shoe. As you put them on, say:

> *Alder leaf inside each shoe*
> *Hide me one and hide me two.*
> *Grounded in your living green*
> *Where I walk I'll be unseen.*

Masculinity

Is the alder a being of primordial masculine power? It would appear so, as there is an ancient Irish legend that names an alder tree as the material from which the first man was forged. Visit an alder tree to increase and align with your own masculine energy or to make peace with the masculinity of others.

Physical Healing

A decoction of tannin-rich alder bark has been used in a number of herbal healing traditions as a mouthwash, gargle, skin wash, and blood purifier. It has a drying action that is said to soothe irritation and inflammation.

To support physical healing in an energetic way—particularly if your challenge has something to do with bodily fluids, infection, or inflammation—visit an alder tree. Sitting or standing in quiet contemplation, take a moment to tune in. Open up to the tree's energy and allow yourself to receive an infusion of his healing vibration. Then deepen this effect by sitting with your spine against the trunk or hugging the tree for a good long moment.

Protection

In *The Fairy Bible*, author Teresa Moorey states that "the alder fairy may fly forth in the form of a raven. He can impart all the secrets of good defense to you." As such, if you happen to be spending time with an alder and a raven appears, consider it a very magical omen. Increase your chances of this happening by placing a shiny object near the tree, such as a mirrored bead or a silver coin. Then when you see the raven, silently express your reverence and respectfully request magical guidance regarding psychic and all-purpose protection.

Magical Correspondences

Element: Air
Gender: Masculine
Planet: Ceres

Almond

*S*prawling almond (*Prunus dulcis*) orchards surround my hometown in California. To this day, when I witness them blossoming forth in their pinkish white splendor, they affect me in much the same way heaven might affect one, were it to suddenly appear in one's backyard.

Considering that almonds are perhaps my main food staple (seriously! I could eat them for every meal and sometimes do), I was shocked to learn that the wild (bitter) almond is highly toxic. So toxic, in fact, that eating just a small amount can be fatal. The domesticated (sweet) almond, on the other hand, is one of the healthiest things you could eat. Here's where it gets even more fascinating: almonds are perhaps one of the oldest domesticated food plants, and botanists think that whoever cultivated them must have known which of the bitter almonds were sweetest. But if they're so deadly to eat, then how did they know? Perhaps there was some sort of mysterious and highly evolved technology afoot, like so much attributed to the earliest teachers of agriculture, such as the pyramids and sacred geometry.

Magical Uses

Beauty

Everything about the almond tree is beautiful: her wizened trunk and branches, her whimsical and otherworldly blossoms, and certainly the delicate taste of her fruit kernel (commonly called a "nut"). Sweet almond oil is an excellent moisturizer that enhances the skin's natural health and radiant glow. Nutritionally, almonds lend themselves to beauty as they are filled with balancing, vitalizing vitamins, minerals, and nutrients such as calcium, magnesium, potassium, vitamin E, protein, fiber, and healthy fats. In fact, simply eating almonds can make for a potent beauty spell. For example:

ALMOND BEAUTY SPELL

Preheat your oven to 350 degrees Fahrenheit. Center yourself by holding your hands in prayer pose and calling on the Great Goddess to bless your magical workings. Place three cups of organic, raw almonds in a medium to large bowl. Add a tablespoon of olive oil and a bit of salt, and stir in a clockwise direction with a wooden spoon until coated. As you stir, mentally direct very bright pink light through the spoon into the almonds. Line a cookie sheet with foil and pour the almonds onto the cookie sheet, spreading evenly. Hold your open palms over the almonds and direct the energy of your words into them as you chant three times:

Goddess of love, Goddess of light
Bless me with your beauty bright.

Bake for ten to twelve minutes or until they are a rich, dark brown. Cool completely, then store in a large jar or other sealed glass container.

Every morning until they're gone, have one-quarter to one-third cup almonds with breakfast (or *for* breakfast). Repeat as desired.

Fertility

One story about the origin of almond trees states that the first sweet almond tree was born of the Anatolian goddess Agdistis, who possessed both male and female identities and came by them honestly. She was the child of such archetypal masculine and feminine deities as Zeus and Gaia. After a cruel prank (in essence, an ancient hate crime) caused Agdistis to castrate herself, her blood spilled upon the earth, and from this, the almond tree burst forth. When Nana, daughter of a river god, gathered almonds from the tree, she became pregnant and gave birth to a son, Attis. The myth continues in most mysterious ways, and indeed the goddess and her progeny were aligned with a widespread mystery tradition, in some ways similar to the Eleusinian Mysteries of Demeter and Persephone.

While the subtle meanings of the myth of Agdistis, Nana, and Attis may not be readily apparent, one can glean from the subtext that almonds are quite magical and have much to do with the fertility of both humans and the earth.

Additionally, almonds have traditionally been featured in iconography of baby Jesus and Mother Mary. And, according to the poet Virgil, copiously blossoming almond trees foretell of an abundant wheat harvest.

Goddess Energy

The pale white blossoms of almonds, as well as the tree's alignment with sustenance, hope, beauty, and fertility, lend themselves to the tree's ancient association with the Great Goddess. This is certainly true in her incarnations as Mother Mary and Cybele (whom some align with Agdistis), but also perhaps in the ancient origins of Judaism and other Abrahamic religions. According to author Fred Hageneder in *The Meaning of Trees*, almond's "archaic Semitic name, amygdala, can be traced back to the Sumerian *ama ga*, which means the Great Mother." He goes on to say that Aaron's staff ("the rod of God") "was said to be handed down from Adam via Abraham, Isaac and Jacob to Joseph who took it to Egypt where Moses obtained it. That Moses should bear the almond of the Great Mother is ironic, because in the Old Testament he is instructed to destroy the ancient cult of the Goddess." Indeed, one wonders about the patriarch wielding such a powerful Mother Goddess symbol as an indication of his divine authority. Could it be a hint—as author Raphael Patai suggests in *The Hebrew Goddess*—that the Divine Feminine was much more present in early Judaism than the Old Testament would have us believe? We may never know for sure, but it certainly seems likely.

Grief

Here's another almond origin story: The Thracian queen Phyllis fell in love with the beautiful youth Demophon, and they were married. Shortly thereafter, Demophon returned to his country of origin and, after being ensnared by the charms of another, did not return in a timely manner. Out of grief, Phyllis died and was transformed into an almond tree. When Demophon heard about it, he realized his error and returned instantly, throwing his arms around his partner's trunk. Then, as an expression of her continued love, she burst forth into bloom.

In many ways, this mirrors the almond's bitter/sweet polarity, which one can't help but notice is the same polarity that characterizes love in all its forms. The more sweetness with which we love, the bitterer the heartache we experience from spurning, separation, loss, or simply the unrealized fears of such things. And yet we love still. Even when it's cold out and there are no leaves on the trees, our hearts can blossom with love, again and again, in every phase of life. Would we trade our sweetest love so as not to feel our bitterest grief? Perhaps we may be tempted, but that would certainly be much too dear a price.

Hidden Treasures

In some places in the world, such as Tuscany, an almond branch has been employed as a Y-shaped dowsing rod to discover hidden treasures.

Hope

As you know if you've ever lived near an almond orchard (or just an almond tree), exquisite almond blossoms burst forth abundantly quite early in the season, on branches still devoid of leaves. This is why, in the Middle East, almond trees have been associated with hope.

Magical Correspondences

Element: Air
Gender: Feminine
Planet: Jupiter

Apple

As I write, I am sipping organic apple cider and gazing at a most transcendent vision: a blossoming apple tree (*Malus domestica*) in my front yard. With pale pink and white petals; brand-new spring leaves in a cool, aventurine shade of green; and the promise of sweet, crisp, nourishing deep red fruits in the fall, it's not difficult to imagine these trees—equal parts earthy and otherworldly—adorning the legendary Avalon, the sacred island of magic and power from the Arthurian legends (popularly believed to be synonymous with Glastonbury in Scotland). The fact that this tree was such an iconic resident of Avalon is demonstrated by the island's alternative moniker: the Isle of Apples.

Magical Uses

Blessings and Abundance

One of the most essential symbols of the harvest, and sacred to the earth and agriculture goddess Demeter, the apple represents an abundant crop and the enjoyment of the fruits of one's labor. From September through Thanksgiving, the nourishing fruit shows up in seasonal imagery representing abundance, sustenance, and nourishment. A beautiful way to draw wealth and prosperity during these months is to display a bowl or a basket of apples in the home or on one's altar. Enjoying apple cider (alcoholic or non) with friends during a fall barbecue or the holidays can be a similarly seamless way to celebrate the sweetness of life and, in so doing, draw even more blessings into your life experience.

Eternal Youth

The Norse goddess Idun presides over both apples and eternal youthfulness. Apparently, the other Norse deities relied on her apples to preserve their relative immortality. This legendary attribute is mirrored in the physical realm: apples support youthfulness through enhancing health. They're rich in vitamins and minerals, support detoxification, improve digestion, and stimulate healthy fluid production in the lungs.

IDUN PETITION FOR YOUTHFULNESS

To increase your youthful appearance and personality, call on Idun. Offer her cinnamon incense and request that she infuse your apples with her magic. Then eat one daily.

Feminine Power

In the Adam and Eve myth, the forbidden fruit from the Tree of the Knowledge of Good and Evil is perhaps most often thought of—at least in the West—as an apple. According to our cultural heritage and the popular imagination, by picking and tasting the sweet and delicious "apple," and then by convincing Adam to do so as well, Eve got herself and her partner cast out of the garden, and set in motion all of the pain and challenges humans experience. Isn't that just like a woman (the unspoken story goes) to be shamefully seduced by the realm of the sensual and then to maliciously (or stupidly) deceive her partner into being seduced as well? (And of course it's no coincidence that the snake was once a symbol of the feminine divine.)

Clearly, it's time to let this archaic abhorrence of femininity die and reclaim our joy in feminine sensuality, wisdom, and independence. What better symbolism for doing so could there possibly be than for a woman to take a defiantly loud, sloppy, satisfying bite of a sweet, voluptuous apple? Indeed, I suggest that you seriously consider incorporating loud and unapologetic apple eating into rituals designed to reclaim cultural and/or personal feminine power.

The Five Elements

Perhaps you have cut an apple in half horizontally and viewed the five-pointed star normally hidden within. This symbol of the five elements—earth, air, fire, water, and spirit—shows up again and again in magical and alchemical literature, indicating the apple tree's alignment with magic, the Goddess, and All That Is.

Love

A member of the rose family and considered sacred to the archetypal love goddess Aphrodite, the apple offers both a gorgeous, heart-opening blossom and a sweet, juicy, sensual treat. Naturally, this makes the apple tree an abundant supplier of love-drawing magical ingredients of the highest caliber and potency. Employ apple seeds, fruit, and blossoms in love-drawing charms, sachets, and baths.

Self-Acceptance

As one of the original thirty-eight Bach Flower Remedies, crabapple flower essence can be extremely helpful for cultivating sincere self-acceptance. In fact, when I was in my mid-twenties, crabapple flower essence helped me shift my inner dialogue from profound self-loathing to profound self-love. If you—like I once did—constantly berate yourself for your appearance, experience embarrassment about your complexion, or feel inexplicably dirty or grimy no matter how much you bathe and scrub, try taking two drops of crabapple essence three times per day under the tongue or in water. (You can find it at most health food stores and online.)

Alternatively, spending quality quiet time with a blossoming apple or crabapple tree can have a similar effect, especially when performed regularly while the blossoms are present.

Sweetness

In his excellent book *The Botany of Desire*, author Michael Pollan convincingly demonstrates that the very existence of the anciently cultivated apple tree can be wholly attributed to our human desire for sweetness. If you could use more sweetness in your life or if you'd like to sweeten your feelings toward another person, visualize an apple filled with bright pink light, request divine support in infusing it with the energy of sweetness, and then mindfully eat it. Similarly, if you'd like to bring out the sweetness in someone else's disposition or cause them to take action on their existing feelings of sweetness toward you, bless an apple with sweetness in a similar way and give it to them as a gift.

Unicorn Alignment

Those with an affinity for unicorns will be pleased to know that, according to author Teresa Moorey in *The Fairy Bible*, "the unicorn lives underneath [the apple tree]." To be sure, there is nothing in the visual world that evokes the sweet, gentle magic of a unicorn quite like the ethereal beauty of a blossoming apple tree. Visit an apple tree in spring to commune with the realm of the unicorns.

Wand Making

Do you feel a kinship with the fae? If so, apple wood might be just the wand material for you. It's said that fairies play beneath blossoming apple trees and that wands made of apple wood can open a portal between this world and the world of the fae.

Magical Correspondences

Element: Earth
Gender: Feminine
Planet: Venus

Ash

A rare variety of ash tree lines many of the residential streets in my California hometown, including the street I grew up on. Not a friendly tree by any means, but also not an unfriendly one, ash (*Fraxinus*) is like a scientist or a soldier staring the great abyss in the face with a somewhat unsettling degree of neutrality and calm.

Please note that while the ash has long been named as the world tree from which the Norse god Odin hung during his spiritual rite of passage, that tree is in fact now believed by many scholars to be a yew.

Magical Uses

Advanced Magic

The wisdom of the ash is aligned with the Druids. At least one Druidic staff made of ash wood has been discovered, and the tree is powerfully aligned with the archetypal, omnipresent, white-bearded magician known as Merlin. For advanced magical knowledge and know-how, often and regularly spend time with an ash tree and request the tree's sponsorship and masterful support.

Broom Making

A broom with a handle made of ash is a powerful magical tool for sweeping away every sort of non-neutral energy and generally clearing the decks. (There's no need to actually touch the floor with it, just glide above it to sweep the energy instead.) Additionally, it can be a magical tool for connecting with the Infinite and safely traversing realms. For this purpose, place an ash broom in your magical circle while meditating or visualizing.

Fairies

It's said that in locations where oak, ash, and thorn all grow, fairies dwell. While fairies are often perceived as sweet, loving little creatures, if you really tune in to them (or read classic fairy tales!) you'll know that, in fact, they are not exactly friendly and not exactly evil either. Rather, like nature, if you treat them well they will reward you handsomely, and if you treat them ill they will punish you in a most uncompromising way. As we've seen, this is an important aspect of the ash tree's wisdom.

Justice

The Greek goddess of justice and righteous revenge, Nemesis, is said to carry an ash branch. And it's no wonder: ash—like the uncompromising silence and vastness of space—has an impersonal, leveling, karma-activating quality that can be magically directed with great effect. For example, if someone has genuinely wronged you, and you are consequently in a legal skirmish of some sort, ash can powerfully assist with your efforts to bring this person to justice. But do be aware that once you enlist ash's support, if you have behaved shabbily in even the slightest of ways, you will also receive your just deserts.

Ash Ritual to Banish Injustice

Visit an ash. Touch the trunk and mentally convey the situation you'd like assistance with. Respectfully gather nine ash twigs. Once you're back home, light a black candle and use it to safely, successively burn each twig in a cauldron or a large pot.

Protection

Highly protective in the most honorably masculine of ways, an ash tree in front of the home can be enlisted to powerfully defend all inhabitants from harm, while simultaneously ensuring that the inhabitants themselves conduct themselves with the highest possible integrity. (To be sure, the inhabitants will still have free will, but they will find that the universe will not give an inch if they knowingly behave unfairly toward another living being.) Additionally, carrying a bit of ash wood (or incorporating it into a charm) will protect against ill will, and will additionally protect from drowning, snakes, and accidents.

Wand Making

Wise, powerful, and adept at nuanced calibration, ash provides an excellent wood for wands created specifically for the purpose of assisting with physical healing.

Magical Correspondences

Element: Air
Gender: Masculine
Planet: Mars

Aspen

*A*nyone who's appreciated the clean, otherworldly majesty of a grove of aspens knows that these trees possess a potent magic all their own. Indeed, the shimmering effect created by the constantly quivering leaves, paired with his elaborate root system that links an entire forest of genetically identical specimens, contributes to the singular wonder and spectacle that is the aspen (members of the genus *Populus*, or poplar).

Magical Uses

Ancestry and Heritage

As mentioned above, the aspen—unlike other trees—reproduces by cloning himself at the level of his root system. This means that every tree in an aspen grove is not only genetically identical, but is also linked to every other tree in the grove via the roots. So while seemingly individual trees live for approximately 40 to 150 years, the entire living entity that is the grove can live tens of thousands of years. (The Pando grove in Utah is believed to have lived for somewhere in the vicinity of 80,000 years!)

Clearly, the aspen is a wonderful teacher when it comes to feeling connected to our ancestry and heritage in a way that nourishes us and gives us a sense of expansive continuity. Magically, we can draw on this power when we feel particularly called to research and/or reconnect with our ancestors and the traditions, beliefs, and customs that make up our heritage. Many of us feel this pull when we reach middle age, and it's often felt by people who were adopted or who have been uprooted in some way from their family's place of origin.

If reconnecting with ancestry and/or heritage is important to you right now, consider making a pilgrimage to an aspen grove and performing the following:

ASPEN ANCESTRY ALIGNMENT PILGRIMAGE

Visit a thriving aspen grove and spend some alone time in quiet contemplation. Become aware that there is a vast root system beneath you, interconnecting all the aspens that surround you as far as the eye can see. Just as this root system has been around long before the aspens you see, it will be around long after.

Know that even if you're not as consciously aware of, or connected to, your ancestry as you would like, it's all there anyway. Your foremothers and forefathers have not only propelled you to precisely this point in time, they're also encoded within your very DNA. Know that no matter what they were like in their physical incarnations, in the realm of light, where they currently reside, they're everlasting and beneficent, and they support you thoroughly and with profound love and approval.

Take as much time as you need to really feel and know that this is true. Before you leave, be sure to thank the aspen grove from the bottom of your heart.

Cleansing and Healing

While in the past some have associated the constantly quivering leaves of the aspen with fear or shame, this is absolutely not energetically accurate. Rather, this quivering indicates the tree's alignment with the air element and with all the invigorating, fresh, cleansing energy that is within his domain. In much the same way Archangel Raphael is associated with both the air element and healing, the aspen's sparkling clean energy is extremely healing to the mind, body, and spirit. Like an immaculate breeze in sunlight, it instantly whisks away all that is heavy, painful, festering, or stuck.

In fact, aspen bark (like willow bark) contains salicin, and has been employed medicinally for its anti-inflammatory and pain-relieving qualities. Magically, simply spending time in the presence of aspens—particularly on a clear, breezy day—can bring about a deep and thorough energy clearing.

Family and Community

Humans thrive—physically, spiritually, and psychologically—when we feel connected to a mutually supportive network of other humans. We also thrive when we feel connected to nature: to the earth and the non-human living beings around us. Aspen has much to teach us in this regard. In addition to the fact that every aspen grove is like one giant, enduring entity connected underground by a network of roots, the aspen is quite the team player from the perspective of the ecosystems to which he contributes. His bark is a host for moss and moth larvae, as well as food for hares, beavers, and other animals. The cover of aspens facilitates the growth of grasses that feed livestock and big game such as deer and elk. Aspens are amazing for reforestation efforts because they grow so quickly and support so much life.

To bolster every aspect of your well-being by strengthening your sense of connection to All That Is, create the following charm:

ASPEN CIRCLE OF LIFE CHARM

Lovingly collect a bit of aspen wood or bark. Draw a circle on it to represent the circle of life with which you're connected and by which you're surrounded, supported, and protected. Place it on your altar.

Mitigation of Heat

Aspen has a very interesting and intimate relationship with fire. Groves of aspen have historically relied on forest fires in order to thrive. While the root system of the grove remains intact during a fire, the tall trees are destroyed, making room for new saplings to grow—something they are only able to do in full sun. In fact, astonishingly, fire prevention is a major contributor to the dwindling of the aspen population in the United States.

On the other hand, the energy of aspen is very cool, and it's been used medicinally to clear heat in the body and relieve fevers. Not to mention, aspen wood is one of the less flammable woods.

Magically, this means that spending time in the presence of aspen can bring about a cooling effect on the mind and emotions. Say you're feeling very passionate, angry, or rushed, for example. Before behaving like a hothead, it would behoove you to take a moment to relax, breathe, and observe aspen leaves as they perform their delicate dance.

Magical Correspondences

Element: Air
Gender: Masculine
Planet: Jupiter

Avocado

*T*he lovely avocado tree (*Persea Americana*) has a cheerful, magical, and reassuring vibe that instantly confers a sense of happiness and well-being. With a fruit that is not only highly nutritious but also the very essence of delicious sensuality; an oil that possesses numerous beautifying benefits; and bark, leaves, and rinds with medicinal properties, it certainly seems like a tree that one would find in paradise. Indeed, avocado is a gift that keeps on giving—which is especially amazing when you realize that all her benefits can be exponentially yours for a lifetime if you simply choose to coax a single avocado pit into becoming a tree.

Magical Uses

Beauty

Am I crazy or can you actually *feel* yourself getting more beautiful while eating a fresh avocado? You can, right? Perhaps this is due to the avocado's vitality-boosting ingredients, but I suspect there's an energetic component as well: the fruit simply radiates vivacity and sumptuous beauty. Furthermore, avocado seed oil is amazing for the skin, hair, and scalp and so is a mashed avocado: try spreading one all over your neck, chest, face, and hair as an all-over beautifying mask.

On the vibrational side of things, a dried avocado pit can be an excellent beauty charm, particularly when paired with an attraction-enhancing scent such as jasmine, sandalwood, or rose. If it's sunny out and you know of an avocado tree, you might simply spend some time in quiet contemplation with the tree, consciously allowing yourself to soak up her beautifying vibes.

Hair Growth

Here's a magical treatment to promote hair growth to be performed on the night after the new moon and then again on the night before the full moon. Before bed, rub avocado oil into your scalp. Then wash your hair in the morning, massaging your scalp thoroughly with the pads of your fingers. Repeat during following moon cycles as desired.

Healing

An ointment of the mashed avocado fruit has been used to help heal wounds and soothe skin irritations. On an emotional level, a nice bowl of guacamole served with tortilla chips can be quite the comfort food to help repair frayed nerves or an aching heart. Or during a waning moon, you might mentally direct any persistent pain or illness into an avocado pit and then bury it at the base of an avocado tree.

Love

Avocado is known for her love-drawing properties. The blossom, also, is love drawing and mirrors its magnetic attraction action in the way that it is (remarkably) both feminine and masculine at once. As such, you might add avocado flower essence to your bathwater or drinking water in order to attract love into your life.

Magic Wands

According to author Scott Cunningham in *Cunningham's Encyclopedia of Magical Herbs*, "Magical wands made of avocado wood are potent all-purpose instruments." If you feel drawn to craft a magic wand out of avocado wood, try affixing a small clear quartz or amethyst point to the end and anointing it with essential oils of neroli and ylang ylang. Tie the handle with silky or satiny green ribbon to support love, vitality, and prosperity: in addition to being everyone's favorite magical intentions, they also happen to be avocado's magical specialties.

Rebirth

The phoenix perennially rises from the flames as an archetypal symbol of rebirth. The wood used to build the fire in this ancient Egyptian legend was that of a persea tree, which is the same family from which the avocado hails.

Additionally, the fruit closely related to avocado (the exact identity of which is now apparently lost to history) was known as the "heart of Horus," a god who would never have been born were it not for his father Osiris's miraculous resurrection at the hands of his mother, the goddess Isis. What's more, Osiris was resurrected after his casket had become hidden in the branches of a persea tree. Perhaps the tree's powerful association with rebirth in Egypt is the reason the wood was included in Egyptian funeral bouquets. However, avocados were also included in ancient Aztec burial sites, indicating that the avocado's association with rebirth seemingly transcends cultures and even spans oceans.

Sexual Attraction

The Aztecs were really intense in their attribution of lust-inducing powers to avocados. So much so that they reportedly believed that one would have quite a difficult time eating an avocado and remaining a virgin. When Spanish explorers introduced the fruit to European settlers, and even when the avocado was gaining popularity in the United

States, this attached a certain fascination, as well as a certain taboo to eating the decadent fruit. In fact, at some point avocado growers felt compelled to run an ad campaign dismissing rumors of the avocado's aphrodisiacal properties in order to increase mainstream acceptance of their product. Today, we know that the avocado is indeed chock-full of nutrients that support one's sexual health. Of course, one can easily perceive that eating an avocado is an exceptionally sensual experience.

Serve avocados to promote sexual attraction in another and/or to increase your own libido or sexual health. And here's a tip that may sound weird if you haven't tried it before: avocados can be employed as the base for an insanely delicious (and insanely healthy) chocolate pudding. Seriously. Like this one that doubles as a love potion you can eat with a spoon:

Choco-Avocado Pudding Potion

The night or morning before sharing this dessert with a love interest (or potential love interest), hold two ripe avocados in your open palms and mentally direct a lovely pink light into them as you set the intention for and visualize what you desire.

Say:

> *Fruit of love and fruit of lust*
> *Please help me in my aim—you must!*
> *If hearts are willing and feelings true*
> *Set passions loose between we two!*

Cut and scoop the avocados and place them, 1 ripe banana, ½ cup unsweetened cacao powder, ½ cup almond butter, a dash salt, ⅔ cup maple syrup, and ¼ cup soy milk in a blender or food processor and blend. When the potion is smooth, fill 4–6 serving cups to the very top. (This way, if things get wild, you'll have extras for later in the evening or the next few nights. It's not ideal for an unsuspecting bystander to snack on one, but if it does happen, it won't be the end of the world…and hey, let's admit it: it might be entertaining.) Cover with plastic wrap or lids and chill for at least six hours. When it's time to serve, top with dairy-free whipped cream and a dusting of cinnamon.

Vitality

The ancient Egyptians believed the persea (related to the avocado) tree to be present in the realm of the gods, and if you're one of the many who enjoys the delectable experience of eating an avocado, you're likely to agree that "food of the gods" certainly fits. In addition to filling you with the vitality that comes from the simple joy of eating something so ridiculously delicious, avocados are filled with potassium, vitamins, healthy fats, and even a good amount of protein. In fact, in West Africa, they're employed as an ultra-nourishing baby food.

When my body feels run down and my digestion seems a bit sluggish, I'll switch to a raw vegan diet for a week or two, and that fixes me right up. Guess what my main "meaty" staple is during this time. You bet: it's avocados. By the end of my little detox, I am feeling downright exuberant. Glowing even! Thanks in large part—I am sure—to this most vitalizing delicacy. Avocados are a health supplement that literally grows on trees.

Wealth

Between the leaf, the rind, and the fleshy pulp, avocados are all shades of green. Not only that, but they are a treasure trove of expansion and sustenance in and of themselves: they nourish us, moisturize us, and even promote fertility in our species through promoting lust and sexual health. And—as I mentioned in the intro—the potential for a lifetime's worth of their amazing benefits is miraculously contained within a single pit.

Indeed, avocados are potent wealth charms in and of themselves: hold one in both hands and charge it with the intention to draw wealth. Then cut it up and put it in your salad. Eating it will allow you to internalize the magic and become a money magnet yourself. You can also incorporate the pits into prosperity rituals and charms, and the flower essence will help turn up the volume on your natural ability to magnetize.

Magical Correspondences

Element: Water

Gender: Feminine

Planet: Venus

Banana

On the Mariana Islands there's a legend about a handsome stranger who asked the chief for his daughter's hand in marriage. After performing every magical feat the chief requested and bringing much wealth to the village in the hopes of winning his desired wife, the stranger became angry and did not return, rightfully feeling that his generosity had finally become overtaxed. Realizing that the stranger (whom she loved) was actually the storm god Uchan, the daughter distanced herself from her greedy father, reached her arms and face up to the storming sky, and became the first banana tree (*Musa*).

Speaking of greed and banana trees, bananas have been the most popular fruit in the nation for some time. Unfortunately, the banana that most of us know and love—a variety called the Cavendish—is currently at risk of extinction. Because of the genetic uniformity of commercial crops, the fruit tree has become dangerously susceptible to a particular fungus. In response, while some banana growers are attempting to find alternative marketable varieties, others are resorting to genetic modification. Therefore, in the interest of supporting alternative solutions and boycotting GMOs (a practice I recommend wholeheartedly for the sake of all humans, animals, plants, and the planet), I suggest only purchasing organic and non-Cavendish varieties of bananas. You know, like little tiny ones, or red ones, or basically any of the other 300-odd banana species in existence. (Before the 1960s, we were all eating a different variety called the Big Mike, which, at that time, finally succumbed to a fungus and was replaced by the Cavendish.)

Please also note that banana's cousins—plantain and ensete—are similar enough to be grouped together with the banana in this section.

Magical Uses
Duality

If any tree is the arboreal quintessence of duality, it's the banana. First of all, he possesses the somewhat rare trait of exhibiting both masculine and feminine flowers on the same tree. He is also a tree of life and death, as well as death and resurrection. The banana grows quickly and fruitfully, and then technically dies as soon as the fruit is picked, although new shoots immediately take the place of the original stem (indicating the fact that the banana is not technically a tree, but actually a giant herb). While we're on the topic of death and resurrection, historically Christians in the Middle East were at one time opposed to cutting bananas. They only broke them with their hands, as it was believed that cut bananas represented and resembled the crucified savior. (It's not clear exactly how.)

As if all that weren't enough to convince us of banana's association with duality, it has been postulated that the banana (and not the apple) was in fact the fruit of the Tree of the Knowledge of Good and Evil, which caused Adam and Eve to suddenly see the world in terms of light and dark, good and bad, and life and death. Perhaps it's no coincidence that the banana grows in locales characterized by exceptionally bright light: the kind of light that casts the darkest shadow.

Magically, the banana's dual nature can help us balance out our own extremes. For example, if you find yourself fluctuating between mania and depression, or if you could benefit from tempering your extroverted activity with some calm receptivity (or vice versa), you might spend a bit of time quietly communing with a banana tree. Banana flower essence taken orally or added to bathwater would also be an excellent medicine for this purpose.

Fertility and Potency

Admittedly, magical properties can be subtle. But if you've ever spent time with a healthy banana tree—particularly one heavy with blossoms or fruit—you probably know what I mean when I say that he may as well be bellowing the words "fertility" and "potency." Although human reproduction doesn't exactly need a boost right now, if you'd like to bless a project, career, or business with fertility, or your personal energy with potency, banana is your man. You might also visit a fruit-filled banana tree, or incorporate bananas into rituals designed for this purpose, or as a much more magical (as well as healthier and less expensive) alternative to Viagra…Speaking of which, I think we're overdue for a cookie ritual!

....

Banana Cookies for Robust Arousal

Preheat the oven to 350 degrees Fahrenheit. Light a green candle. Place the following ingredients in a large bowl and mix them with a wooden spoon in a clockwise direction: ½ cup flour, ¼ cup maca root powder (an herbal aphrodisiac), ½ cup organic sugar, 2 cups rolled oats, ½ teaspoon baking soda, ½ teaspoon baking powder, ½ teaspoon salt, and ¼ teaspoon cinnamon. As you mix, envision bright green light (the color of banana leaves) filling the mixture. Hold a barely ripe (not green but not freckled) mini banana in both hands and project this very bright green light into it as you chant three times:

Desire bright, desire true
Robust arousal shall carry us through.

Then place it in a food processor with $1/3$ cup olive oil, $1/2$ cup agave nectar, and 1 tablespoon vanilla extract. Blend while imagining the potent, arousing magic of the banana being released. Combine the wet mixture with the dry mixture. Add a package of chocolate chips and stir, visualizing even more vibrant green light filling the dough. Line a large cookie sheet with parchment paper and divide into twelve big cookies. Press lightly to flatten. Bake for eleven to fourteen minutes or until lightly browned around the edges. Cool and enjoy, or share with a lover.

Luck

It's been said that being married beneath a banana tree bestows a generous helping of luck. Truly, from an energetic perspective, all that vibrant growth and fruitfulness feels very lucky indeed. If your luck could need a boost, visit a banana tree. Relax in quiet contemplation and then request an infusion of the banana's lucky energy. When you get the sense that the tree agrees, gently sandwich a leaf between your flat palms and allow yourself to absorb the bright green, luck-filled vibes. Feel the energy filling your body via your hands: first through your arms, to your heart, and then throughout the rest of your body.

In Southern India, food is sometimes served on a banana leaf. If you have your own banana tree or know someone who does, you might gather a leaf lovingly, empower it with your intention to infuse yourself with luck, wash it thoroughly, spread it on the table, and serve yourself an Indian meal on it. You could also share a banana leaf meal with others to enhance the luck of a group.

Representation of People and Divinities

As in the legend related at the opening of this section, as well as in the Christian tradition of seeing bananas as representing Jesus on the cross, in a number of cultures the banana has been in some way been synonymous with both humans and gods. In Micronesia, there's a legend about a ghost giant named Kot forming servant women out of bananas, which he first orders to fall from a tree. Also indicating the banana's penchant for symbolizing humans is the fact that banana bunches grow in groupings called "hands."

The volcano goddess Pele was said to have gifted Hawaii with its first banana tree. Considering that banana stalks have been employed in Hawaii as a substitute for human sacrifices, and Pele was not one of the volcano deities to whom humans were sacrificed, one wonders if her gift of the banana tree was a way of offering a kinder alternative.

Magical Correspondences

Element: Earth
Gender: Feminine and masculine
Planet: Pluto

Baobab

While the name *baobab* (BAY-oh-bob) might not exactly be a household word in the United States, for those of us interested in the magic of trees, it certainly ought to be. As you'll see from the magical qualities listed below, baobab (*Adansonia*) is a spiritual superstar of the arboreal world, ranking right up there with time-honored celebrities such as oak, palm, peach, and sequoia.

A native to Madagascar, Australia, and the Arabian peninsula, the baobab can grow to an immense size and live for up to 3,000 years.

Magical Uses

Ancient Awareness

Simply gazing at a baobab tree, or even an image of a baobab tree, is likely to invoke a very ancient feeling—perhaps due to genetic memory or even a past life. Indeed, the

The Trees 53

baobab appears otherworldly in a most ancient way, like a fern, a trilobite, or a ptero-dactyl. Not only that, but baobabs are also a species that can grow to be extremely old. Indeed, there are some alive on earth today that have been here since biblical times.

Along similar lines, the size of a baobab can be so immense that it quickly reminds us of how small and temporary we actually are. With all of this ancient vastness in mind, baobab can help us connect with past life and genetic memories for the purpose of heal-ing. For example:

TREE TRUNK TIME TUNNEL

Sit with your spine straight, close your eyes, relax your body, and take some deep breaths. Begin to feel that you're standing in front of a giant baobab just before sunset. Bring to mind a present difficulty or challenge, and set the intention to travel back in time to a source of this challenge. In your mind, speak this intention to the tree, whom you know hears and understands. Then walk respectfully to the other side of the giant trunk and notice a door or another kind of portal in the trunk. Open the door (if neces-sary) and walk inside.

Once inside the hollow trunk, feel yourself being sucked downward or upward, through a time tunnel, knowing that wherever you land will be perfect. In time, you feel your feet gently yet firmly land upon something solid, again inside a tree trunk (but possibly a different species of tree). Feel around for a door and push it open. When it opens, allow yourself to be in another time and place, and even another body and life-time. Be aware that this may be your own previous lifetime, or the lifetime of an ancestor with whom you share DNA. Explore this lifetime and learn what you need to know with regard to your present challenge. When this feels complete, find your way back to the door in the tree trunk and step inside. Feel yourself transported back to the baobab through the tree trunk time tunnel.

When you arrive to the interior of this original tree, ask the tree for help transmuting the old challenge or hardship into pure positivity and blessings. Feel the tree bathe you in light, shifting the old pattern into a beautiful new one that perfectly complements and supports your most ideal life flow in every way. Thank the tree from the bottom of your heart. Feel for the door, push it open, and exit. Come back into the present moment. Open your eyes.

Divine Communion and Blessings

An alternative name for the baobab is the "upside-down tree," as her top half appears to be a bottom half—her trunk a large taproot and her branches spreading roots. In fact, there are numerous legends about the tree falling top down from the divine sky realm, and lodging its top half into the earth. As such, the baobab may be thought of as a gift from, and gateway to, the sky realm and all its power. Spend time with a baobab to receive wisdom and gifts from angels and the Great Mystery. Incorporate baobab ingredients—bark, flowers, fruit, or leaves—into rituals designed for the purpose. If you can locate or create a flower essence or other vibrational essence created from the baobab, it will be powerful medicine for aligning with the Divine.

Grounding and Earth Wisdom

In addition to her alignment with the sky realm, the baobab is deeply aligned with the power of the earth. Another of her alternative monikers is "tree of life," and she does indeed resemble that culturally ubiquitous symbol of a pillar between the worlds, and a key to the wisdom and beauty of both. Spend time with a baobab (or simply visualize one) to get grounded in the physical world: to awaken your senses and receive access to the ancient knowing that resides eternally within the earth and your own body.

Knowledge

There is an African saying that "Knowledge is like the baobab tree. No single human can embrace it." If building your library of knowledge is important to you right now—for example if you're a college student or interested in deepening your magical repertoire—you'll receive great benefits from reminding yourself that you'll never know it all and there's always more to learn. After all, it really is all about the journey and the joy of learning, and not about the destination or the aim of knowing all there is to know. To bless your studies and formally commit yourself to a lifelong pursuit of knowledge and wisdom, you might try spending time with a baobab tree and—inwardly or aloud—communicating your intention to offer yourself up to this path. Respectfully request assistance and support, and affirm that you will remain a passionate seeker, in a state of constant curiosity. Then offer a symbolic gift to the tree, such as a shiny coin or a clear quartz point.

Natural Abundance, Sustenance, and Generosity

Although Madagascar is one of the poorest countries in the world in terms of monetary wealth, it is blessed with the considerable abundance of the baobab tree (as are the other regions where it appears). Baobab fruit is delicious and exceptionally nutritious. It tastes like sherbet, and astonishingly turns into something like candy inside its slightly fuzzy, coconut-like shell by dehydrating all on its own. Baobab's bark is medicinal, and the shoots and leaves are edible like vegetables. As if all that weren't enough, the trunk stores a huge amount of water, something that is invaluable for humans and other animals in extremely dry climates… The majestic baobab is a "tree of life" indeed!

Call upon your alliance with the baobab tree for sustenance and gifts of abundance from the universe. You might call to mind an image of the baobab and feel deeply supported and loved by this ancient and generous being as you remember that you are perfectly provided for in every way. The baobab reminds you that just as she offers her many gifts, the universe is your source and will produce exactly what you need exactly when you need it, as long as you trust that this is so.

Spiritual Power

All of baobab's other magical gifts—ancient awareness, divine communion, earth wisdom, knowledge, natural abundance, and spirit world alignment—lend themselves to the magical gift discussed in this section: spiritual power. There is an African legend about a son who takes an entire baobab tree up from its roots and presents it to his father. According to author Moyra Caldecott in *Myths of the Sacred Tree*, in doing so he symbolically "takes the whole teaching of the spirit world and brings it back with him to use when it is his turn to lead the tribe."

While actually uprooting a baobab tree is both prohibitively difficult (not to mention harmful to the environment), there are a number of ways you might incorporate baobab's essence in order to initiate yourself into greater levels of spiritual and magical power. For example, for this purpose you might:

- Spend time with a baobab, request an infusion of magical and spiritual power, and then allow yourself to receive it by feeling yourself soaking up the energy of the tree.

- Take a vibrational essence made from baobab or add it to your bathwater.

- Mindfully eat baobab fruit.

- Incorporate parts of the tree into rituals or charms designed for the purpose.

- Visualize standing before a baobab tree, and honoring her intense magic and power. Then see the tree shrink, while retaining her concentrated energetic essence. Finally, place the tree within your heart, and feel her flood you with increased spiritual power.

Transitioning To and From the Spirit World

Baobabs are considered potent portals between this world and the spirit world. Consequently, in some areas, the hollow trunk of cracked baobab trees have been employed as vertical tombs, particularly for members of the tribe who were particularly revered.

Baobab's alignment with the otherworld is also mirrored in the fact that its flowers are pollinated by nocturnal animals such as bats.

The upside-down nature of the baobab lends itself to seeing beneath the obvious surface and bringing what lies beneath into the light.

With all of this in mind, you might incorporate the baobab into rituals or meditations designed for mediumship (communicating with people who have transitioned) or for supporting a loved one as they transition from this realm to the next.

Travel

Time travel, travel from the realm of heaven, and travel between the worlds of the living and the transitioned … it seems we have a theme! Along the same lines (although slightly less mystical), for harmonious travel in the physical world, tie a bit of baobab bark into a muslin bag and stow it in your suitcase or carry-on.

Magical Correspondences

Element: Spirit
Gender: Feminine
Planet: Neptune

Bay Laurel

*S*ometimes called "bay," sometimes called "laurel," and sometimes called "bay laurel," this aromatic, sun-loving tree (*Laurus nobilis*) is the very embodiment of fame, victory, and success. In ancient Greece and Rome, victors wore laurel crowns, a tradition continued until the present day by Italian high school grads. Additionally, the word "laureate" (indicating a high level of mastery and recognition) comes from *laurel*, as does the expression "resting on one's laurels."

Magical Uses

Fame

Bay laurel is aligned with fame in its most purely positive sense: how do you want to be known and seen in the world? And what, exactly, would you like to be known *for*? After all, we're all going to be seen and known *some* way, and it's not wrong for us to desire to be respected for the talents and skills we care about.

Bay Leaf Fame Charm

Gather and dry a bay leaf, or purchase an already dried one from a grocery store (just look in the spice department). Light a red candle when the waxing moon is in a fire sign (Aries, Leo, or Sagittarius). Visualize, sense, and feel that you are known and seen in precisely the ways you'd like to be known and seen. Feel the joy that comes from being recognized for excelling at what you love to do. When this feeling reaches a peak, draw the Kenaz rune (<) on the leaf with a black pen, and then use a tiny paintbrush to anoint the leaf with a tiny bit of clove essential oil. (Make sure not to touch the oil to your skin, as it will burn.) Keep the charm on your altar until your vision is realized, and then let it go into a moving body of water.

Masculinity

Have you ever noticed that "bay rum" is often the scent of choice when it comes to naturally scented products for men? Perhaps that's because—in addition to being sacred to the god Apollo—bay smells deliciously manly. Aromatherapeutically, it instills confidence and aligns one with one's most beautifully realized potential. While bay is indeed a tree with a potently masculine solar energy, we all contain both masculine and feminine aspects. As such, bay can be helpful for anyone who wants to enhance the masculine qualities of directionality, action, and single-minded focus.

Prosperity

Bay's expansive, bright, highly positive vibration lends itself to the attraction and accumulation of wealth. For this purpose, on the full moon create a generous wreath with sprigs and branches of bay, and then hang it on your front door. Or on the new moon empower four dried bay leaves in bright noonday sun, and then place them in your wallet or cash box.

Protection from Harassment and Unwanted Advances

According to Greek myth, the nymph Daphne—despite the best attempts of her father, the god Eros—preferred to remain single in order to concentrate on her love of nature. When the god Apollo fell madly in love with her and pursued her, she transformed into a laurel tree to escape him. As such, much like a matron saint of unwanted sexual advances, Daphne can help when you're experiencing this type of harassment. For this purpose, try the following ward:

Bay Laurel Harassment Ward

Hold a single bay leaf (fresh or dried) between your two flat palms and place your hands in prayer pose at your heart. Feel, imagine, and sense a bright sphere of blinding sunlight surrounding you and shielding you from all negative effects of harassment and unwanted advances. Call on the nymph Daphne to support you in this intention, and remind yourself that you are not in any way deserving of such treatment. Vow to yourself that, starting now, you will refuse to tolerate it or take it to heart. Then place it in a drawstring bag, along with a hematite stone, and wear it around your neck so that it rests over your heart. Thank Daphne for her help. Wear as needed. If you feel you could use extra support in this area, touch the charm with your right hand.

Success

In the Bible, as well as the ancient and present-day Mediterranean, the laurel is synonymous with victory and success. Add one or more bay leaves to any magical working performed with the intention to manifest any variety of success.

Magical Correspondences

Element: Fire

Gender: Masculine

Planet: Sun

Beech

*J*ust yesterday, my partner, Ted, and I took a summer walk in the historic town of Lexington, Missouri, and we encountered the most beautifully lush, sprawling, purple-leafed trees. It turned out they were a variety of beech (*Fagus*)! Who knew?

In the past beechnuts have been an important food source for humans and livestock, though they're not popularly employed for this purpose at the present time.

Magical Uses

Healing Our Deepest Wounds

The compassionate beech is ruled by the planet Chiron, associated in astrology with the concept of the "wounded healer." Magically, the beech supports us in finding, shedding light on, and eventually healing the source of our deepest pain. While this can be excruciating, in terms of evolution, harmony, and personal growth, there is nothing better that we could be doing with our free time. Not to mention, it's ultimately much less painful than perpetually avoiding and tiptoeing around our most fundamental issues.

If you're ready to face your fears and uncover your deepest wounds, spend time alone with a beech. Relax, take some deep breaths, and open yourself up to this intention. Then freewrite in your journal about everything unhealed within your heart and allow yourself to receive guidance from the beech on exactly how to go about healing these things. Or if you're already in the middle of such a deep-healing excavation, spending time with a beech will be like receiving a bolstering energy healing from a revered guru and master healer.

Sensitivity

A very sensitive tree, beech bark doesn't heal once scarred, and initials carved into his trunk never disappear. Additionally, the beech doesn't thrive in polluted areas and can be especially susceptible to aphids and fungal infections. As such, he is a sympathetic ally for those of us who are empathic, allergenic, or just plain sensitive to harshness or negativity. To heal your aura, recharge your batteries, or to learn how to manage your sensitivity in order to exist more harmoniously in this modern world, spend time in quiet contemplation with a thriving beech.

Additionally, beech can be a helpful ally for those who would like to deepen their sensitivity and increase their openness to the thoughts, feelings, and needs of others. For example, if you feel that your tough exterior shell keeps you from manifesting a romantic relationship or connecting as deeply with others as you would like, spending time in quiet contemplation with a beech can help remedy this condition. Intensify the effects by placing your attention on your breath: simply notice as you breathe in and notice as you breathe out. When you notice that your mind has wandered from the breath, simply bring it back, over and over again, as necessary.

Magical Correspondences

Element: Earth
Gender: Masculine and feminine
Planet: Chiron

Birch

*I*n the Celtic mind, the elegant birch (*Betula*) was associated with birth, death, and rebirth. This lithe tree was also associated with the balance between the physical realm and other realms, including the realm of the fairies and the realm of the dead. Aligned with the element of fire as well as the watery, ethereal moon, and possessing both masculine and feminine energy at once, the birch is clearly a tree of polarity. This is true in the material sense as well: she appears delicate and light but is actually unusually hearty and adaptable.

Magical Uses

The Divine Feminine

Corresponding with goddesses no less powerful and revered than Brighid, Frigga, Freya, Venus, and the Morrigan, the birch is truly an arboreal emissary of the Great

Goddess and feminine/lunar mysteries. Indeed, it's added to sabbat fires as a representation of the Great Goddess.

Healing Depression and Anxiety

Some say that depression is a side effect of being overly attached to the past, while anxiety is a side effect of being overly attached to the future. By bringing inspiration, tranquility, and beauty to our present moment experience, birch can help with both.

For this purpose, take the homeopathic medicine (called "Betula") or spend time in quiet contemplation with a birch.

Renewal and New Growth

The rune Berkana (appearing like a pointed capital letter B) is named after birch, and—like springtime—indicates a time of renewal, rebirth, verdant expansion, freshness, and new growth. What's more, maypoles were made of birches. It's believed that this tradition began when Christianity began forbidding people to perform springtime fertility rites (read: exuberant orgies) among the birch groves.

Remember, too, that new beginnings are also always a sort of death to what went before. In much the same way that the daffodil—as one of the earliest spring flowers—is associated with birth *and* death, as well as the passage between these two domains. Birch is aligned not just with renewal, but also with mortality and the land of the dead. In fact, in Celtic burials, the body was covered with birch branches as it was conveyed to its final resting place.

In the practical sense, birch demonstrates renewal in the way that she is among the first to appear after a fire or other land disturbance. This paves the way for other plants and animals to eventually return and thrive as well.

BIRCH CHARM FOR BEAUTIFUL NEW BEGINNINGS

To release the old and make room for a beautiful new beginning in any area of life, visit a birch tree at sunrise on a new moon. Offer a bit of ale or red wine by pouring it around the tree's base, and then silently communicate what you're ready to let go of and what you're ready to welcome into your life. Lovingly gather a small amount of the tree's papery bark. With a gold pen or gold paint, draw the rune Berkana (shaped like a pointed capital B) on the bark. Place it on your altar or keep it with you until your new beginning manifests.

Magical Correspondences

Element: Fire

Gender: Masculine and feminine

Planet: Moon

Bodhi

Also known as the sacred fig, or *Ficus religiosa* (and also the peepal), the magnificent bodhi tree is tremendously sacred to Buddhists because the Buddha sat beneath one as he obtained enlightenment. It's also said that for the entire week following his enlightenment, he stood still, gazing at it lovingly. Although the original tree under which he sat is believed to have been cut down by a queen who was jealous of the attention paid to it by her devout husband—and two of its successors have been cut down by subsequent monarchs—a descendant of the Buddha's bodhi, dwelling in its original location, is visited by Buddhists pilgrims to this day. (And descendants at other Buddhist monasteries are also pilgrimage sites.)

But even before the Buddha's time, the bodhi was sacred to Hindus, and it is said that both Buddha and Vishnu were born beneath one. The fact that the bodhi's leaves tremble even when no wind is blowing has traditionally been seen as a sure indication of his divinity.

Magical Uses
Enlightenment

Bodhi translates to "enlightenment," just as *Buddha* means "enlightened one." As mentioned above, when the Buddha first experienced his famed enlightenment, he was sitting beneath a bodhi tree. In the words of Moyra Caldecott in *Myths of the Sacred Tree*, near the conclusion of his forty-nine-day meditation

> [h]e could feel the great tree drawing nourishment and energy from the earth. He could feel it drawing nourishment and energy from the air and sun. He began to feel the same energy pumping in his heart. He began to feel that there was no distinction between the tree and himself. He was the tree. The tree was him. The earth and the sky were also part of the tree and hence of him.

If, like the Buddha, you desire to call in more spiritual enlightenment and awakening, try meditating under a bodhi tree, performing a visualization exercise incorporating a bodhi tree (similar to the Buddha's enlightenment experience described above), or simply sitting in quiet contemplation with one. Perhaps it's no coincidence that elephants— beings who noticeably exude a calm and awakened state of consciousness, and who have been associated with the Buddha—munch on the leaves of bodhi trees.

Fertility and Masculinity

Since such archetypal masculine divinities as Vishnu and Buddha were both legendarily born beneath the bodhi, it should come as no surprise that bodhi trees have traditionally been employed to help bring about the conception of a male child. While this might not be applicable to our frequent, modern-day lack of preference for one gender over another (not to mention our perilously overabundant human population), we can see it as a part of the bodhi tree's association with both fertility and masculinity. From an energetic perspective, masculinity may be seen as the active, projective principle as opposed to the passive, receptive (feminine) principle, while fertility may be seen as a synonym for prosperity and abundance. As such, to bless a project with forward, active movement and fruitfulness you might visit a bodhi tree and lovingly connect by placing your palms on the trunk. Then, when you feel ready, state your intention and lovingly request the tree's assistance.

If you're "birthing" a new project or life condition, you might like to perform a blessing by lightly holding two of a bodhi tree's neighboring branches and allowing yourself to receive an infusion of strength and fortitude.

Healing

Traditionally, the bodhi tree has been magically employed to help support physical healing on behalf of an ailing friend or family member. For this purpose, visit a bodhi tree on seven consecutive days and—after petitioning the tree for a miracle healing for your loved one—offer one cup of water to the tree seven times on each of the seven days (for a total of seven cups of water each day).

Nature Spirits

The constant movement of the bodhi tree's leaves is a beautiful indication of the tree's magical aliveness, as well as the potent presence of nature spirits within and around him. To connect with nature spirits (such as fairies and the unique personality that animates each individual tree), visit a bodhi tree and relax comfortably while gazing at his leaves. Allow yourself to receive healing energy and intuitive messages through the greenery's infinite dance.

Rainmaking

Offering water to sacred trees and requesting their assistance in "rainmaking" (or magically bringing about rain) has taken place in numerous cultures. According to a Sri Lankan text known as the Mahavamsa, offering water to bodhi trees for this purpose is an extremely ancient practice. The text also relates this rainmaking chant, which it says originated more than two thousand years ago: "May the rains fall in time, may the harvest be bountiful, may the world be prosperous, may the rulers be righteous."

If your region could use some rainfall, and if you'd like to perform a blessing ceremony for the world along with your rainmaking efforts, bring pure water in a clay vessel to a Bodhi tree. Empower it with love as you imagine it filled with bright white light, and then offer it to the tree. Then speak the above chant once, making sure to do so clearly, mindfully, humbly, and with love.

Protection

The bodhi tree's divine alignment and active positivity provides a potent protection boost. While simply spending time with a bodhi tree can increase the natural protectiveness of your personal energetic field, walking around the trunk in a clockwise direction nine times will have a particularly protective and purifying effect.

Wisdom

If you're in need of a little wise guidance, or you'd like to increase your own personal wisdom on any given issue, you need look no further than a living bodhi tree. A true guru of the tree kingdom, simply spending time with a bodhi tree can offer the counsel you need. For this purpose, visit the tree as you would a spiritual master. Kneel near the trunk and silently offer up your challenge or situation through your thoughts and emotions. Then simply relax and be with the tree until you feel centered, grounded, and calmly certain about how to proceed.

Magical Correspondences

Element: Air
Gender: Masculine
Planet: Neptune

Boswellia

*T*his medicinal tree is best known in magical circles for its famously fragrant sap with which you are almost certainly acquainted. It was a gift of the magi, it's a staple at Catholic churches, and it commonly goes by the name of frankincense.

Aligned with the very brightest, strongest, and most positive energies, frankincense (*Boswellia serrata*) has been magically employed for millennia to align with the Divine and bring powerful healing and purification on all levels.

Magical Uses
Healing

Boswellia is an ancient healing remedy that's been used for skin, joints, respiratory ailments, mouth and throat challenges, and general inflammation. On the emotional and spiritual level, frankincense (when used as an incense or anointing oil) can support all forms of healing (including physical) by establishing a clear and positive atmosphere and calling in the fortifying presence of the Divine.

Purification, Consecration, and Sacred Space

In ancient Egypt frankincense was burned as an offering to Ra, the sun god. Indeed, the resin, particularly when burned as incense, possesses a purity, brightness, and strength reminiscent of sunlight itself. Smudge with frankincense to purify a person, an object, or a location.

Similarly, as the Catholic Church is well aware, anointing with the oil or smudging with incense can serve as a powerful consecration ritual: it can be employed to dedicate a person, an object, or a place to divine purposes and elevate the object of the ritual to the realm of the sacred.

Protection

With such a clear, powerful, and vibrant energy, frankincense protects against negativity by dissuading what is not of its vibration. Additionally, it possesses an actual aspect of conscious, alive divinity. This establishes a strong shield of positivity through which no malevolent energies would dare to pierce.

To protect yourself or another, anoint the forehead, heart, belly, and hands with essential oil of frankincense. To protect a space, anoint every door and window on the outside with the oil and smudge the inside with the incense.

Magical Correspondences

Element: Air
Gender: Masculine
Planet: Sun

Buckthorn

If ever a tree were a Taurus with an Aries rising, it's the buckthorn (*Rhamnus*). With a grounded, masculine, up-and-at-'em type energy—and even a name reminiscent of both bull and ram horns—the feisty little buckthorn is an excellent magical ally not just for starting projects, but for stubbornly seeing them through to their fabulous finish.

Magical Uses

Getting Stuck Energy Moving

Medicinally, buckthorn is most often employed as a laxative—but please do not wildcraft unless you are a card-carrying expert: fresh buckthorn is toxic! Still, when dried and aged properly, buckthorn is a gentle herbal laxative safe to use—in the correct dosage—even for most children. (To be on the safe side, research thoroughly, consult a holistic health professional, and purchase from a reputable source.) When used as a laxative, it has the added benefit of purifying the liver and blood.

And this is not the only way buckthorn gets energy moving! Buckthorn has also been employed for exorcisms. I suspect this would be particularly useful when what needs to be exorcised is some sort of trapped or stagnant energy within a space.

Similarly, if you're having trouble motivating for any reason, try magically employing buckthorn to get you up and get you moving. For example:

Buckthorn Clutter Clearing Kick Start

If you want to clear clutter but you just can't seem to get started, offer a shiny silver dollar to a buckthorn by placing it at the tree's base. Then lovingly snip a small branch. Once home, sweep the air around your body. Then move through each room and area of your home in a counterclockwise direction, sweeping the air as you do so. Give the branch back to the earth by placing it on the ground outdoors, and then choose one small area to clear, such as your medicine cabinet or the top drawer in your dresser, and clear it. If you'd like to continue clearing after that, feel free. Otherwise, choose another small space to clear tomorrow, and another on the following day, again and again, until your clutter is cleared.

Starting a New Project or Endeavor

In addition to possessing a powerful initiatory energy, buckthorn has magical staying power. So if you're starting a new project or endeavor—like writing a book or launching a business—buckthorn would be an excellent magical ally.

New Project Buckthorn Blessing

On a new moon at noon, visit a buckthorn tree. Empower a polished stone with your intention, holding it in bright sunlight (if possible) as you do so. Feel, imagine, and sense yourself feeling harmonious and joyful as you launch your project, work on it faithfully, and experience the type of success you'd like to experience with it. Pour all these confident visions and empowered feelings into the crystal. When this feels complete, bury the crystal at the base of the buckthorn and pour an entire bottle of red wine around its roots.

Wish Granting

In *Cunningham's Encyclopedia of Magical Herbs*, the author says:

> A charming legend concerning the buckthorn says that if one sprinkles buckthorn in a circle and then dances within it under a full moon, an elf will appear. The dancer must notice the elf and say, "Halt and grant my boon!" before the creature flees. The elf will then grant one wish. I cannot make any guarantees that this will happen, however.

Still, I think we can all agree that it's certainly worth a try.

Magical Correspondences

Element: Earth
Gender: Masculine
Planet: Mars

Carob

While native to the Mediterranean region, all throughout my childhood an aged carob tree (*Ceratonia siliqua*) contributed to the cool shade of my grandparent's California backyard. I'm told that my Italian immigrant great-grandmother (whom my father, uncles, and aunt called "Nona") regularly ate the tree's dried, chocolaty carob pods like crackers.

Magical Uses

Healing Dreams

In many ways we work things out in our dreams, and we can magically employ our dreams to gain insight and actual healing in the areas of mind, body, spirit, and emotions. As a tree governed by the planet Neptune, carob can support intentions related to healing dream work. For example:

CAROB POD HEALING DREAM CHARM

To receive guidance and actual healing through the medium of your dreams, visit a carob tree at night when the moon is in Pisces. Offer a full bottle of beer or ale to the tree by pouring it around the roots, and then lovingly gather a single carob pod. Sleep with the pod under your pillow whenever you'd like to experience healing via your dreams.

Honoring Past and Future Generations

There is a Jewish legend about a wise man in Israel who saw an elderly man planting a carob tree and asked him why he would do such a thing. After all, the old man wouldn't be around in seventy years when the tree finally began to cast shade and bear fruit. The old man responded that he was planting it for his grandchildren to enjoy. The wise man then promptly fell asleep for seventy years, woke up, and observed the man's grandson not just enjoying the tree his grandfather planted, but also, in turn, planting a new one for *his* grandchildren to enjoy.

If it's your intention to leave a positive legacy for future generations—your own grandchildren or other people's grandchildren—plant a carob tree and tend to her lovingly, knowing that even though you may not be around to benefit from the tree's nourishing pods and cooling shade, future generations certainly will.

Nourishment

As my Italian great-grandmother apparently knew, carob pods are a nourishing food. An excellent source of vegan calcium and iron, carob has been consumed since ancient times. Manuscripts as ancient as the Bible, Talmud, and even the Epic of Gilgamesh demonstrate the importance of carob as a food source, and carob is featured in the Egyptian hieroglyph that translates to "sweet." Even today, carob syrup is a popular, healthy sweetener in places throughout the Mediterranean and Middle East.

Magical Correspondences

Element: Earth

Gender: Masculine and feminine

Planet: Neptune

Catalpa

*N*ever having known about them before, what a wondrous treat it was to make the acquaintance of the wizened, mystical catalpa trees (of the family Bignoniaceae) in my Missouri front yard. As I write, brand-new velvety, paper-thin leaves burst out from the ends of their branches like spring green magnolia blossoms.

Magical Uses
Embracing Uniqueness
With an uncommon energy entirely his own, catalpa marches to the beat of his own drummer. His presence emboldens us to do the same. Spend time with a catalpa, take the flower essence, or visualize the tree during meditation when you're ready to step into your singular variety of power, discover and/or celebrate your peculiarities, and fully embrace yourself in all your unique glory.

Esoteric Studies

The roots of catalpa's wisdom reach deep into the darkness, and his branches stretch toward the ethereal light of the mysterious, the ancient, and the veiled. Interestingly, the qin—a Chinese stringed instrument traditionally made with catalpa wood and played for its silence and pauses as much as for its sound—is symbolically and culturally associated with scholarship. Spend time with catalpa or work with the flower essence when you're immersed in esoteric studies of any kind. He can help build a bridge across the ages and bring what is shrouded and cryptic into the clear light of understanding.

Expressing Creativity

The catalpa's ability to help us express creativity is threefold. By tapping into our uniqueness, dunking us into the realm of mystery and enchantment, and aligning us with spirit and the spirit realm, he places us precisely where we need to be to express our creativity in the most fluent and satisfying of ways. This energetic creativity assistance is mirrored in the physical realm: catalpa wood is used in instrument making because of its resonance and tone.

....

CATALPA CREATIVITY CHARM

After communing with and expressing appreciation toward a catalpa tree, lovingly gather seven fallen catalpa twigs and tie them together with silver string. Carry or place on your altar for magical assistance with all things creative.

Spirit Summoning

In Shintoism a traditional practice involves summoning a spirit (or kami) with a bow or a one-stringed lute made from catalpa wood. Because the catalpa is aligned with the realm of spirit, the tree can also be enlisted in other ways to connect with unseen allies of any variety, including angels, fairies, deities, and ancestors. For example:

OTHERWORLD CONNECTION RITUAL

Visit a catalpa at midnight during the dark moon. Safely light a white tealight candle in a jar and carry it in your left hand as you place a moonstone at the tree's base as an offering. Then touch the trunk with your right hand and request support connecting with beneficent beings in the otherworld. Be very present as you allow yourself to receive an infusion of energy from the tree. When this feels complete, thank the tree and return home.

Magical Correspondences

Element: Spirit

Gender: Masculine

Planet: Uranus

Cedar

A powerful ally of pure divine light, when we seek spiritual cleansing, healing, or guidance, we need look no further than the cedar. Considered to be profoundly sacred since time immemorial, in ancient spiritual literature—time and time again—cedar is aligned with divinity and divine wisdom.

While there are a lot of trees that feature the word "cedar" in their name, this section focuses on the "true cedars" of the fragrant *Cedrus* genus. This includes the Atlas cedar, Cyprus cedar, Deodar cedar, and Lebanon cedar.

Magical Uses

Breaking Spells

Occasionally you may find that you have cast a spell that you eventually wish to undo. Because you've determined that it's not in alignment with your truest good, you might imagine this unwanted spell (to employ the cosmology of Star Wars, as I love to do) as a "disturbance in the Force." From this perspective, you can see how the cedar—which you might say is an arboreal representation of the Force itself in all its purely positive glory—can undo this disturbance and reestablish a natural harmony and flow.

CEDAR EXTRA STRENGTH SPELL-BREAKING RITUAL

To break a spell that you have cast, visit a cedar alone the night after a full moon, when the moon is visible in the sky. Light a candle or bring a lantern if necessary to see. Call on the Divine in a way that feels powerful for you, and then bring the old spell—along with all its unwanted results—to mind. Really tune in to this unwanted energy as well as its effects. Hold this in your mind as you gather forty cedar twigs (naturally fallen if possible) and then bind them together with hemp twine, then tying it in nine knots. This bundle now represents exactly what it is that you'd like to undo.

Now, cut the twine decisively with scissors as you say, "The spell I cast is now undone."

Walk counterclockwise around the trunk of the tree, slowly scattering the twigs as you say:

Though this spell was tied up tight
I fully dissolve it on this night.
The natural flow clearly resounds
As all effects are now unbound.
Beloved cedar, all thanks to thee
The spell is broken; so mote it be.

When the twigs are all dispersed, brush your aura downward with your hands and then flick your fingers toward the ground nine times as you continue to walk counter-clockwise around the tree. Finally, rest your back against the trunk and feel the cedar lending you his energy, creating a powerful, cleansing flow from your feet to the crown of your head and back down again. Thank the tree again from the bottom of your heart.

Clarity and Focus

Essential oil of cedar is quite possibly unsurpassed in its ability to relieve tension and anxiety, clear the mind of extraneous thoughts, support crystal-clear clarity, and facilitate sustained mental focus. In no small way, the scent of cedar does this through eliciting inspiration; so often it's not that our minds *can't* pay attention to something, it's that they won't because they're just not inspired by the topic. Cedar helps us to uncover what's interesting about the topic at hand, so that our minds naturally want to apply themselves. This makes cedar oil a great magical ally when it comes to learning, studying, writing, and test taking. (Of course, if you're forcing your mind to apply itself to something that doesn't naturally interest you in any way, cedar won't be able to help. Incidentally, if this is the case, you might want to question whether you're on a path that's actually suited to you.)

For this purpose, diffuse essential oil of cedar, or put ten to twenty drops in a small mister of purified water, shake well, and mist the room.

Sacred Space

Considered to be sacred since very ancient times, one only needs inhale the scent of essential oil of cedar to understand the tree's ability to create sacred space within and around us. Indeed, both the tree and the fragrance establish great clarity and profound alignment with the realm of the Divine through uniting the realms of heaven and earth, much like the proverbial Tree of Life. Perhaps this is why cedar was the wood of choice in the ancient world for temples and altars throughout the Mediterranean and Middle East. To establish sacred space in any room or area, mist the space with water containing cedar oil (as above), diffuse essential oil of cedar, or burn cedar incense.

Strengthening the Energy Field

Cedar's energy is extremely positive and powerful, and can lend an infusion of strength and brightness to your personal energy field. This can be helpful for anytime you feel run-down energetically, such as after a trauma or an illness, or after completing a particularly draining project or activity. Try spending time with your spine against a cedar trunk, diffusing essential oil of cedar in your space, or adding a few drops of cedar oil to your bathwater.

Wisdom

Archetypal wisdom superstar King Solomon chose to feature cedar wood prominently in the building of his temple. In ancient Sumeria, cedars were honored as dwellings of the spirit of wisdom in the form of the god Ea. Indeed, cedar is an appropriate emissary of wisdom, as he is Divinity in tree form, and all true wisdom does not come from cleverness, but rather from an infusion of divine energy and presence.

If you need divine guidance on any issue or challenge, visit a cedar and sit in quiet contemplation, allowing yourself to align with the realm of the Divine. Notice your breath and consciously relax with each breath, breathing out tension and breathing in nourishment. In time, you'll find that you have access to precisely the wisdom you seek.

Magical Correspondences

Element: Air
Gender: Masculine
Planet: Sun

Chaste Tree

Also known as vitex and lilac chaste tree (*Vitex agnus-castus*), herbal healers consider chaste tree berries to be one of the most important herbs for balancing female hormones and promoting all varieties of reproductive and menstrual health. By affecting the pituitary gland, the herb activates the body's own ability to regulate itself, which can (for example) help lengthen short moon cycles and shorten long ones, promote fertility and breast milk production, and remedy all varieties of unpleasant premenstrual symptoms such as headaches, acne, and cramps.

Magical Uses

Attracting Bees

Bees—creatures sacred to the Great Goddess (aka Mother Nature)—*love* chaste tree flowers. Plant a chaste tree (or several) in your yard to promote the well-being of this extremely helpful insect and endangered precious resource.

Sexual Balance

The chaste tree got her name because in ancient times she was employed to dissuade sexual urges. For example, during the festival of Thesmophoria (in honor of the goddess Demeter), when sex was forbidden, Athenian women placed the leaves and branches on their beds to prevent their partners from making advances and maidens wore the flowers to protect their chastity. Similarly, it's said that Christian monks of ages past wore girdles of the wood and chewed the berries to support them in upholding their vows of celibacy. However, today herbal healers have employed chaste tree berries to *increase* fertility and sex drive. In fact, according to anecdotal evidence, it appears that taking the herb medicinally supports one in experiencing a balanced relationship with one's sexuality according to what is currently needed—whether that means increasing sex drive, decreasing sex drive, setting better sexual boundaries, or letting down one's guard.

While chaste tree berries definitely have an effect on hormones, extensive medical testing has been inconclusive about exactly how and why this occurs. What is clear, however, is that chaste tree's specialty (magical *and* medical) has to do with female sexual balance of all varieties: physical, mental, emotional, and spiritual.

To experience these benefits, spend time with a chaste tree, take the flower essence, or consult with a holistic healing practitioner for guidance on how to employ the berries.

Magical Correspondences

Element: Water
Gender: Feminine
Planet: Ceres

Cherry

Clearly, those who don't believe in magic have never stood under a blossoming cherry tree (of the *Prunus* genus) in sunlight, soaking in the almost impossible beauty of the boughs as they gently tremble under a bright blue sky. Could there be a more heavenly visual experience in this material world? If so, I haven't yet encountered it.

Magical Uses

Divine Orchestration

Allied with the realm of the angels—particularly the cherubim—cherry trees possess an energy notably akin to "cherubic fire." (While cherubs appear in more recent times with winged children, when cherubs appear in the Bible they take the form of grown women with wings and serve as highly positive protectors and guides.) Similarly, the fairylike beings called the "Vila" often appear near cherry trees, and cherry trees play the role of guardian in some fairy tales.

Essentially, the fiery, heavenly energy of the cherry tree helps bring us into powerful alignment with our most auspicious possible alignment and flow. For this purpose, sit in quiet contemplation with a blossoming cherry tree or take cherry flower essence.

Goddess Energy

In addition to being ruled by the planet Venus and sacred to the goddess of love, the cherry tree is a symbol of the Japanese goddess Konohana-sakuya Hime, who is considered a divine foremother of the human race. Indeed, the cherry tree is a potent powerhouse of divine feminine energy and can assist us in getting in touch with the goddess within. In other words, she can help us radiate our divine beauty and embrace our sensuality, magnetism, receptivity, and sensitivity. For this purpose, place cherry blossoms on your altar or empower a bowl of cherries in sunlight and mindfully eat them.

Love

An important aspect of many Japanese wedding celebrations, every component of the cherry tree vibrates at the frequency of love. Bless a romantic relationship by spending time together under a blossoming cherry tree or by planting two cherry trees in your yard. You can also create a love-drawing charm by placing two dried cherry pits in a pink drawstring bag, anointing it with rose absolute, and using a safety pin to pin it to the inside of your clothes so that it rests against your skin.

Power and Strength

Popular for furniture, interior details, musical instruments, and carving, the deep red of cherry wood conveys a sense of the tree's energetic potency. Similarly, the mahogany-colored flesh and skin of some varieties of the fruit reveals its sanguine magical signature. Spend time in quiet contemplation with a cherry tree to bolster your personal power and strength, or bless nine cherries before mindfully eating them.

Sweetness

Not all cherries produce edible fruit, but the ones that do produce *very* edible fruit. So edible, in fact, that the phrase "life is a bowl of cherries" is used to communicate that life is sweet and filled with enjoyment for its own sake. A maraschino cherry in a cocktail or on top of a dessert is the quintessential symbol of pleasure and satisfaction. And children of all ages are enthusiasts of cherry-flavored candy and snow cones, as well as the actual candy-like fruit itself. To add more sweetness to your life, spend time with a cherry tree or bring one or more into your yard. Or, of course, you can always simply eat cherries.

Magical Correspondences

Element: Fire

Gender: Feminine

Planet: Venus

Chestnut

The beautiful chestnut (*Castanea*) can live to be more than a thousand years old, and some species can get quite huge. With luxurious shade and nuts that can be a reliable food source even for prolonged periods of time, this ancient tree is a divine and miraculous blessing to all who benefit from its many gifts.

Magical Uses

Abundance

Chestnuts have been cultivated since ancient times in both east and west and, like a grain, is considered a major food staple. (In fact, some cultures may have survived almost exclusively on chestnuts, at least at certain times.) Also like a grain, chestnuts are magically aligned with sustenance, and therefore abundance and prosperity.

In the Bible, Jacob puts a peeled chestnut twig in his livestock's water source to promote their healthy and abundant procreation. (In ancient times, an abundance of healthy livestock was a major indication of wealth.) In Japan, chestnuts are eaten at New Years' for success and good fortune.

Employ chestnuts in a meal to activate prosperity, or empower your household's wealth by placing a chestnut twig in your watering can before watering your plants.

Attracting Animals

Deer love chestnuts, and other animals, such as squirrels and birds, are attracted to chestnut trees as well, as they provide both shelter and sustenance. Plant chestnut trees in your yard if you'd like to attract animals, or spend time with a chestnut tree if you're in the mood for a little animal communication.

Relieving Worry

The Bach Flower Remedy made from white chestnut blossoms helps relieve excess worry and frenetic thinking. Additionally, some American Indians made infusions of chestnut leaves to relieve that perennial worry symptom: the headache. Certainly, a lush chestnut tree in the breeze instantly soothes the spirit and calms the mind.

Interestingly, the Christian mystic Hildegard von Bingen stated that chestnuts promote longevity. Perhaps this is related to the chestnut's ability to relieve that primary health hazard known as stress by quieting a worried mind.

Transforming Karma

There is a Korean legend about a boy who a traveling Taoist predicted would be eaten by a tiger at a young age. However, the prediction also came with a remedy: plant and care for one thousand chestnut trees. This the boy did, and when he turned twenty, a stranger knocked on his door and demanded his life. Upon learning about the chestnut trees, however, the stranger died on the spot just after his true identity as a tiger was revealed. This allowed the boy to live a long and successful life.

In Taoism, it's believed that many things contribute to our destiny and our good fortune, and this includes our deeds. In this story, by cultivating one thousand chestnut trees that otherwise wouldn't have existed, the boy counteracts his fate by nurturing so many living beings—and harvesting so much sustenance for his fellow creatures in the process—that he effectively transforms his fate.

While one thousand might be just a tiny bit too many, if you feel that intense karma transforming is needed, you might plant one to three chestnut trees in your yard or a nature area (provided they're beneficial to the ecosystem and you have the approval of the stewards of the land). Tend to them lovingly and make sure they thrive.

Magical Correspondences

Element: Spirit
Gender: Masculine/Feminine Balance
Planet: Mercury

Cinchona (Fever Tree)

The cinchona, or fever tree (of the Rubiaceae family), is known in its native Amazonian region as quina-quina, which, tellingly, translates to "bark of barks" or "medicine of medicines."

While cinchona bark is an ancient herbal remedy with a wide range of healing benefits, it's best known to Western medicine as the source of quinine, an effective cure for malaria. Though this life-saving healing property was almost certainly known to South Americans since long before it was discovered by Europeans in the 1600s, according to *Malaria Journal* (May 2011), "The discovery of quinine is considered the most serendipitous medical discovery of the seventeenth century and malaria treatment with quinine marked the first successful use of a chemical compound to treat an infectious disease."

Quinine is also the definitive ingredient in tonic water, and it is added in very small amounts to a number of commercial beverages for its bitter flavor. Interestingly, under a black light, tonic water and other beverages with quinine appear fluorescent blue.

Please note: Quinine and cinchona bark should not be consumed by pregnant women and should only be used medicinally under expert supervision, as excessive dosage can cause serious harm and even death.

Magical Uses

Digestive Support

In some cases, herbal healers recommend a tincture from the bark of the cinchona tree as a bitter tonic to activate digestive juices and remedy sluggish digestion. (A commercially available homeopathic remedy for indigestion containing cinchona is available from the brand Hyland's.)

Emotional Clearing and Detoxification

Medicinally, cinchona bark has been used for heart healing and fever reduction, and to dry excess moisture from the system. These physical properties, along with the bark's antifungal and antibacterial actions, mirror the tree's energetic ability to help heal grief and heartache, and to detoxify festering emotional wounds. Indeed, when life seems to have given you a "bitter pill to swallow," this bitter-tasting tree can support you in first accepting the bitterness, and then transforming that bitterness into a tonic for permanent wholeness, power, and wisdom.

For this purpose, visit a cinchona tree—preferably in a place where you can be alone—and offer her a pinch of organic or wildcrafted tobacco. Sit in quiet contemplation with her. Silently present your emotional challenges and old hurts, and then allow yourself to feel and express your feelings as fully as you possibly can. Imagine that the pain and toxins that you feel are being drawn out of you, and into the soil for neutralization and transmutation.

Alternatively, you can create an emotional detoxification potion like the following:

....

Tonic Water Emotional Detox Potion

On a bright, sunny day when the moon is waning and in an air sign (Aquarius, Gemini, or Libra), prepare the following potion outdoors in full sunlight. Conjuring up gratitude for the cinchona tree pour a small glass of chilled tonic water. Add five drops of willow flower essence (one of the Bach Flower Remedies, available at most health food stores). Without touching the glass, direct your cupped palms toward it, being careful not to cast any shadow on it. Visualize the potion filled with a blindingly bright sphere of detoxifying light (like a miniature sun) as you say:

> *Medicine of medicines, make me clean*
> *Infuse me with pure light of green.*
> *With this drink to clear the old*
> *My heart's true healing shall unfold.*

Then feel the magic working as you drink every last sip.

Protection

As the cinchona tree resonates with the potent, highly positive, fiercely protective energy of the Great Goddess in her earth mother aspect, cinchona bark can be an excellent addition to protection sachets and spells.

Relaxation

"Antispasmodic" and "muscle relaxant" are listed among cinchona bark's many medicinal monikers. From a metaphysical perspective, this aspect of cinchona's wisdom translates into support with stress that manifests as headaches, cramping, spasms, and general physical tension. To receive an energetic infusion of support for any of these types of concerns, spend time in quiet contemplation with the tree while breathing consciously and allowing your thoughts and worries to settle. Additionally, a homeopathic remedy made from cinchona is commercially available and can be taken for the purpose. (Responsibly prepared homeopathic remedies contain very diluted amounts of the actual plant and are generally safe.)

Magical Correspondences

Element: Earth

Gender: Feminine

Planet: Ceres

Coffee

*A*ccording to legend (and perhaps some smidgen of fact), an Ethiopian goatherd discovered coffee. This goatherd (whose name was Kaldi) noticed that his goats became particularly wired when they grazed on a certain small tree. After relaying his findings to a local clergyman, the clergymen roasted the tree's seeds, brewed them with hot water, and served the resulting beverage to monks, who suddenly found themselves able to meditate and study until late in the night.

Today, as you surely know, coffee (*Coffea*) is *very* big business. As you may also know, because of unfair business practices and slave labor, it's a good idea to look for the "fair trade" symbol before purchasing your coffee.

Magical Uses

Abundance

With creamy white blossoms that look and smell luxuriously like jasmine, vibrant red "cherries" that glow with happiness, and glossy green leaves that flutter abundantly like so much paper currency, the lovely coffee tree undeniably resonates at the frequency of wealth. In practical terms, this is mirrored by the fact that coffee is such a huge commodity all over the world, and by the fact that literally billions of people fuel their money-making efforts with a ready stream of freshly brewed java.

If you can visit an actual coffee tree (which would probably mean that you're in Africa, Hawaii, or South America), spending time in quiet contemplation with one would be an excellent way to increase your wealth consciousness and help magnetize abundance. Just relax, breathe, appreciate the tree's unique beauty, and feel yourself receiving an energy infusion directly from the tree.

Goddess Energy

Beloved author Isak Dinesen wrote, "Coffee, according to the women of Denmark, is to the body what the Word of the Lord is to the soul." (Incidentally, she and coffee had an intimate relationship: she owned and managed a coffee plantation for a time, as she wrote about in her delightful autobiographical novel *Out of Africa*.) Indeed, not just the beverage but the tree herself possesses a seemingly divine energetic charge, with a vibration reminiscent of a divine feminine powerhouse such as Pele or Ishtar. And like all plants with five-petaled blossoms, she is sacred to the Goddess.

Speaking of goddesses and coffee, have you heard of the coffee goddess Caffeina? It's more than likely that she's a recent addition to the roster of popular divinities, but she's quite appropriate for our modern age. If you're a coffee lover, consider creating an altar to her in your kitchen or creating and framing a postcard-sized image of a goddess rising from a cup of coffee and hanging it near the place where you prepare your coffee. You can also take a moment to thank her and sing her praises just before drinking your first morning cup.

Productivity

Like a gift of a single red rose given with the intention to enhance romantic love, there are some magical ingredients that are so potent, even non-magical people make use of them. As modern-day workplaces are well aware, a coffee bean potion (aka *coffee*), drunk to increase productivity, definitely works like a charm.

While coffee has many health benefits, it can also increase stress and anxiety and can cause stomach problems because of its high acidity. But did you know that cold brewing your coffee and straining it through a paper filter makes it much healthier? It cuts the PH by up to 75 percent and removes many of the harmful components. Plus, it's delicious! Here's how to make a coffee potion that's better than the average joe:

COLD BREW COFFEE POTION FOR PRODUCTIVITY AND WEALTH

Combine one cup of coarsely ground fair trade coffee with four cups of cold or room temperature water. Place in the fridge for fourteen hours. Put a basket filter in a strainer and strain. Store in the fridge, and use as a concentrate: mix one part coffee with two parts non-dairy milk. Sweeten to taste with agave nectar or maple syrup, and sprinkle with cinnamon.

Magical Correspondences

Element: Fire
Gender: Feminine
Planet: Mars

Coral

The exotic and fiery-flowered coral tree (*Erythrina caffra*) is the official tree of my longtime home of Los Angeles, California. Considering how few residents of Los Angeles are actually from Los Angeles, it's perhaps appropriate that the coral tree is, in fact, a native of South Africa.

Considered by the Zulus to be an extremely auspicious and magical tree, it has traditionally adorned the graves of their tribal chiefs. Warning: Coral trees are toxic.

Magical Uses
Attraction

Although not noticeably scented, coral tree's red flowers are abundantly nectar-filled and attract all sorts of pollinating birds. Insects, as well, are attracted to the coral tree, both nesting within it and feeding off of it. In Africa, women wear jewelry made from its seeds, thus increasing their powers of attraction. To increase your attractiveness or your ability to attract positive qualities of any kind, spend time with a coral tree (particularly a blossoming one) or incorporate the seeds or flowers into rituals.

Luck

Children in the coral tree's native Africa have been known to collect the seeds, calling them "lucky beans." (But please do *not* eat them, as they are toxic.) Incorporate the seeds into rituals designed for the purpose or create a simple luck charm by tying nine coral seeds into a piece of bright red-orange felt and carrying.

Fame

The sun-drenched climate in which the coral tree thrives and the fiery appearance of his flowers—not to mention the traditional belief in some circles that burning the wood will attract lightning—indicate the tree's notable ability to help fan the fires of fame. (No *wonder* Los Angeles adopted the coral tree as its own!)

If you'd like to be more seen and respected in any given arena, lovingly connect with a blossoming coral tree. When you're ready, communicate your desire to the tree via thoughts, visions, and feelings. Then relax and allow the tree to bathe you in wisdom related to manifesting your intention. Feel, imagine, and sense this wisdom filling your aura with magical, fame-magnetizing fire. Alternatively (or additionally), you might direct your intention into a bit of wood from a coral tree, and then safely burn it in a fireplace, campfire, or fire pit. As it burns, visualize bright, fiery light filling your entire body and aura.

Magical Correspondences

Element: Fire
Gender: Masculine
Planet: Jupiter

Crepe Myrtle

The delicate, lush appearance of the flowering crepe myrtle (*Lagerstroemia*) belies her heartiness and her penchant for dry, warm climates. This contrast is part of her charm: like a well-groomed southern belle sparkling with perfection even in the sweatiest and dustiest of scenes, the tree's verdant leaves and fresh blooms unfailingly breathe balance into the austere desert landscapes she adorns.

Magical Uses

Longevity

They may appear fragile upon close inspection, but in truth, few blossoms last longer than the crepe myrtle's, regardless of the fact that they bloom in the hottest summer months of some of the warmest climates. As such, crepe myrtle's magical gift is one of staying power: this includes literal health and longevity, as well as the longevity of relationships, business partnerships, organizations, and other such institutions. For physical longevity or longevity in any other area, plant crepe myrtle and enlist her help or create the following longevity charm:

CREPE MYRTLE LONGEVITY CHARM

Lovingly gather a crepe myrtle blossom. Tie it in a scrap of muslin along with a hematite, nine evergreen needles, and a cat's naturally shed whisker. Anoint it with essential oil of tea tree. Hold it in your right palm and bathe it in bright sunlight as you say:

For timeless ages I'll [we'll/this will] joyfully stay
Nine times nine, forever and a day,
Happy, healthy, wealthy, strong
My [our/this] life's span is vast and long.

Place your left hand over the charm and cup it in both hands. Bury it near a threshold that you regularly cross.

Love

The crepe myrtle's ability to thrive in otherwise parched climates is reminiscent of true, long-term romantic love. Plant crepe myrtle near your home to ensure your committed relationship stays fresh for the long haul. (Be aware that this will only work if the relationship is for your truest good. Otherwise, the presence of the tree may speed its dissolution.)

Magical Correspondences

Element: Water
Gender: Feminine
Planet: Saturn

Cypress

*L*ike the Queen of Swords in the tarot deck, cypress's personality is swift, concise, and uncompromising. Aligned with both the planet Mercury and the element of air, she is especially suited for magical work involving communication, thought, and healing the emotions through purifying and releasing old wounds.

Technically, *cypress* is the name of a large family of conifers that includes junipers, sequoias, and redwoods (each of which possesses its own section in this book). Here, we'll specifically discuss those trees of the family Cupressaceae with the word "cypress" in their name, such as the Monterey cypress, Leyland cypress, and Italian cypress.

Magical Uses

Clarity

With such a meticulously clear energetic signature, cypress can help when we desire clarity on any given issue or challenge or just a greater level of mental clarity in general.

Simply sitting in quiet contemplation with a cypress tree would be an excellent way to receive this benefit. Bring along a fluorite crystal for added intensity.

Emotional Healing

Long recognized as an ally for those who are grieving, the cypress tree indeed cleans and clears grief and other emotional wounds in an uncommonly potent way. Once we've acknowledged and felt our feelings fully, cypress's detached wisdom allows us to simply release them and dissolve them into the sky, like morning dew drops in dry summer heat.

....

CYPRESS DEEP EMOTIONAL DETOX

When the waning moon is in an air sign (Aquarius, Gemini, or Libra) and the sun is shining visit a cypress tree. Sit comfortably with your spine relatively straight and take some deep, conscious breaths. Relax your body and center your mind as you gaze at the cypress and come into alignment with it. Pour clear water into a glass bowl and hold the bowl in both hands. Still relaxing, get in touch with the feelings that you'd like to detox-ify from your system. Feel them as fully as possible, and mentally direct the energy of them into the water. Cry if you need to, or just get into the flow of the feelings as best you can. When you feel that you've poured your feelings into the water as completely as possible, stand up and pour the water around the base of the tree, setting the intention to fully release all attachment to these feelings as you do so. Finally, touch the trunk of the cypress and allow yourself to tap into her deep wisdom and strength. Inwardly thank her from the bottom of your heart.

Longevity

Some cypresses can live for up to a thousand years, and many varieties can withstand harsh and extreme weather conditions. Energetically speaking, cypress possesses a wise and Zen-like disposition, teaching us through example to adopt a healthy and sustainable relationship with the unavoidable stresses of life. These qualities combined make cypress an excellent magical ally for intentions related to longevity and sustained physical health. For this purpose, spend time in quiet contemplation with cypress, plant cypresses in your yard, or bring a small potted specimen—such as a lemon cypress—into your life. A potted cypress would also be an excellent gift for a convalescing loved one.

Writing and Speaking

The gift of language falls within cypress's domain. As such, magical intentions related to writing and/or speaking with clarity and power can be greatly fueled by cypress's clear vibration. For example, for public speaking, or before anytime when you desire for your words to be particularly resonant and persuasive, lightly brush your throat and third eye (forehead) with a sprig of cypress (provided you are not allergic). Similarly, you can enhance your writing efforts by tapping your keyboard and both hands (or your notebook and writing hand) with a sprig of cypress before you begin.

Magical Correspondences

Element: Air
Gender: Feminine
Planet: Mercury

Dogwood

*W*hile the flowering dogwood just happens to be the state tree of Missouri (where I sit as I write), lucky for everyone else there are all kinds of dogwoods for all kinds of climates! Like man's best friend with whom he shares his name, the dogwood (*Cornus*) comes in many sizes and species. Also like our canine buddies, he's adorable, friendly, and emotionally supportive, and he's been historically employed for a number of practical purposes.

Magical Uses

Boundaries

Though extremely friendly, the dogwood can be enlisted to protect you from what you choose to exclude. He can also help you determine whom and what should be excluded. In other words, much like a dog will growl at a guest to indicate something isn't quite right, magically working with dogwood can tip you off or emanate "back off" vibes when someone or something is not in alignment with your vibration.

For protection and boundary setting, you might plant a dogwood near your home. As you tend to the tree and build your relationship with him, begin to communicate your wish that he support you in only allowing positive visitors and conditions to enter your space. For an inner shift that will allow you to more naturally set healthy boundaries with yourself and others, take two drops of dogwood flower essence under your tongue two to three times per day. Naturally fallen parts of the tree (such as leaves or bark) can also be carried for the purpose.

Dog Communication and Healing

Although some say that the name dogwood evolved from "daggerwood"—an allusion to the historic use of the tree's wood to make knife handles—I'm not so sure. Even if that *is* the origin of the tree's name, "dogwood" stuck for a reason. After all, the dogwood's personality is loyal, helpful, playful, and loving. He isn't mysterious, independent, or coy like some trees, but he will energetically jump up on your lap and lick your face.

As such, if you want to communicate more clearly with dogs, visit a dogwood tree. In addition to silently communing with the tree, you might also request a bit of the tree's bark or wood. Be sure to explain to the tree exactly why you want it, offering an agate (by placing it near the tree's base) as an advance gift of gratitude. Then, when you receive a sense that it's okay, gather a bit of wood or some bark and carry it to facilitate your canine communications.

The dogwood can also be magically employed for support with healing a dog companion. Visit a dogwood and request energetic support with this intention, and/or place parts of the tree (flowers, wood, or bark) in the same room as a convalescing dog.

Endurance

In the Victorian language of the flowers, the dogwood tree means "endurance." Plant a dogwood tree in your yard or sit in quiet contemplation with a dogwood tree to cultivate enduring physical and/or emotional strength or to help a romantic or family relationship to endure.

Healing the Emotions

When your emotions need healing—even if your heart is downright broken—it's hard not to feel like you're on the mend when a loving, cheerful dog is smiling at you adoringly and giving you the message that you're never alone. Spending time with a dogwood tree (particularly a blossoming one) can have a similar effect. Additionally, if you need a good cry and you know of a dogwood tree where you can spend time without being disturbed, go sit against the trunk or under the branches and bawl your eyes out. Part best friend, part emotional purgative, the dogwood tree is an excellent ally when it comes to getting the heavy grief out and leaving you clean and light.

Love Divination

To divine whether or not someone shares your attraction, visit a blossoming dogwood not long before the sun goes down. Tell the tree whom you admire and in what way (via your feelings rather than your words), and request that the tree support you in gathering intelligence about whether or not he or she feels the same. If you sense that the tree is okay with it, respectfully snip a blossom, leaving two rose quartz crystals near the tree's base as a thank-you gift. Return to your home and place the blossom on top of your mailbox. (You can do this even if you have a shared mailbox. If you have a mail slot or for some other reason can't set the flower on your mailbox, place it on some other outdoor surface such as a wide fence post, fire extinguisher box, or balcony railing.) In the morning, if the blossom is still in the exact same place, your feelings are not reciprocated. If it's blown off, fallen off, or (better yet) has mysteriously disappeared, it's a sign that the object of your affections feels the same.

Miracles

Anne Morrow Lindbergh famously wrote, "After all, I don't see why I am always asking for private, individual, selfish miracles when every year there are miracles like white dogwood."

Still, when you're in need of a more personal miracle (i.e., when the options you perceive do not seem to offer a key to the outcome you desperately desire), a dogwood blossom can be an excellent magical ally. For example:

"Dogwood, Send Me a Miracle" Ritual

If you're lucky enough to find a blossoming dogwood when you need it, offer the tree a green or a blue crystal by placing it near the tree's base just before 4 p.m. Then lovingly request a blossom for the purpose of manifesting the necessary miracle. If you get an inner sense that it's okay, right at the stroke of 4 p.m., respectfully snip a blossom and wrap it in clean white cloth. Thank the tree, return home immediately, unwrap the blossom, and place it in water on your altar. Leave it there until the miracle appears, and then return to the tree. Place the blossom and pour out the water at the base, thanking the tree heartily as you do so.

Physical Healing

Various species of dogwood have been employed for a wide range of medicinal purposes throughout the world. For example, the bark extract from some dogwoods have been used as a substitute for quinine (from cinchona bark) for fevers. A Japanese variety of dogwood is used in Traditional Chinese Medicine for a number of reasons, including dizziness and incontinence. Additionally, a dogwood native to the area near the Black Sea yields a fruit called the "cornelian cherry" (not really a cherry) that is reportedly delicious and also high in vitamin C. As such, it's been employed like orange juice to support the immune system in warding off colds and flu.

Magical Correspondences

Element: Spirit
Gender: Masculine
Planet: Saturn

Dragon's Blood Tree

*Y*ears ago I lived on the upper floor of a tiny Hollywood guesthouse, and a dragon's blood tree lived in the front near the mailbox. She was a whimsically funky sort, somewhat like a mysterious, self-sufficient, and exotically beautiful aunt. This unique tree looks something like a giant mushroom and emanates a potent vibrational combination of love, magic, and fierce protectiveness.

While we'll refer to them interchangeably in this section, it should be noted that two separate but similar species of *dracaena* are commonly called the dragon's blood tree: *Dracaena draco* and *Dracaena cinnabari*. *Dracaena cinnabari* is an endemic, highly endangered species from the small Socotra Archipelago, and *Dracaena draco* is a native of the Canary Islands. In addition to sharing spiky leaves and a unique, umbrellalike shape, both can be cultivated in some coastal and desert locations, and both have a deep red resin used in incense and dye that is often called "dragon's blood." (Although the endangered status of

Dracaena cinnabari makes *Dracaena draco* the only one of the two that can be responsibly purchased in this form.)

Please additionally note that there are other botanicals—such as *Jatropha dioica* and *Croton lechleri*—that also yield a resin sold as dragon's blood. This section is not referring to those.

Magical Uses

Activation

Like her famously prompt (and even impatient) astrological ruler, Mars, the dragon's blood tree does not dillydally: she's compelling, she's quick, and she means business. That's why her bright red resin can be employed to put the rush on any magical endeavor or intention, or to instantly turn up the volume on your magic's potency. For this purpose, hold your realized intention in your mind's eye. As you feel as if it's already come to pass, burn a stick of dragon's blood incense, add a bit of the resin to an incense mixture, or throw a pinch of it on a fire.

The powdered resin can also be used as an all-purpose activation formula. For example, you might sprinkle it in your wallet for fast money, on a picture of you and your partner to help you move through any stagnation in your relationship, or on your legal documents to help move things forward in any dealings that seem to be at a stalemate.

Clearing, Cleansing, and Hex Breaking

Perhaps dragon's blood incense and powder are most famous in magical circles for their ability to energetically clean and cleanse interior spaces: to help remove any lingering negativity or stagnation, to clear unwanted presences, and to help wayward spirits move into the light. This fame is well deserved, especially because the dragon's blood tree's extra benefit of protection creates an aura of positivity that lasts long after the clearing itself. Incense mixtures also containing white sage and/or frankincense can be especially effective for this particular magical use.

Additionally, in climates where she thrives, the actual tree herself can be employed for this purpose. For example, planting a dragon's blood tree in the yard after an intense spiritual clearing of a formerly haunted or otherwise energetically challenged home can help preserve the effect of the clearing and prevent the return of what was cleared.

Dragon's blood incense can be used as a smudge smoke for cleansing one's personal energy field or removing a perceived hex or a curse of any kind, and the powder can also be added to bathwater for the same purposes.

Love

Provided your intentions are pure, clear, and respectful of everyone's free will, dragon's blood can be employed for love. There are a number of ways you might do this. Here are some:

- Burn dragon's blood incense to persuade an estranged partner to return. (Make sure to do so with the intention that he or she will only do so if it is in alignment with his or her true will and most authentic good.)

- If you feel that you're losing yourself in a relationship because you're handing your power over to your partner more than you would like to, you might magically employ the resin (or the tree herself) to help you regain your footing and ground yourself in your own power. For this purpose, you might spend time with a dragon's blood tree or light a red candle and a stick of dragon's blood incense on your altar during the full moon.

- To protect and bless your relationship, you might lightly sprinkle a pinch on your wedding rings before the ceremony or on the threshold of your newly shared home.

Moon Cycle Support

Dragon's blood tree can be an excellent magical ally for any type of challenge related to your moon cycle or female reproductive health. Try visiting a tree, offering a libation of red wine, and spending time in quiet contemplation, allowing yourself to receive an energetic infusion of strength, vitality, and healing. You might also take a sea salt bath by the light of a red candle while burning dragon's blood incense.

Protection

Dragon's blood tree and dragon's blood resin are both highly protective and create an aura of potent positivity that absolutely nothing of ill intent can abide. Spend time with a tree to strengthen your natural protection, cultivate a tree on your property, or burn the incense for this purpose. Of course, a pinch of the resin along with a clove of garlic in a protection sachet would be an unbeatable companion when you feel compelled to traverse an energetically challenging location (such as a hospital, courtroom, or Hollywood casting call).

Magical Correspondences

Element: Spirit
Gender: Female
Planet: Mars

Elder

lder (*Sambucus*) may be physically small, but she's a magical giant. Magnificently wise and elegantly aloof, her complex spiritual vibe can be compared to the mysterious Moon card of the tarot deck, the austere high priestess of Avalon, the deliciously dark queen of the fae, and the wild old crone of the crossroads.

With a vibration both positive and fickle, she must be employed with caution both magically and otherwise. To illustrate, consider that the berries of some elder varieties are delicious and nutritious additions to jams and drinks, but they are also a source of highly toxic cyanide if they aren't heated properly first.

Magical Uses
Blessings

Like a fairy godmother's kiss, elderflowers bestow blessings of magic, beauty, and luck. To bless and consecrate an object for magical use or to bless an interior space for magical work, elderflowers or an elderflower infusion would be an excellent ally. This is particularly true if you have a connection to the fairies and the moon. For example, you might bathe a crystal in elderflower tea, sprinkle dried elderflower over a new wand, or use a fresh flower to fling small bits of spring water around the perimeter of a magical circle.

To bless a journey or new endeavor, brew a potion of elderflower tea, add honey, and mentally direct white light into the cup. Drink just before you embark.

Fairy Communication

It's said that standing under an elder during Beltane, Midsummer, or Samhain bestows the ability to see fairies and/or the Elf King. Perhaps this is because elders are residents of fairyland: elders and fairies certainly have a very similar vibe and magical signature. For example, fairies and elders are both selective about whom they magically work with and for what purpose. You can't just walk up to an elder tree and invoke her help for any reason. You've got to approach respectfully and you've also got to pass her magical inspection: she must approve of your intentions, demeanor, and overall vibe or—like fairies—she may cause problems for you rather than help solve them, or if you're lucky she will just give you the cold shoulder.

What's more, elders attract native birds and butterflies, and the valley elderberry longhorn beetle uses elder wood as a cozy egg-laying and incubation site. And what do birds, butterflies, and beetles have in common? They're all fairies ... No, I'm not just saying that they're aligned with fairies, I'm saying they're *actually* fairies. The next time you encounter one of these beings while you're alone, make a point of connecting with them in a way that goes beyond the usual. Really see this being in the present moment. Let go of human preconceptions and fully enter into her world. Let your consciousness speak her language. This is an intuitive and instinctive exercise rather than a logical one. Once you've completed this assignment, I'm pretty sure you'll get it. (And bonus: you'll speak fairy!)

Feminine Power

Mysterious, changeable, and emotional, the elder feels no shame in exhibiting qualities that have been dismissed by our patriarchal culture as overly feminine. Indeed, they are the very things that characterize and fuel her considerable power.

Because cosmic balance requires that we reinstate our respect for the feminine principle if we are to heal ourselves and save the world from destruction, this aspect of the elder's wisdom is particularly of the essence at this point in history. Can you feel it? We Goddess-embodying women and Goddess-honoring men are being called to step into our power and embody our role as medicine people. As the elder will whisper to you if you approach her with respect and take the time to listen, the Goddess, indeed, is rising.

Graceful Shifts and Transitions

Elder has been associated with ideal transitions from the physical to the spiritual realm, and because of this symbolism, she has traditionally been included in funerals and cemetery landscaping. Elders are also traditionally considered portals to other worlds, and places where spirits and fairies can pass through.

Healing

Elder is used extensively in herbal medicine, particularly for the flu, colds, and other respiratory issues. Intriguingly, while her flowers and berries are harvested in spring and fall respectively, she's associated with the Celtic tree month that starts on November 25 and continues until December 22 (also known as flu season). She's also been traditionally employed for help with rheumatism, another challenge that has been known to worsen in winter.

ELDERFLOWER HEALING POTION (TO AVERT OR TREAT A COLD)

To stop a cold before it starts, or at least to lessen its symptoms, brew a cup of elderflower tea at the earliest possible sign. Combine with a heaping spoonful of clover or wildflower honey (local is best) and some lemon juice (ideally fresh), and let stand for ten minutes or so. Cut a peeled garlic clove into tiny pieces, and swallow each piece like a pill, using the tea to wash it down. If there's any tea left, finish that too.

Intuition

Crowns containing elder twigs—particularly when worn at Beltane—are said to facilitate clairvoyance. The vibration of the berries as well as their deep blue/purple pigment are in alignment with energy of the third eye chakra (the energy center related to intuition that resides in the center of the forehead). Additionally, the white of the blossoms corresponds with both the moon and the crown chakra (the energy center at the top of the head that has to do with divine alignment and connection), both of which are strongly associated with intuition.

Try drinking a single glass of elderberry wine or a solitary cocktail with blueberry juice, club soda, and Saint Germain (a French liqueur made from elderflowers) before any sort of oracular or divinatory work to help unlock your intuitive gifts. These beverages might also be good choices for Beltane or Midsummer rituals, particularly if you'd like to bolster your intuition for the purpose of communing with the fairies.

Magic

One of the trees most associated with magic, the elder has been called the "witch tree." In fact, it was actually believed that witches were synonymous with elders, and that one could transform easily into the other. Elder is aligned very closely with the magical Germanic deity Hulda (also known as Mother Holle), and devotees danced ritually in circles around her trunk.

Music

People from diverse cultural groups—including Native Americans, Celts, and rural Californians—have made elder sticks into flutes. These have been used as magical tools, as when played with clear intention, the music that comes out of them can bring about energetic shifts.

Protection

Like a seasoned warrior, elder can be a highly protective ally . . . *if* you're on her good side. Otherwise, she can be a formidable foe. It is considered extremely unwise to cut down or take wood from an elder without a request and a promise to the Elder Mother (a spirit who protects and watches over all elders, avenging their unjust treatment). Author Charlotte Sophia Burne, in *The Handbook of Folklore*, says this request and promise was traditionally stated as "Old Girl, give me some of thy wood and I will give the some of mine when I grow into a tree."

While I'm not sure I would recommend that you make any binding promises to the Elder Mother, I would certainly think it wise for you to do everything in your power to avoid cutting down one of her children. When gathering any part of the elder tree for magic or any other purpose, I strongly advise that you follow your intuition in order to choose an appropriate, respectful gift to give her in return. A moonstone would be a good option, as would a bit of shiny silver, a round vanilla cake, or a loaf of freshly baked bread.

Elder can be a choice component of protection amulets of all varieties. The power that watches over the elders themselves—traditionally personified as a spirit such as Mother Holle or the Elder Mother—can be invoked to fiercely guard and shield people and animals as well. You'll just need to successfully interweave the energy of a living tree with the energy of the being you wish to protect. Only do the following ritual if you know of an elder tree that you can visit privately, and that is not in danger of being cut down or moved.

ELDER MOTHER PROTECTION

Cleanse a moonstone in a natural body of running water, and gather a glass bottle full of that water. If you're protecting a person other than yourself, ask the person to hold the stone in both hands and to consciously send a bit of their personal energy into it. If it's an animal, set the stone near the creature while it is sleeping so that it will absorb a bit of the animal's essence while it sleeps. If you're protecting yourself, send your own energy into the stone. Gather a bit of hair, a fingernail, or a naturally shed claw of the being you wish to protect. Visit an elder tree under a full moon when the sky is clear. Kneel and respectfully connect with the elder tree, admiring her beauty and magic. Offer the bottle of clear water as a libation, pouring it around her base. Then place the charged moonstone at her base, along with the hair, fingernail, or claw.

If the protection is for someone other than yourself, speak the following words:

Under protection by this tree
Safe and shielded my beloved shall be.
As long as this tree stands and grows
They shall be watched over wherever they go.

If the protection is for yourself, it will go:

Under protection by this tree
Safe and shielded I'll always be.
As long as this tree stands and grows
I shall be watched over wherever I go.

Magical Correspondences

Element: Spirit
Gender: Feminine
Planet: Moon

Elm

*I*f there is a single archetypal tree—an image that pops up in one's mind when one hears the word "tree"—it just might be the elm (*Ulmus*). An ancient, varied species that has flourished throughout Asia and Europe for millions of years, it's almost certainly imprinted in our genetic memory as a longtime friend and adored arboreal earthling.

Magical Uses

The Divine Feminine

The beloved Ainu goddess Kamui Fuchi, by some counts, was the daughter of an elm tree. In Norse mythology, the first woman, Embla, may have been fashioned out of elm wood. Kamui Fuchi is known as an emissary between the realm of humans and the realm of the Divine, and Embla was the genesis of human femininity as created directly by the god Odin. As such, the elm seems to embody not just the archetypal Divine Feminine, but also the borderland where the Divine Feminine meets humanity and human femininity is born from the Divine.

Spend time in quiet contemplation with an elm to connect with the Great Goddess and/or to awaken and embody the Goddess within.

Healing Depression

As a Bach Flower Remedy, elm is useful for healing depression stemming from the feeling that there is too much to do and no possibility of doing it all. This is particularly true for those of us who feel called to work toward healing Mother Earth and her inhabitants. You might think of this as an aspect of the tree's alignment with Saturn: the planet of limitation. The word *limitation* gets a bad rap, but in truth, boundaries are indispensable. For example, if we take it one day at a time and put one foot in front of the other, we can accomplish far more than if we set unmanageable goals and become paralyzed before we even begin. Besides, small accomplishments are often not as small as we may think: simply smiling at a stranger can set in motion a huge wave of positivity, the profound and long-term effects of which we may never comprehend, but which are real nonetheless.

If you can sense that this aspect of elm's wisdom will support you in unsticking your emotions, lifting your mood, and fueling your motivation, visit an elm and sit in quiet contemplation. You might also (or instead) take the flower essence regularly for a month.

Nymphs

Not only was the Greek name for elm derived from the name of the tree nymph Ptelea, elm is also a tree that often appears side by side with nymphs in ancient literature. Legendary mountain nymphs planted elms on the graves of the deceased, and elms were reportedly neighbors of altars and sacred wells devoted to nymphs.

To connect with the beloved nature spirits known as the nymphs, create an altar to them in the shade of an elm tree, using mostly objects found in nature and maybe one or two other items such as a chalice, statue, or bowl.

Transitions

In Homer's *Iliad* mountain nymphs plant elms at burial sites. This indicates the tree's alignment with harmonious transitions, such as the transition from the world of the living to the otherworld and realm of light. From the physical perspective, elm wood is quite flexible, and elms can thrive in a wide range of soils.

As such, elm supports magical intentions related to gracefully traversing any type of transition, including birth, death, moving, changing jobs, and ending or beginning relationships. When you're going through a period of rapid and immense change of various types, elm can help you come into the present moment and feel nourished and supported no matter what you're experiencing in the external world. To receive this sort of support, spend time in quiet contemplation with an elm or take the flower essence.

Magical Correspondences

Element: Water

Gender: Masculine and feminine

Planet: Saturn

Empress Tree

This gorgeous tree (officially known as *Paulownia tomentosa*) blossoms with an abundance of robust, foxglove-like, pale pink to lavender flowers that possess a powerful, sweet scent reminiscent of jasmine. Of course, there's way more to love about the enchanting empress tree, but if you ask me, that alone is plenty.

Other names for the empress tree include princess tree and foxglove tree.

Magical Uses

Expansion

One of the fastest-growing trees in existence, and a tree that takes root and thrives almost anywhere, the empress tree can fuel our own desires for expansion in any life area. If you're finished playing small and you want to expand your capacity to experience wealth and success, for example, the empress tree can help. She can also help with expanding your magical power or expertise, expanding your network of friends and allies, or really any other expansion-related magical intention.

For this purpose, spend time in quiet contemplation with an empress tree and request her support or try this:

....

Empress Tree Expansion Petition

When the moon is waxing or full, visit an empress tree and spread a white cloth or sheet on the ground beneath her. Take a moment to relax and tune in to the tree's energy. Then hold a white pillar candle in your hands and visualize/imagine/sense experiencing expansion in precisely the way you want to experience it. Really feel as if it's already happening. Place the candle on a holder and light it. For at least five minutes (and up to twenty), rest under the tree, breathing consciously and letting your mind relax. Allow any guidance or support to flow into your mind, body, energy field, and emotions. (This may happen above or below your conscious awareness.) When this feels complete, thank the tree and extinguish the candle. At home, place the candle on your altar and light it again at intervals until it's burned all the way down.

Love

Inhale the scent of a blossoming empress tree and you will feel as if love is truly in the air. Indeed, if you want to irresistibly magnetize an exciting romance, it's a good idea to spend time in quiet contemplation with an empress tree in spring, consciously absorbing her powers of sweetness and attraction. (Be sure to thank her afterward, inwardly or aloud, and perhaps even with a bit of red wine.)

In China, a picturesque historical custom involved planting an empress tree after the birth of a girl. Because the tree is so fast growing, the tree matured at the same rate as the girl, making it obvious to all who passed when the daughter of the house was ready for marriage. At that time, the tree would be cut down and carved into her wedding chest and other objects for her dowry.

Rebirth

The empress tree is associated with the phoenix in Chinese tradition, possibly because she survives fires by sending out new growth at the roots, and because she can be cut down to a stump and still burst forth with new shoots in the spring, again and again. As such, the empress tree can help when we have recently undergone what felt like total destruction in one or more life areas, and desire to be reborn into a stronger, more resilient, and more radiant form than ever before.

Plant or spend time with an empress tree to align yourself with her rebirthing wisdom and medicine, and allow yourself to ride the tide, surrender to the destruction of the past, and be reborn in a powerful and dynamic new form.

Magical Correspondences

Element: Fire

Gender: Feminine

Planet: Venus

Eucalyptus

Although eucalyptus is one of Australia's most famous natives, perhaps no other tree reminds me more potently of my home state of California, a state where—particularly in the coastal areas—the lofty silvery gray-green trees have been naturalized so thoroughly since being introduced in the 1850s that you notice them (and smell them) everywhere.

But you needn't have grown up in a tropical locale to be familiar with the scent of eucalyptus. A popular ingredient in cough drops, chest rubs, and other cold remedies, her fresh and purifying aroma reminds many of us of healing from every variety of respiratory congestion, from sniffles to coughs to sinus infections.

A tree that draws copious amounts of water from the soil and is simultaneously highly flammable (due to its oil), *and* a tree that is usually situated in bright, sunshiny locales located next to large bodies of water, eucalyptus has a uniquely dynamic elemental makeup that is simultaneously potently aligned with both water and fire. This is mirrored in a healing dynamic that is both warming and cooling at the same time, a sensation that can be noticeably detected when inhaling the scent of the essential oil or using medicine or body products that contain it.

You may be surprised to learn there are hundreds of varieties of eucalyptus trees, although only a portion of these appear in places other than Australia.

Magical Uses

Abundance

How's this for an abundance charm: researchers have found that eucalyptus trees actually prospect for gold, as they draw particles of this most precious metal up through their roots and out into their very leaves. They also send their roots very deeply into the earth to tap right into abundant water sources as they concurrently soak in sunlight at an uncommonly rapid rate, effectively fueling their vitality and expansion from both above and below. Not to mention, their lush, potent scent helps instantly align us with a feeling that's both energizing and relaxing, which places us right in the emotional center of prosperity consciousness. This can be of particular help when we seem to have been mired in depression, stagnation, or fear with regard to finances.

To give your finances and wealth consciousness a boost, diffuse the essential oil in your space or anoint your wallet with it (or simply place a fresh leaf or two in your wallet or near your financial documents). Here's another idea: on a new moon, place ten to twenty drops of eucalyptus oil in a small dropper bottle and fill the rest of the way with a carrier oil such as jojoba or sweet almond. Hold it in both hands and visualize very bright green or teal light with golden sparkles filling and surrounding it, empowering it with the energy of wealth. To experience greater prosperity, anoint your palms lightly with it first thing every morning until the new moon. (If you have sensitive skin, add fewer drops of essential oil into the mix or skip this step.)

Cleansing and Clearing

As mentioned above, eucalyptus is associated powerfully with the highly cleansing elements of water and fire. In much the same way that the trees are sometimes planted in swampy areas to clear excess moisture and reduce the threat of malaria, eucalyptus helps clear mucus and infection from the respiratory tract. Energetically, this action is mirrored by the trees' ability to clear negativity from, and raise the overall vibration of, a space or person. For this purpose, create a small broom from fresh branches and sweep the air while moving in a counterclockwise direction throughout a space, or sweep the person's aura (i.e., invisible energy field). Alternatively, diffuse the essential oil in a space, mist with water into which you've added a few drops of eucalyptus essential oil, or inhale the scent. Adding a few drops of the essential oil to cleaning supplies or body products (provided your skin is not overly sensitive) can also provide a cleansing and clearing action.

Fame

Because they're so packed with oil, eucalyptus trees are so flammable that they have been known to literally explode when exposed to fire. In feng shui and in the popular vernacular, fire is associated with fame. For example, when someone is becoming well-known, we say that they are "on fire," "about to catch," or "exploding." The old cliché "I can see it now—my name in lights" also paints a fiery picture, as does the very fact that we refer to celebrities as "stars." Perhaps it's no coincidence that eucalyptus trees have made themselves right at home in Hollywood, though Southern California certainly doesn't need any more flammable material in its forests.

Because of this fiery tendency of eucalyptus, as well as their proclivity for growing and spreading quickly, this tree makes for a good magical ingredient when it comes to rituals related to fame. Employ leaves, bark, sticks, branches, or oil in spells related to this purpose. For example:

Eucalyptus "On Fire" Ritual

To help increase your visibility and reputation in any given area, lovingly gather and dry nine eucalyptus leaves. When the moon is between new and full, and when it's in the sign of Leo, stand before a raging campfire, fire pit, or fireplace and hold the leaves in both hands. Visualize and feel yourself surrounded in a ball of bright, golden-orange, fiery light. Call to mind positive images and feelings associated with receiving the type of recognition you desire. To make sure that your fame is purely positive and doesn't veer into infamy, make an inner vow that you shall use your fame for love and positivity rather than for ego desires. Then place the leaves in the flames. As they burn, say:

Leaves of fire, burning bright
Surround me in your gorgeous light.
I vow to be a force of good
And to spread love like fire on wood.
My flames of fame shall now be fanned
As my name spreads throughout the land.

Healing Depression and Raising the Spirits

Energetically, depression might be compared to a swamp, as it feels stagnant and leaves unfavorable conditions in its wake. In the same way the eucalyptus draws swamp water up and away, transmuting it into vibrant, fragrant life, eucalyptus can help draw out the energetic and emotional toxins and replace stuck, depressed feelings with those of euphoria and health. This can help get energy moving and propel one out of a rut. For this purpose, spend time in quiet contemplation with a tree, add a few drops of the essential oil to your bathwater (as long as your skin isn't too sensitive), or diffuse the essential oil in your space.

Physical Healing

Popularly, eucalyptus is perhaps best known for its healing ability. When I feel like I might be catching a cold or an infection, one of the first things I do is diffuse the essential oil in the space in order to strengthen my immunity and neutralize the challenging effects of any bacteria or viruses. Traditionally, the Aborigines employed it in healing infections and fevers, and its fame has now spread throughout the world for this purpose. A popular ingredient in cough drops, cold medicine, cold and throat remedy teas, and chest rubs, it helps open the airways of the lungs, has an antiseptic action, and helps clear mucus from the lungs. It also helps sooth skin and muscle pain with its unique warming/cooling action.

Repelling Insects

I love it when our elders pass down folk wisdom. Once when my cats had fleas, my dad counseled me to place eucalyptus leaves under the rug (a recommendation he had in turn received from my grandma), so I did. While I also used the flea medicine my vet prescribed, I'm sure the leaves didn't hurt in keeping the fleas from coming back, and they certainly smelled good. Similarly, eucalyptus oil is often an ingredient in natural insect repellents, which I so prefer to the highly toxic, nonaromatherapeutic, and earth-hostile versions. When guarding against insect infestations of any sort, you might also diffuse eucalyptus essential oil in your space, along with any combination of peppermint, citronella, and/or clove.

Stress Relief

Have you ever hung out with a koala? I haven't, but I wish I had! I hear they are extremely mellow. As we know, they basically eat and hang out in eucalyptus trees all day. So if you want to get rid of stress, you might make like a koala and hang out with eucalyptus or just diffuse the essential oil in your space. (But don't eat the leaves! Koalas have some sort of evolutionary superpower going on where they can do such a thing without receiving any toxic effects. We, however, have no such power.)

Soothing Grief

In addition to eucalyptus's recognized ability to soothe pain, eucalyptus's energetic clearing action can help expectorate the tears and draw out the emotional toxins related to grief and heartbreak. Additionally, while eucalyptus leaves are a silvery gray-green, the scent and energy of the tree is more like a vibrant bright green, similar to the color associated with the heart chakra. While time really is the only real cure for loss-related pain, eucalyptus can help soothe the heart and smooth the path to healing.

Magical Correspondences

Elements: Water, Fire
Gender: Female
Planet: Saturn

Fig

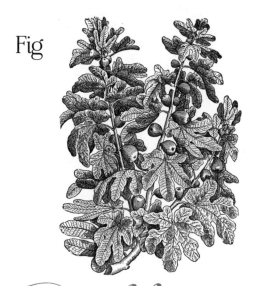

My childhood home in rural California had an old fig tree (*Ficus carica*) in the backyard, with a trunk that bent at a 90-degree angle twice—so that it grew vertically, then horizontally, and then vertically again. I loved that tree dearly and spent many magical hours in that yard, relishing fresh figs after picking them with a tin can and a blade perched on a long wooden stick (something we called "the fig picker") and frolicking among giant, vibrantly green, slightly fuzzy leaves.

The fig has been cultivated for food since very ancient times, and dried figs have been discovered at a human archaeological site that dates back to around 5,000 BCE. The grain and agriculture goddess Demeter is associated with the fig tree, and a grove of fig trees dedicated to her was located near the Eleusinian sanctuary. Indeed, you might spend time with a fig tree to connect with this most magical goddess, and incorporate the tree into meditations and visualizations if you feel guided to explore her deliciously endless mysteries.

Magical Uses

Attraction

Simply empowering a fig with your own positive energy (i.e., holding it in your hands and mentally sending bright light into it) and giving it to a romantic partner is an excellent way to increase the attraction between you. As a matter of fact, the fig has been employed as an aphrodisiac and is associated with both Aphrodite and Hathor (goddesses of love and pleasure) as well as Dionysus, a god of intoxication and sexuality.

....

CHARM YOUR LOVER WITH A FIG

In order to avoid undesirable karmic repercussions, I suggest doing this with a partner who is completely on board with the idea of the two of you bewitching each other and who fully desires to participate (and likes figs). By candlelight, begin by each holding a clean fig in your open left palm and cradling your left hand in your right while facing each other. Consciously connect with the energy of the fruit in your hands as you chant together:

> *Seduced by my sweetness*
> *Drawn to my arms*
> *Enthralled by my presence*
> *Bewitched by my charms.*

Offer the fig to your partner (so that you are feeding it to each other), and mindfully enjoy.

Divination

To choose between two options, or two possible courses of action, place a symbol, image, or representation of each one on your altar (even something as simple as words or phrases written on slips paper—like "yes" and "no" or "Phoenix" and "Albuquerque"—

will work fine). Place one freshly picked fig leaf beneath or near one symbol, and another beneath or near the other. Light a stick of incense and call on the Divine in a way that feels powerful for you, perhaps invoking a specific divinity associated with the fig tree, such as Demeter, Juno, or Hathor. Bring to mind your thoughts and concerns, and then offer up the challenge to the Divine, requesting clarity about the best path to take. Relax completely, trusting that you will receive the guidance you seek. Then leave the altar as it is, keeping an eye on it over the next one to five days to see which leaf stays fresh longer. The fresher leaf will indicate the divine recommendation. If they both wither quickly, explore additional options. If they both stay fresh for an uncommon length of time, both options are viable.

Fertility and Potency

Dionysus—in addition to being the Greek god of intoxication and sexuality—was a god of fertility. Statues of him and phalluses associated with him were fashioned out of fig wood. Additionally, the ancient Greek word for testicles is the same as the plural word for figs. Certainly, fig trees, including their fruit and leaves, possess a palpably lusty and potent vibration. If you know how to whittle, create a phallus out of fig wood as a potency or fertility charm, or just eat a fig or two for the same magical purpose. If possible, and weather permits, another excellent (and exceptionally fun) option would be to dance naked under a fig tree as the full moon shines brightly in the night sky.

Grounding

After rituals or intuitive work, or really anytime you feel like you could use some grounding in the physical world, try indulging in a small feast of figs. They'll help balance your energy and blood sugar while energetically anchoring you and aligning you with the energy of the earth.

Luck

In ancient Rome, the fig tree was considered quite lucky. It goes back to the legendary beginnings of Rome, when the ancient city's founders, Romulus and Remus, were famously nursed by a wolf beneath a fig tree. Similarly, the matron goddess of Rome and protector of the state's prosperity, Juno, was associated with the fig tree, especially in her fertility goddess aspect. To bless a project or a group with luck, serve figs, eat figs, carry a fig leaf, or decorate with fig leaves.

Magical Power

Sexual energy has a lot to do with attracting and manifesting desires. Therefore, in many ways, sexual potency is synonymous with magical power. Because we're talking about sexual potency in a vibrational/energetic sense (i.e., one's attractive power and intensity rather than one's ability to "perform" or reproduce), this is true for those of all genders, ages, and sexual orientations. Because of the fig tree's fertile and potent vibe, simply spending time with a fig tree, particularly when it's done with respect and clear intention, can increase one's magical power considerably. This effect intensifies profoundly when the tree is flourishing near your home.

Remote Communication

To communicate a message or emotion to someone who is off the grid or otherwise unable to connect in the usual ways, or if you just prefer to connect by magical means, stand outside on a windy day and hold a fig leaf between both palms. Concentrate on what you'd like to communicate, sending the energy of your message into the leaf. Hold the leaf over your head and mentally connect with your desired recipient. When a gust of wind reaches a peak, release the leaf. (Rest assured that the leaf need not travel far physically in order for the message to be received.)

Travel

To ensure that you or someone you love will return from a journey safely, empower a fig leaf with that intention. Hold it between both hands and visualize yourself or your loved one returning home joyfully and in high spirits. Then place it on your altar or mantel. After the completion of the journey and the return home, gratefully release the leaf in the wind, float it on a moving body of water, or place it at the base of a tree.

Vitality

If your energy is flagging, your health needs bolstering, or your enthusiasm is waning, you might simply consume that hearty little purple fig with its sweet, bright scarlet, seed-filled flesh. In addition to its considerable magical benefits, the fruit is packed with minerals, fruit sugar, and fiber, and it's been used medicinally as a detoxifier, laxative, and blood tonic.

Magical Correspondences

Element: Earth
Gender: Masculine
Planet: Sun

Aligned with the Great Goddess and spirit of the forest, the pungent and mystical fir (*Abies*) possesses a magical energy like no other. A popular choice for a Christmas tree, fir's many varieties can often be recognized as distinct from other conifers by the flattened look of her needles and the way they are relatively soft to the touch.

Magical Uses

Abundance

Fir's delicious fragrance and the way she appears green and thriving all year round speak to her verdant, abundant energy and her ability to help us magnetize abundant wealth. For this purpose, spend time in quiet contemplation with a fir when the moon is between new and full, and then offer her a silver dollar by placing it at the base of her trunk.

Rebirth and Regeneration

Like the planet Pluto that is her ruler, fir is about intense regeneration, which by its very definition requires destruction and disintegration as a mandatory prerequisite. This is much like childbirth, which requires intense pain and complete annihilation of the way the lives of the parents and child were before the child's delivery into this physical world. Indeed, fir needles have been burned to mitigate the pain of childbirth and smooth the child's transition out of the womb. Perhaps not surprisingly, the fir was associated with Osiris, the Egyptian god who was famously destroyed and resurrected, as well as Artemis, the Greek goddess who is known (among many other things) as an overseer of childbirth.

Shadow Work

We all encounter times when it would benefit us to gaze into our shadowy depths and bring what we most fear about ourselves out into the light. Fir—a tree that is used even by self-proclaimed non-magical folk to shine light into the darkest and coldest time of the year (as a Christmas tree)—is an excellent ally for times like these.

When you feel called to engage in this form of brave self-exploration and excavation, consider initiating your shadow work by aligning your energy with that of a fir tree. Do this by simply sitting in quiet contemplation with one. Watch your breath as it goes in and out until you feel very still. Then naturally open up to the fir's energy and feel yourself receiving an infusion of strength, courage, and wisdom. Imagine that the fir is blessing you with a metaphorical lantern that you can use to shine light in the darkest recesses of your innermost self.

Magical Correspondences

Element: Earth
Gender: Feminine
Planet: Pluto

Fringetree

This native to the southeastern United States owes his name to his most delicate, wispy, and otherworldly white flowers. Resembling clouds from a distance and feathers or fringe up close, the spring blooms of the fringetree (*Chionanthus*) give one the sense that one is safe and all is well.

Magical Uses

Divine Protection

This tree may be physically little, but his consciousness is vast. Simply gazing at (or even just visualizing) a fringetree—particularly one in bloom—reminds us that we are never alone, and that we have friends in high places. That's why fringetree is an excellent magical ally to invoke for protection and safety, particularly when we are navigating through uneasiness and anxiety.

Fringetree Protection Ritual

Place a framed picture of a blossoming fringetree on your altar and light a white pillar candle and a stick of frankincense incense. Breathe deeply and imagine yourself in the presence of the tree. When this visualization feels strong, allow yourself to receive an energetic infusion of divine protection and let your consciousness shift to the awareness that you are safe and all is well. Alternatively, if you know of a fringetree in bloom nearby, visit and offer him a small clear quartz and a libation of blessed water. Then request his assistance and receive the infusion as above.

Harmony and Ease

The more aligned we are with the Divine, the more harmonious we feel and the more things seem to flow easily and effortlessly for us. This is the wisdom of the fringetree, who—if we choose to allow this—distinctly bestows the sense that we are already experiencing heaven on earth. So, if your life seems to be beset by struggles and hassles, visit or visualize a fringetree, incorporate him into your magic, or take the flower essence.

Interestingly, this soothing and smoothing action of the fringetree is mirrored in the physical realm in the way that his roots and bark were once employed by Native Americans to treat congestion and skin infections.

Prosperity

"Prosperity is your natural state," says the fringetree. "Remember this, and all the riches and blessings you desire are already yours." For prosperity magic that is equal parts pleasant and powerful, visit a fringetree in spring or summer. Spread a blanket beneath him and recline, gazing at his beauty and allowing him to shower you with his wisdom. Feel every cell and atom of your mind, body, and energy field shifting into resonance with true divine prosperity.

Magical Correspondences

Element: Air
Gender: Masculine
Planet: Jupiter

Ginkgo

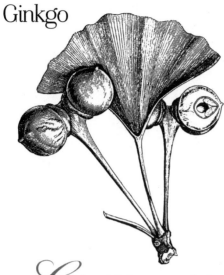

*G*inkgo biloba, or maidenhair tree, is quite literally the most ancient of all tree species still alive today. The sole survivor of the more than 250-million-year-old ginkgo family, he evolved long before flowering plants. This unique fernlike lush green living fossil turns a beautiful goldenrod color in the fall. He is revered in Buddhist, Taoist, and Confucian traditions.

Magical Uses
Ancient Wisdom

In addition to being the most ancient of living tree species, individual ginkgos can live for up to 2,500 years. Some planted by temples in Asia are believed to be more than 1,500 years old. In China he has been called the "grandfather-grandchild tree" due to the fact that his maturing process is roughly equivalent to that of three human generations.

In the same way that these trees have carried their unique living DNA blueprint into the present time, they have also carried a most profound wisdom and power forward from the earth's incomprehensibly ancient past. Indeed, the ginkgo's energy is primordial and pure, like the dawn in the clearest and most open of skies.

This energy is so potent, in fact, that simply gazing at the tree for a brief moment can nourish your wisdom and presence with an awe-inspiring depth. Taking a longer moment to tune in and sit in quiet contemplation has even more lasting and far-reaching benefits.

Hope

Would you believe that there was a small number of ginkgo trees within a one-mile radius of the atom bomb dropped on Hiroshima in 1945, and that these trees not only survived the blast, but also continue to thrive to this day? It's difficult to comprehend, but it's reportedly true! In fact, monuments to world peace are now placed near some of the trees, and the ginkgo is thought of as "the bearer of hope."

Luck

It's almost impossible to think of anything with more auspicious energy than a ginkgo tree. If you have the tiniest amount of intuitive ability, you will sense the tree virtually pulsating with pure positivity and luck.

....

BAD LUCK BANISHING/GOOD LUCK CONJURING RITUAL

On a full or new moon, empower nine clean, shiny coins (dimes or pennies would work great) in sunlight, and place them around the base of a ginkgo. If you sense that it's okay with the tree, lovingly cut a sprig with clippers or large scissors and inwardly thank the tree profusely. Then simply sweep your body and aura with the sprig. As you do so, feel bad luck departing quickly and good luck arriving abundantly and in full force. Thank the tree again and place the sprig near his base.

Protection from Fire

Ginkgo is a magical fire protector (certainly the tree's survival of the atom bomb seems to indicate a supernatural power) and is believed to have protected temples near which he's planted from fires that would otherwise have destroyed them. In addition to holding moisture in his leaves that may naturally discourage flames, it's postulated that his sap may be a powerful flame retardant. For magical fire protection, plant ginkgos near your home.

Wealth

Ginkgo's lushness, his longstanding and deeply rooted wisdom, his luck, and his amazing survival abilities all lend themselves to his ability to magically confer and encourage wealth. To release blocks to abundance and align yourself with the infinite generosity and supply of the universe, spend time in quiet contemplation with a ginkgo tree.

Magical Correspondences

Element: Spirit
Gender: Masculine
Planet: Sun

Hawthorn

*H*awthorn (*Crataegus*) may be small, but she's also one of the most magical trees in the Western traditions. Running through the folklore and herbal healing wisdom of countless cultures and continents, she's associated with love, fairies, the Great Goddess, and the divine marriage between the Goddess and the God.

To this day, the British royal family's Christmas table is adorned with a flowering sprig of Glastonbury thorn. Related in myth to both Jesus and King Arthur, hawthorn is a descendant of the same biannually flowering tree that was legendarily born of Joseph of Arimathea's staff when he placed it in the ground at Glastonbury.

Magical Uses
Embracing What Is

Magically, hawthorn is highly protective, in large part because of her ability to bring us fully into the present moment. After all, when we're fully present, we're both relaxed and alert, which makes us ready to defend ourselves swiftly and effectively.

Medicinally, hawthorn has been employed in a number of cultures and continents to support digestion. This mirrors her ability to help us "digest" and harmoniously assimilate what is true in any given moment. By helping us surrender to what really is—not what "should" or "shouldn't" be—we release resistance and move through challenges in the most ideal of ways.

Fairy Communication

Hawthorn has long been considered a tree associated with fairies and the border between the realms. Her flowering branches are used to decorate on Beltane, when the veil between the human world and fairyland is the thinnest. Consequently, she's also aligned with the sacred union of the pagan Goddess and God that is traditionally celebrated on this day.

Furthermore, the hawthorn is dear to the fairy realm because of her many contributions to the care and feeding of wildlife. By providing food, shelter, and nectar, she supports the lives of many varieties of birds, mammals, and insects.

Heart Healing

Medicinally, hawthorn has been used to strengthen the physical heart. Author Fred Hageneder states in *The Meaning of Trees*, "Trials have shown that it helps in the treatment of high blood pressure and mild to moderate heart failure, while also helping to reduce the anxiety associated with these conditions."

Magically, hawthorn's vibration has long been employed to heal broken hearts. For example:

HAWTHORN HEALING WATER FOR A BROKEN HEART

To facilitate and speed the healing of a broken heart, gather two bottles of clean drinking water and visit a blossoming hawthorn tree. Sit or stand comfortably and breathe consciously as you relax your body and come into the present moment. When you feel grounded and centered, hold both bottles and say a prayer of blessing. Call on angels or simply the Divine to bless the water with pure, vibrant white light. Envision the water pulsating with this light. As an offering, pour one of the bottles around the base of the tree. Then request that the tree bless the other bottle with a vibration that will support the healing of your broken heart in exactly the way that is most needed. Trust that the tree responds according to your wish. When you feel ready, drink the water. As you do so, feel it filling you with a beautiful healing and balancing light.

Protection from Vampires

According to Serbian legend, if you want to kill a vampire with a stake, it must be made of hawthorn. Apparently, this is due to the vampire's allergy to the wood, which is reminiscent of the famed aversion to garlic.

Of course, vampires in the movies drink blood, and there are actually some people who enjoy doing so; though usually not the blood of nonconsenting adults. Self-aware psychic vampires are also often quite ethical about receiving consent. The problem, how-ever, are the people who greedily prey on others by draining their energy in the form of money, vitality, or power. If, for any reason, you feel that you are uncomfortably close to unpleasantly predatory vampires of this variety, you may want to carry the following charm:

....

HAWTHORN VAMPIRE WARD

Lovingly gather a hawthorn twig under the bright noonday sun. Empower a clove of garlic in this same sunlight, and then tie both into a bit of deep red flannel. When you need protection from vampires, carry it in your pocket or use a safety pin to secure it under your clothes.

Weddings

As a member of the rose family and a plant with a five-petaled flower (making her sacred to the Goddess), hawthorn is associated with joyful commitment and lasting romantic love. Flowering hawthorn branches were traditionally employed in wedding ceremonies and were used to adorn altars to Hymen, the Greek god of marriage celebrations.

To precipitate a proposal or to bless a proposal you're planning to make, place flowering hawthorn on your altar on a Friday during the waxing moon.

Wishes

If you discover a hawthorn growing near a sacred well or a natural spring, you can confide in her a wish. Then tie a small bit of ribbon or colored yarn around one of her branches to demonstrate that you fully release the ideal unfolding of your wish to her infinite wisdom.

Magical Correspondences

Element: Earth
Gender: Feminine
Planet: Ceres

Hazel

Extremely sacred in a number of cultures, the verdant hazel (*Corylus*) is often found growing alongside holy wells in England. In addition to being aligned with the gods in a number of ancient pantheons, the hazel's delicious, protein-rich nuts have been a treasured food for millennia.

Magical Uses

Communication

The Greek god of communication, Mercury, received a caduceus of hazel as a gift from the god of harmony. It's said that he used it to bestow blessings of peace and communication upon humankind.

To facilitate harmonious communication or to counteract the challenges associated with Mercury retrograde periods, lovingly gather a hazel branch. Use it to bless a room or a building by sweeping the air around the perimeter of the space while moving in a clockwise direction. For the same purposes, lightly tap communication devices (like phones and computers) with a hazel wand.

Immortality

With delicate blossoms in late winter or very early spring, German tradition aligns the hazel tree with immortality. Sacred to the god Thor, the wisdom of the hazel reminds us of our true eternal nature and divine spark of infinite light. To align with this wisdom, spend time in quiet contemplation with a hazel tree.

Dowsing

Hazel branches are a traditional choice for "Y rods," which are used to dowse for underground water and buried treasure. It's said that they're most powerful when cut from the tree between sunset and sunrise while facing east. It's also said that cutting the rod the day before Midsummer makes it particularly potent.

Magic

Very much like the Magician card in the tarot deck, hazel is like a lightning rod with the ability to draw magic from the heavenly invisible realm and bring it into the earthly realm of physical manifestation. Indeed, according to tradition, Jewish magicians wielded wands of hazel.

Hazel also teaches about the balance of duality: of yin and yang, masculine and feminine, light and dark, and about consciously employing this duality in order to create positive change. This is an important key to both Eastern and Western magical traditions.

To receive magical wisdom and power from a hazel, hug a hazel tree or sit with your spine resting against the tree. Feel the tree's energy moving your own energy from the crown of your head to your feet and vice versa. In addition to empowering you with the unique magic of hazel, this will align and activate your chakras and subtly balance your energy field.

Wisdom

For the Celts, hazelnuts were powerful symbols and receptacles of wisdom. In fact, the Salmon of Knowledge, a fish who could live despite being eaten, was a regular mortal salmon until he ate nine hazelnuts from the trees that grew around the Well of Wisdom that was his home. After eating these hazelnuts, the salmon possessed all the wisdom of the world. Later, when a servant boy named Fionn mac Cumhaill (pronounced Finn McCool) was asked by his master to cook the fish, he checked with his thumb to see if it was cooked, burned his thumb, and then licked it. At that moment he was imbued with all the wisdom of the world too, and he grew up to be a legendary hero.

Hazelnut Wisdom Spell

To magically summon more wisdom, roast exactly nine hazelnuts by cooking them at 350 degrees Fahrenheit for thirteen minutes. Cool completely. Hold them in your right hand and charge them in bright sunlight as you say:

> *Wisdom deep and wisdom wide*
> *Be my rudder, be my guide.*
> *Fill me with a knowledge vast*
> *And understanding that shall last.*

Then, one by one, eat them.

Magical Correspondences

Element: Spirit
Gender: Feminine and masculine
Planet: Mercury

Hemlock

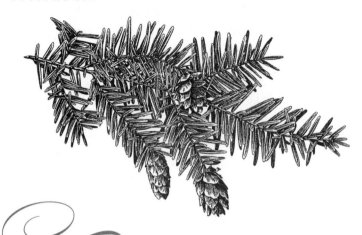

*T*otally unrelated to the infamously poisonous plant (although reportedly possessing a similar scent), the intensely magical hemlock tree (*Tsuga*) is a gorgeous, lush, nontoxic evergreen, native to North America and Asia. Some hemlocks grow quite tall and can live up to 900 years.

Magical Uses

Cleansing

The hemlock's lovely scent and ancient, steadfast vibration lend themselves to the tree's intense spiritual cleansing properties. A branch or wand of hemlock would be an excellent tool for any type of magic related to energetically cleansing a person, animal, object, or space.

Fire Magic

When working magic involving an actual fire—such as a bonfire or a fireplace—try throwing a tiny pinch of dried hemlock needles on the fire and watch them spark up and awaken the spirit of the fire. Similarly, this can be done to activate any sort of energy when you empower the dried needles with your intention before casting them to the flames.

Secrets and Mysteries

Aligned with both the goddess Hecate and the god Pluto, the hemlock is powerfully associated with what is unseen, what is hidden, and all that lies beneath the obvious and the known. Spend time with a hemlock when it's your intention to delve into your depths and to chip away at the mystery of who you really are. (What really motivates you? What is your spiritual lineage? Who have you been in previous lives?) Hemlock can also be an excellent ally for those times when you are exploring spiritual mysteries and unlocking the secrets of the stars.

Additionally, when you wish to cast a veil over your motives or shroud yourself in an enticing web of mystery, try bringing hemlock into your magical work. If, for example, you feel you need a little armor in the form of a magical disguise or a bit of a softening and smudging of the broader brushstrokes of your personality, or if you just want to appear charmingly mysterious for any given social occasion, try this:

....

VEIL OF MYSTERY CHANT

Visit a hemlock at night (if necessary, bring a flashlight to get there and a candle to light once you're there) and offer her an entire bottle of chardonnay by pouring it around her roots. Then place your hands on her trunk. Feel yourself absorbing the tree's mysterious majesty as you say:

Beloved Hemlock, for one night
Adorn my true and simple light.
Like your secret depths so rare
May my peculiar charm ensnare.

Thank the tree from your heart, then go forth and mesmerize! You have until sunrise the next morning. (And please be careful with your ability to enchant: you'll want to be sure not to manipulate anyone into doing anything they wouldn't normally do.)

Shadow Work

Finally, the hemlock tree is a most superb ally when it comes to looking at the shadow: the part of our own personality made up of every true thing about ourselves that we deny or prefer not to claim. We all have a shadow, so it's nothing to be ashamed of. But the more we bravely shine light into our shadow self, the more of our true power we reclaim. Over time, the relationship between the bright half and the shadow half becomes easier and more fluid, and we no longer have to dread looking into the dark. This is a key aspect to embodying the fullness of our joy, true destiny, and magical authority.

For support with bravely plumbing your shadowy depths, spend time with a hemlock tree, or bring hemlock into your visualizations. Additionally, you might light a fire and throw a bit of dried hemlock needles onto the flames in order to symbolize transforming the stuck and hidden parts of yourself into lightness, brightness, and power.

Magical Correspondences

Element: Fire
Gender: Feminine
Planet: Pluto

Hickory

*H*ickory—the mere name of this tree is a poem that conjures up images of mystical natural settings and soul-cleansing fires with billowing, fragrant smoke.

While magical writers have, in the past, classified hickory as a masculine tree—perhaps because of the famous strength of her wood and her generally imposing energetic character—my impression is that *she*, in fact, represents the immense fortitude of the feminine body, mind, and emotions. After all, who is fiercer than a protective mother figure, and what is more awe-inspiring than the amazing power of the female body to move through the ever-changing cycles of menstruation and endure the ordeal of childbirth?

Note: This section covers typical and Asian hickories of the family Carya. For pecan hickories (also of the family Carya), see "Pecan."

Magical Uses

Childbirth Support

Hickory wood is exceptional in its combination of strength and solidity, although the living branches are quite flexible in the breeze. This is mirrored by hickory's energetic ability to help fortify our minds, bodies, and spirits while simultaneously supporting us in moving with the changes and allowing *what is* to be. As such, hickory can be magically employed to help support the childbirth process. For this purpose, within a month or two before giving birth, visit a hickory tree and sit or stand in quiet contemplation. Through your thoughts and feelings, convey your upcoming challenge to the tree, and request an energetic infusion of both fortitude and flexibility.

Land Nourishment

In addition to nourishing any given area with her strong and wise presence, hickory provides food for squirrels, moths, and beetles, and her leaves lend beneficial minerals to the soil. Plant hickory (or thank existing hickory) for lending a sense of lushness and fertility to the land. (Because of the feng shui law that the condition of our space mirrors the condition of our life and vice versa, this, in turn, can help nourish your degree of wealth and prosperity.)

Protection from Legal Difficulties

Like a no-nonsense judge, hickory's vibration is intolerant of legal unfairness or undeserved hassles. That's why she can help cut through the red tape and shield you from unnecessary litigation. For this purpose, empower a hickory nut in sunlight and mentally charge it with the intention to protect you from any and all legal difficulties. Place it on your altar or carry it in your pocket.

Transitions

In addition to supporting the transition of childbirth (as mentioned on page 160), hickory has been employed to help transitioned spirits find their way to the light. For this purpose, burn hickory incense or throw a hickory log on the fire.

Magical Correspondences

Element: Air

Gender: Feminine

Planet: Mars

Holly

An extremely ancient and widespread plant, the holly (*Ilex*) is drenched in mystery and tradition. The Druids decorated with holly at the winter solstice, the Romans employed the branches in their Saturnalia celebrations, and to this day Brazilian rainforest inhabitants enjoy a sacred, energizing tea from the leaves of a holly species called yerba mate. (Do be aware that many holly varieties are poisonous to humans, however.) Even in the mainstream imagination, holly is associated with magic; her wood was used to fashion Harry Potter's wand.

Magical Uses

Energy

Since very ancient times, glossy-leaved, red-berried holly has been magically employed during the coldest, darkest time of the year as a way to ignite the spirit and feed the inner flame. Yerba mate, an energizing tea, is made from a variety of holly leaf containing caffeine and theobromine (which is also in chocolate), as well as minerals and amino acids. Luckily, this tea—which bestows not just energy but also a mildly euphoric state—can now be purchased at most health food stores. (When purchasing, do make sure it's organic, fairly traded, and sustainably harvested.)

Fairies

An ancient belief states that fairies inhabit holly trees and that bringing a branch into the home brings fairies in with it. Similarly, planting a holly tree in your yard can summon fairies, and spending time with a holly tree can align you with the realm of the fae.

Positivity

Flower essence pioneer Edward Bach described the holly flower essence remedy as being helpful for "those who are sometimes attacked by thoughts of such kind as jealousy, envy, revenge, suspicion…Within themselves they may suffer much, often when there is no real cause for their unhappiness." Flower essence therapists recommend taking the essence regularly to support an open heart and a general attitude of positivity and openness.

Additionally, simply spending time with a holly tree or bringing her leaves, branches, or berries into your home (or placing them on your altar) can help infuse you and your household with this purely positive vibe. This can be particularly helpful when it's your intention to banish bickering, arguing, gossiping, resentment, negative expectation, or any other indication of discord.

Protection

There is a long-standing and widespread tradition of employing holly to repel all forms of negativity, danger, and ill intent. It's said that throwing holly in the direction of a wild animal will cause the animal to stop attacking, and that a holly in the yard will protect from both evil and lightning. In ancient Persia and India, water infused with holly bark was used to bless newborn children; as a modern incarnation of this ancient practice, you might gently anoint the head of a newborn with a little water into which you've added a drop or two of holly flower essence.

Interestingly, birds sometimes use spiky-leaved holly trees as literal protection from predators by taking refuge in their branches. This is especially convenient for the species of birds that thrive on the tree's fruit, which is toxic to humans but not to birds.

Victory

In both myth and history (and in both Europe and the Americas) holly wood has been used for arrows and spears. With little berries (actually "drupes") that resemble—both energetically and literally—the warrior planet Mars, holly has a fierceness that lends itself to victory.

....

HOLLY VICTORY CHARM

To achieve victory on behalf of any sort of worthy cause, place nine holly berries in a red drawstring bag during the full moon, then carry it close to you.

Magical Correspondences

Element: Fire

Gender: Masculine and feminine

Planet: Mars

Hornbeam

*W*hat a beautiful little toughie is the hornbeam (*Carpinus*)! In addition to being radiant with power and magic, her wood is some of the hardest around. It has been historically employed to make wagon wheels and chariots, and in more modern times it has been featured on the elegant doors of the Rolls-Royce. Also, when used for fuel, her wood burns quite hot and for an exceptionally long while.

Magical Uses
Boundaries

Aligned with both earth and sun, and with a bright, hot, and long-burning fire, the hornbeam's essence reminds me of the Celtic fire goddess Brighid. Like Brighid, you can call on hornbeam for help with creating fiery boundaries through which negativity or anything that is not in alignment with your energy cannot cross. For example:

Hornbeam Fiery Boundary Ritual

Anytime you need to establish a really powerful and positive boundary, you might lovingly gather a fallen stick from a hornbeam, simply offering a few heartfelt words of thanks in return. When you're back home (or wherever you're staying), safely build a fire in a fireplace or a fire pit. When it's really burning, hold the stick in both hands. Get really clear on the boundary you want to set: what is allowed to cross it and what is not. (This can work with people, situations, or dynamics.) When this feels really strong in your mind, body, and spirit, toss the stick in the fire. As it's burning, say:

> *Hornbeam, by your sacred name*
> *Surround me in a wall of flame.*
> *What I choose to allow shall stay*
> *And what I choose to reject shall stray.*
> *By forest, sunlight, sky, and sea*
> *As I will it, so shall it be.*

Hold the vision for a bit longer as the fire warms you. Feel strong in your conviction to set this boundary and know that for as long as you actively choose to keep it, it shall remain.

Enthusiasm

Hornbeam flower essence is often taken under the tongue or in water for a dose of bright-eyed enthusiasm, particularly when one's energy is flagging due to a lack of joy in one's daily tasks. One of the original thirty-eight remedies created by flower essence pioneer Dr. Edward Bach in the 1930s, it can be found at a large percentage of health food stores to this day. Try taking two drops under the tongue twice a day for a month. Pair with white chestnut essence if your frenetic thoughts are adding to your exhaustion or with wild oat essence if you're pining for a life path that will bring you more natural enthusiasm.

Protection

Due to its protective benefits, Hildegard von Bingen, a renowned herbalist of the 1100s, recommended sleeping under a hornbeam if one found it necessary to sleep in a forest. In addition to the fiery boundary ritual, for protective purposes you might plant one or more hornbeams in your yard and request that they protect your home from any and all ill will or negativity from both seen and unseen worlds.

Solving Puzzles

Hornbeams have traditionally been employed as hedges in labyrinths. In his 1838 book *Arboretum et Fruticetum Britannicum*, author John Claudius Loudon writes that "the object in planting a labyrinth is to form a puzzle, first to discover the centre, and afterwards to find the way out again." If possible, wandering through a labyrinth fashioned of living hornbeam can be an excellent way to shed bright light on anything that's been puzzling you. Similar benefits can be found by simply visiting a hornbeam with your challenge in mind, and then relaxing and tuning in to the wisdom of the tree.

Magical Correspondences

Element: Earth
Gender: Feminine
Planet: Sun

Jabuticaba

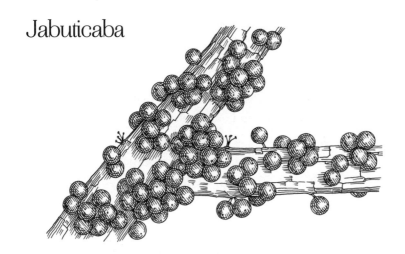

ave you ever seen fruit growing along a trunk, in addition to branches, so that the entire tree looks, incredibly, like it's dripping with giant black pearls? If so, you've probably been to Brazil and seen a jabuticaba tree (*Plinia cauliflora*, also known as a Brazilian grape tree). Before the sweet, grapelike fruits appear (which are used to make jelly and wine), white flowers line the trunk like snowy chrysanthemumlike sea creatures. And these truly unique tropical beauties can go through near-constant blooming and fruit cycles, providing delicious, sweet fruit year round. Talk about magical—not to mention reminiscent of something you might find in Willy Wonka's edible landscape!

Magical Uses

Nourishment

With her near-constant, uncommonly abundant supply of delicious fruit, jabuticaba is truly a representative of the divine earth mother, offering us sweet nourishment and hydration directly from her very body. Spending time with a jabuticaba or meditating on her image, one can see quite clearly that Mother Earth indeed wants to provide an abundance of sustenance and sweetness for her beloved children.

Sweetness

Speaking of sweetness, jabuticaba is literally dripping with it. A powerful symbol and literal representation of the true sweetness of nature and of life itself, spend time with jabuticaba, eat her fruit, or visualize her to summon more sweetness into your life and to enjoy the sweetness that already surrounds you.

Tortoise Alignment

Jabuticaba is derived from the word in the archaic Tupi language meaning "turtle" or "tortoise," likely because tortoises gather at the base of the tree for a sweet feast of fallen fruit. Visualize or spend time with a jabuticaba to align more deeply with your tortoise friends or to glean insights into speaking their language. If possible, enjoying some of the fruit with a tortoise would be an excellent way to increase your magical and emotional bond. You might also adorn your home or altar with artwork depicting the gorgeous jabuticaba if tortoise communication or alignment is one of your magical goals.

Magical Correspondences

Elements: Water, Earth, Spirit
Gender: Feminine
Planet: Ceres

Jacaranda

Like a sunrise, a monarch butterfly, or a rainbow around the moon, a jacaranda (of the Bignoniaceae family) in bloom is one of those rare sights so laden with miraculous beauty that it never fails to make your heart swell and your breath catch. And a street lined with these purple-flowered, feathery-leaved creatures? It's like being in a dream. A native to Central and South America, this celebrated beauty of the tree world is now present in nearly every tropical climate on the planet.

Magical Uses

Beauty

According to legend, the creator god in the Guarani pantheon, Tupa, asked the trees how they wanted to be when they were grown. Without hesitation, the jacaranda simply requested to wear lilac during a portion of each year. Truly, her purple flowers are her most memorable feature. When in bloom, she isn't just a tree with purple blossoms: she's an ethereal being that is completely bedecked in a delicate and otherworldly violet.

Could an actual unicorn sighting be more inspirational? *As* inspirational, surely, but *more*? I tend to think not. (Do you suspect I'm guilty of exaggeration? I guarantee that those who have seen a jacaranda in bloom can confirm.)

Alice Walker wrote in *The Color Purple*, "I think it pisses God off if you walk by the color purple in a field somewhere and don't notice it. People think pleasing God is all God cares about. But any fool living in the world can see that it is always trying to please us back." Indeed, just as the Divine provides wholesome food to nourish our bodies, the Divine provides an abundance of beauty to nourish our spirits. Receiving, allowing, and embodying this divine beauty is an essential component of the wisdom and magic of the jacaranda.

To inspire yourself with divine beauty and to glean some of the jacaranda's beauty for yourself, spend time with a blossoming jacaranda. You might also bless a bottle of water and then offer it to the tree with love, requesting an infusion of beauty.

Healing

While I don't recommend trying this at home unless you know an expert on the practice, the jacaranda's bark and leaves have been employed for soothing the skin, treating syphilis and gonorrhea, healing ulcers, and supporting the lungs and respiratory system. What I *can* recommend is visiting the tree, whether in bloom or not, in order to soothe stress, bolster the immune system, lift the spirits, and receive a powerful infusion of healing energy. Taking the flower essence can also support both physical and emotional healing of all varieties, particularly when stress relief and relaxation are important concerns.

Music

In Brazil guitars have been fashioned out of jacaranda wood, and the author Alejandro Dolina writes of a legendary jacaranda tree in Buenos Aires that can be persuaded to whistle tango songs. Additionally, celebrated Argentine poet, writer, and composer María Elena Walsh has composed a song in the tree's honor. To enhance your musical abilities and get support in developing any music-related art (including playing, singing, composing, or dancing to music), visit a jacaranda. Express your desire for her musical assistance, and offer her a bottle of excellent white wine by pouring it around her roots.

Scholastic Success

In South Africa and Australia jacaranda blossoms are associated with study, scholastic success, and passing one's exams. Visit a blossoming jacaranda or take two drops of the flower essence under the tongue two to three times per day for support with these intentions.

Wealth

While jacarandas are energetically watery and delicate, they also have a quietly lush and expansive quality. These two aspects lend themselves to that understated sort of elegance exhibited by those who are so comfortable with themselves and their wealth that they have no need to be obvious or flashy. That's why you might magically employ jacaranda not for a quick-fix sort of wealth magic, but rather for the kind of wealth magic that will shift you into a more longstanding, sustainable sort of affluence.

....

Jacaranda Wealth Charm

Press a jacaranda blossom between two two-dollar bills in a large book until dry. Roll the four-dollar sandwich toward yourself into a scroll, tie with a narrow purple ribbon, and anoint with essential oil of juniper. Place it near your financial documents or in the far left corner of your home or business (when facing the space from the front door).

Magical Correspondences

Element: Water
Gender: Feminine
Planet: Jupiter

Joshua Tree

Joshua Tree National Park in Southern California is one of the most magical and mystical places on earth. The tree for which it's named, a palmlike/cactuslike variety of yucca (from the agave family) that is unique to very specific and limited areas in the southwest, punctuates the dry, dusty desert landscape, calling to mind an alien planet from a sci-fi novel. Still, despite his prickly, otherworldly appearance, the Joshua tree (*Yucca brevifolia*) is considerably comforting in his own earthy, desolate way.

Sadly, some scientists believe that this already rare treelike plant is gravely endangered by climate change. It's also believed that his ability to spread was severely hampered 13,000 years ago when the Shasta ground sloth became extinct, as this creature may have been the primary disperser of his seeds.

Please note that Mohave yucca (*Yucca schidigera*), as well as other species of yucca, are in many ways similar from a magical perspective.

Magical Uses
Protection
The Joshua tree's spiky and prickly nature, as well as his amazing ability to protect himself in harsh desert conditions, and his powerful alignment with bright sunlight and the element of fire, all combine to make him a fiercely protective ally. For a quick infusion of protection, visualize yourself as a Joshua tree. Feel your strength and fortitude, and tap into the fiery energy that emanates from (and almost constantly beats down on) the Joshua tree, effectively establishing an impermeable force field of pure positivity and light.

Purification
Just as relentless sunlight can act as a bleach that will make even the darkest cloth pale, and as even a relatively short time in bright daylight can literally disinfect an object and render it clean, the Joshua tree's blindingly bright energy can purify even the darkest, heaviest, and most toxic of energies. If serious energetic purification is called for, you might want to make a pilgrimage to visit Joshua trees. For example, plan a camping trip to Joshua Tree National Park or visit somewhere else where they appear, such as the Mohave National Preserve or at certain relatively adjacent areas in California, Arizona, Utah, or Nevada.

Gazing at the creamy white, surprisingly lush and abundant blossom of the Joshua tree (or another type of yucca) is another way to benefit from the intensely purifying vibrations of the plant.

Shapeshifting
Perhaps a part of the reason Joshua Tree National Park is famous for its drug trips, Joshua trees and other yuccas are known for their ability to help with shapeshifting. If this is a magical objective of yours, try visualizing a Joshua tree strongly in your mind before

you begin to get in touch with the energy of the animal whose form you'd like to take. Then call on the animal and visualize/imaging/feel yourself shifting into his or her form. In your mind's eye or as a physical exercise, explore your environment and experiment with existing in this other shape. When you feel ready, consciously shift back into your human body.

Transmutation of Challenges

Just as fire transmutes the deadest, driest, most seemingly useless stuff into radiant heat and light, Joshua tree can help you find the amazing blessings and superpowers hidden within the most challenging traumas of your past. For this purpose, empower a bottle of water with all the sadness and negative feelings related to your challenge and then offer it to a Joshua tree, pouring it out around the base. Envision, sense, and/or feel any negativity or stagnation surrounding these issues being immediately transformed by the plant into pure positivity, nourishment, brightness, and dynamism.

Magical Correspondences

 Element: Fire
Gender: Masculine
Planet: Ceres

Juniper

*J*unipers (*Juniperus*) and humans go way back and are likely, also, to go way forward. Employed medicinally and as fuel and lumber since very ancient times, this vigorous, fragrant, and beautiful little evergreen appears in a number of climates and fulfills countless ecological functions.

Magical Uses

Blood Sugar and Appetite Regulation

According to an article in the medical journal *Diabetes Care*, some Navaho Indians employ juniper to treat their diabetes. Juniper's wisdom is certainly both healing and balancing, and it would be wise to sit in quiet contemplation with a juniper when it's your intention to balance your blood sugar, regulate your appetite, or work with your body's wisdom to help prevent or alleviate diabetes or hypoglycemia. Diffusing essential oil of juniper berry can also be helpful for these purposes.

Healing

According to author Andrew Chevallier in *Encyclopedia of Herbal Medicine*, three cups of an infusion of juniper berries, cornsilk, and marshmallow (five grams each) can be a useful antiseptic for healing urinary infections when drunk throughout the day. Juniper is also said to alleviate digestive discomfort, relieve water retention, and help with arthritis. In fact, some people consume raisins soaked in gin (a beverage that contains and is named after juniper) as a simple home remedy for soothing arthritis.

The essential oil of the berry can also be helpful: according to the book *Aromatherapy for Everyone* by PJ Pierson and Mary Shipley, you might add a few drops to an ounce of carrier oil (such as sweet almond or jojoba) and rub on the skin over the womb area to alleviate menstrual cramps. When you or someone you love is experiencing a cold or a flu, diffuse essential oil of juniper berry to help purify the environment and promote a robust immune response. Diffusing the essential oil can also help heal headaches. In *Aromatherapy for Healing the Spirit*, Gabriel Mojay states that "juniper oil's warming, invigorating effect benefits chronic tiredness, cold hands and feet, lower backache, and oedema (fluid retention)." Please note that juniper should not be used during pregnancy.

Survival

Traditionally, juniper is employed for protection against all number of things (including but not limited to negativity, stagnant energy, ghosts, demons, intruders, challenging childbirth experiences, animal attacks, illnesses like the bubonic plague and leprosy, and people with malevolent intent), but I think this aspect of juniper's magic would be better described as survival. Indeed, in addition to protecting against a variety of challenges relating to or potentially causing death or dire injury, juniper has been a pillar of habitable human ecosystems for millennia. Not to mention, junipers are survivalists themselves: some species grow in extremely cold climates, while others can thrive in desert sands, and still others can live as long as a thousand years or more. No matter where they are, they bring benefits to the entire ecology, protecting from erosion and providing nourishment for birds and certain species of moth larvae, some of which will eat nothing else.

Beautifully, in *A Natural History of Western Trees*, author Donald Culross Peattie writes this about Utah junipers in the Grand Canyon:

> …*when you step gingerly to the edge and look down into the vast emptiness, you see this juniper far below you, dotting the bridle trail, clinging to perilous ledges, springing out of crevices in the rocks…a symbol of undefeated life in an abyss of death.*

More proof of juniper's alignment with survival: the Chinese juniper is often used in the bonsai tradition and is associated with surviving for a particularly long period of time (also known as longevity). Additionally, juniper berries were found in King Tut's tomb, possibly to promote survival into the afterlife.

Aromatherapeutically, juniper gets our energy moving, breaks us out of ruts, and infuses us with fresh perspective: important aspects of survival of all varieties.

Carry juniper berries or employ any part of the tree in charms created for the purpose of survival. Plant juniper near your home to promote the longest, healthiest possible lives for all residents.

Terraforming
Speaking of survival, according to a direct intuitive communication I received from the tree, juniper is aware of the potential need for terraforming other planets (i.e., making them habitable for humans), and he wants us to know that he is here to help. So if you're a scientist who works in this arena or you know someone who is, please spread the word and pass along juniper's desire to volunteer for the job. His adaptability to a

number of climates and multidimensional support of other organisms makes him quite the desirable candidate.

Magical Correspondences

Element: Air

Gender: Masculine

Planet: Gliese 667 Ce (a potentially habitable planet in the Alpha Centauri solar system)

Kamani

The kamani tree (*calophyllum inophyllum*) is a tree of many, many names. So many, in fact, that it was difficult for me to choose which one to use to title this section. Kamani (his Hawaiian name) is an island dweller and appears most often at seashores and near coral reefs. His other names include bitaog in the Philippines, ati in Tahiti, fetau in Samoa, damanu in Fiji, nyamplung in Indonesia, and penaga laut in Malaysia. In the United States and Europe, he's also known as Alexandrian laurel, Indian laurel, beauty leaf, and beach calophyllum. (And that's not even all of them.)

Perhaps because he does have so many names and is not easily recognizable by one single moniker, this handsome beach dweller with his sweet, citrusy smelling leaves is not quite as famous as he deserves to be. This is especially true when you consider his sacred status in so many cultures, as well as his staggering array of potent medicinal and cosmetic benefits.

Please note that the commercially available nut oil is usually sold as tamanu oil, after the name of the fruit.

Magical Uses

Acclimatization

Only 120 plants on the planet produce what are called "drift seeds"—seeds that float along saltwater waves while remaining viable, giving them the ability to take root and thrive on islands relatively distant from their origin. Kamani is one. This quality—along with his ability to remain healthy (once grown) in harsh winds, sandy soil, and even salt-water—mirrors his spiritual and magical wisdom related to acclimating to new and even seemingly challenging environments.

Interestingly, there is a legend about a rebellious son named Sunan Nyamplungan who was banished from the island of Java by his father. He set adrift on a boat, bringing with him two walking sticks. When he found himself on an unpopulated island (now Karimunjawa), he placed the walking sticks in the ground and they immediately transformed into kamani trees. These trees, which share his name in this region (nyamplung trees), are now present on this archipelago in great abundance. They are honored as sacred, protective trees and guardians of the island, just as Nyamplungan has become a protective spirit who watches over the island in the form of a giant bat. Clearly, Nyamplungan shares a spiritual and mythological essence with his namesake tree, which is also cast off from his parent and set adrift upon the seas, transforming almost instantly from a stranger in a strange land to a flourishing local icon and magical protector.

Magically, kamani can be helpful for times when you need support with acclimating to a new home, job, relationship, or phase of life. For example, in Fiji parents have rubbed the nut oil on their children's legs to support them as they learn how to walk.

Additionally, kamani specializes in supporting those who feel cast off or isolated from their family and place of origin, as well as those who find it necessary to acclimate to a seemingly harsh environment. For this purpose, you might spend time with a kamani, inhale his fragrant blossoms, incorporate parts of the plant into rituals or charms created for the purpose, or anoint your palms, heart, and belly with a bit of the nut oil (tamanu oil).

Beauty

Kamani's botanical name is derived from the Greek words for "beautiful leaf." And this is very fitting, as in addition to the actual beauty of Kamani's leaves and flowers, the nut oil is prized as a beautification ingredient. Indeed, while some cultures have known about them for centuries, the spa and cosmetic world is becoming more and more aware of the beautifying properties of the nut oil (tamanu oil), which has been used to treat scars and acne, as well as to increase skin moisture and radiant health.

Additionally, in the Philippines women have traditionally enhanced their beauty by simply wearing the tree's beautiful flowers in their hair.

....

KAMANI BEAUTY POTION

Place ten to twenty drops of tamanu oil in a small glass bottle or jar. Fill it the rest of the way with coconut oil that has been warmed until melted and combine. Hold it in both hands and envision very bright white light coming down from the crown of your head, to your heart, down your arms, and out through your palms into the oil. Envision this light filling and activating this oil as you say:

Tamanu and coconut now combine
To bless me with a beauty fine.
Like dancing light upon the sea
A stunning vision I shall be.

Conjure up the feeling that you associate with feeling beautiful and radiating your beauty for all to see and enjoy. Direct this feeling into the oil.

To enhance your beauty, use this potion as a moisturizer or a mask, or just lightly anoint your forehead, wrists, and throat.

Note that the potion will gain a more solid consistency in cooler room temperatures.

Clairvoyance and Intuition

As I mentioned, the protective spirit Nyamplungan, who shares his name with the nyamplung (kamani) tree, appears as a giant, protective bat. Bats are associated with clairvoyance and intuition, as they are required to "see" in the dark (using sonar and other sensory stimuli), and they are very attuned to subtleties. What's more, traditional uses of parts of the kamani tree (neither of which I recommend trying at home) have involved both healing the eyes and—where enemies are concerned—blinding people. Clearly the tree is aligned with seeing and not seeing, or seeing clearly what is not visible to the physical eyes.

To enhance your clairvoyance or any other type of intuitive ability, you might:

- Spend time in quiet contemplation with a kamani tree, particularly at sunrise or sunset.

- Add a few drops of tamanu oil to your bathwater.

- Take a vibrational essence made from the flower or tree (provided you can find one from a trusted source or create one safely).

- Inhale the scent of the blossom.

Divine Alignment

In Hawaii, Tahiti, Samoa, and a number of other areas, the kamani tree is considered holy: it's planted in and around sacred places, and its wood is used to carve sacred relics.

In the Polynesians, it was once believed that the gods hid in kamani trees to observe people making sacrifices to them. To align with the Divine realm for spiritual purposes or to request support in any life area, spend time in quiet contemplation with a kamani tree, place a bit of kamani wood on your altar, or respectfully gather a blossom and bring it into your home. You might also bring kamani into your yard to bless your outdoor space and consecrate it to the Divine.

Forgiveness

In Samoa there is a legend about a king who found that one of his two wives had poisoned the child he had with his other wife. In response, he ordered that she be placed in a kamani tree and that the tree be set on fire. When the tree refused to burn, sparing her life, the king called it the "tree of life" because it had chosen to rescue the woman from certain doom. The woman was promptly placed on a different island and lived the rest of her life free from punishment. (Notice how this legend, like the legend in the "Acclimatization" section above, mirrors the kamani seed's action of drifting from one island to another and taking root in the new locale.)

One wonders whether the tree knew something the king didn't (perhaps that the woman was actually innocent), but whether or not the legendary woman was guilty as charged, the legend illustrates that the kamani tree is aligned with forgiveness and pardon, even in the face of a seemingly unforgivable crime. If your magical intention involves forgiving yourself or another for a particularly egregious action, kamani might be just the ingredient for you. Try spending time with a kamani tree, placing his blossoms on your altar, or taking a sea salt bath and then anointing your heart and belly with the seed oil (tamanu oil).

Healing and Regeneration

Here is where tamanu oil really shines: it's truly a panacea when it comes to skin issues. It's been used to help heal burns, cuts, scrapes, sores, wounds, insect bites, allergic reactions, scabies, rashes, acne, old scars, and even extreme conditions like chemical burns, post-surgical wounds, leprosy, and cancer. The amazing thing about it is that it doesn't just heal: it disinfects, combats inflammation, and helps actually regenerate the tissues. (Notably, this magical quality is mirrored in the way that the tree itself helps heal and regenerate compromised coastal areas by knitting loose sand together with its roots to discourage erosion and help ecosystems rebuild. In fact, kamani trees were employed in just this way after the tsunami on the coast of Samoa in 2009.)

On Fiji the kamani is called *dolno*, which translates to "no pain." While island countries have known about this veritable miracle cure for centuries, its growing popularity in other locations has been relatively recent. Unlike many essential oils, tamanu oil is more like a mild carrier oil, like sweet almond or jojoba, although it does have a light, comforting, myrrh-like scent. It can be rubbed directly onto the skin. Do be careful when purchasing it to make sure that it's pure, organic, and cold-pressed.

In addition to physical healing, you might magically employ tamanu oil if you have an emotional wound such as intense grief or heartbreak that could use a little miraculous healing. For this purpose, say an invocation or prayer and ritually anoint your heart, belly, and brow. If the tree grows in your area, you might plant one or more of them in your yard to heal and regenerate after serious loss or intense emotional pain of any kind.

Magical Correspondences

Element: Spirit
Gender: Masculine
Planet: Pluto

Kapok

The majestic, heavily buttressed kapok tree (*Ceiba pentandra*) is revered across a number of cultures and continents. To the Mayans he's none other than the tree of life: the Axis Mundi that holds up the cosmos and serves as the central pillar that links the underworld, land, and sky. According to authors Rosita Arvigo and Nadine Epstein in *Rainforest Home Remedies*, "In Mayan, the tree is called *yax che*. *Yax* has three meanings—green, first, and sacred. *Che* is tree."

Magical Uses

Altered Consciousness

While you absolutely must not try this at home, it's worth noting that kapok bark is added to some recipes for the famed spiritual hallucinogenic brew known as ayahuasca. Additionally, it's been employed in herbal medicine as an aphrodisiac and headache cure. As headaches are often related to blocked or challenged spiritual perception, and our ability to connect with our sexuality is all about opening up and allowing ourselves to feel, these qualities also point to the kapok's ability to sensitize us to new ways of seeing, perceiving, and being in our bodies. This enhances our magical abilities and brings all sorts of benefits to our everyday life.

Spend time in quiet contemplation with a kapok tree to expand your awareness and enhance your spiritual perception.

Divine Masculine

In alternative spirituality and holistic healing circles, a lot of attention is given to the Goddess and the Divine Feminine, in large part because for some time now our culture has been glorifying masculine energy to the point of imbalance. But in truth, neither polarity is inherently better than the other, and it's most ideal when the two energies are in dynamic equilibrium by continually complementing and balancing each other.

One of the most healing aspects of kapok's energy is his exceptionally balancing expression of Divine Masculine energy. With his expansive and visible roots, he is anchoring while simultaneously providing strong structure and taciturn spiritual sustenance. (In other words, he's the strong, silent type.)

To embody your own masculine energy in a most balanced and healthy way, or to open yourself up to attracting a masculine partner with a very high level of integrity, spend time in quiet contemplation with a kapok tree. Relax and allow yourself to absorb and mirror his strong and silent vibration.

Integrity

Interestingly, in many of his native lands, the kapok is associated with both divinity and unfriendly spirits who are believed to be hiding or trapped inside certain individual trees. However, the tree does not actually house unfriendly spirits, but rather provides a reflection of the willfully unclaimed and destructive aspects of a person encountering the tree. In other words, if one is out of integrity in any way—behaving greedily, for example, or concealing the truth from oneself or others—those unsavory traits will be reflected back to the perceiver by the tree. If one fails to recognize that what he perceives is an aspect of himself, he will project that aspect upon the tree, and possibly believe that the tree is housing an undesirable spirit of some kind.

This magical property of the kapok tree can be very helpful for those who want to call upon their integrity and step into the role of hero. For example:

Kapok Integrity Ritual and Hero Initiation

Visit a kapok tree and offer three slices of bread by placing them at the base of the tree. Relax and come into harmony with the vast, quiet energy of the tree. Know that any fears or challenging feelings that arise are actually windows into unhealed aspects of yourself. The kapok tree is simply acting as a mirror that will allow you to shine light into the dark places and bravely release what holds you back from serving the planet in the most helpful and honorable of ways. Relax and surrender to this natural spiritual and energetic process, releasing the need to understand what is happening with your linear, logical mind.

Magical Correspondences

Element: Spirit
Gender: Masculine
Planet: Jupiter

Katsura

The katsura tree's divine beauty and elegance make him a very popular ornamental not only in his native countries of China and Japan, but also throughout the world. His lush, heart-shaped leaves are purplish red in spring and green in summer. In fall they turn a gorgeous gold, and—as if showing off— they begin to emanate the fragrance of warm caramel or toasted maple scones.

While similar in many ways to the redbud (and sometimes called "the Japanese redbud"), katsura (*Cercidiphyllum*) is a separate species. When identifying, simply look to the leaves: katsura leaves are opposite, while redbud leaves are alternating.

Magical Uses

Lunar Alignment

A Japanese legend states that katsura trees grow on the moon. Indeed, the tree's vibrant energy is also both ethereal and otherworldly. To align yourself and your magic with the rhythm and harmony of the moon, or to request initiation into the lunar mysteries, spend time in quiet contemplation with a katsura tree when the moon is visible in the sky.

Fame

With his elegance, allure, and kaleidoscopic mystique, katsura obviously has much in common with a perennially popular celebrity. As such, if it's your intention to attract attention and increase your fame, katsura is an excellent ally to enlist. For example, you might try the following ritual.

....

KATSURA FAME RITUAL

When the moon is in Leo and between second quarter and full, wash a moonstone in saltwater and rinse thoroughly. Visit a katsura tree and empower the moonstone in the light of the moon. Relax, tune in to the tree, touch the trunk with love, and request that he support you in increasing your fame and positive recognition. Place the moonstone as an offering at his base. Spend a bit more time in communion with the tree, and allow yourself to receive an infusion of the tree's irresistible fascination and mystique.

Magical Correspondences

Element: Fire

Gender: Masculine and feminine

Planet: Venus, Moon

Larch

A deciduous member of the pine family, the elegant larch (*Larix*) turns yellow in the fall just before she sheds her needles. While she appears in a more diminutive form in non-native areas, she's a towering luminary in her sprawling native forests in Canada, Russia, and Scandinavia.

Magical Uses

Confidence

Flower essence pioneer Edward Bach wrote that larch essence (available at most health food stores) is an ideal medicine "for those who do not consider themselves as good or capable as those around them, who expect failure, who feel that they will never be a success, and so do not venture or make a strong enough attempt to succeed." To remedy this condition, try taking two to three drops under the tongue or in water twice per day for one month.

In addition to or instead of employing the flower essence, try spending time in quiet contemplation with a larch tree, setting the intention to absorb a generous helping of confident and self-assured energy from the tree. Be assured that the tree has an endless supply of such energy and will be quite happy to share.

Protection

Larch pitch literally protects from water when used in waterproofing, and larch wood is also somewhat resistant to fire. Historically, the tree's been associated with protection from serpents as well as fire and water, and can be employed for a number of protective magical purposes. Associated with the planet Saturn and the element of spirit, the larch is an excellent ally when it's your intention to set a protective boundary with the help of the Divine.

In *The Meaning of Trees*, author Fred Hageneder writes:

> In Alpine legend, the larch is the abode of the Saeligen, the 'Blessed Ones,' graceful otherworldly beings who are kind to people and protect animals…[T]he Saeligen maidens have been described as spirit beings dressed in white or silver, dancing under old larch trees and singing the sweetest music.

The Realm of Heaven

Even though Westerners often associate "heaven" with monotheism, virtually every religion and culture has a version of the heavenly realm. For example, Buddhism has Nirvana, Hinduism has Moksha, and Wicca has the Summerland. Because the tree is so potently aligned with the beneficent and loving realm of spirit, and ancient pagans employed larchwood in cremations to help send the transitioning soul to the most beautiful and heavenly of realms.

Magical Correspondences

Element: Spirit

Gender: Feminine

Planet: Saturn

Lemon

The scent of lemon's creamy white blossoms makes your knees weak, and the fruit is the very quintessence of clean freshness. Not to mention her glossy evergreen leaves and petite frame are refined perfection! Interestingly, while the lemon's cousin the orange is aligned with the sun and radiates energy outward, the beguiling lemon is lunar, leaning toward the more receptive, feminine end of the spectrum.

Lemon trees (*Citrus x limon*) are native to China, made their way to Europe through ancient Rome, and later spread throughout the Middle East. I find it interesting that they were first cultivated in Europe in the Italian city of Genoa, as they remind me of my Italian grandmother, who hailed from that region, not only because she loved all things lemon but also because she was small, strong, elegant, and formidable all at one time.

Magical Uses
Bliss

The presence of a lemon tree in a landscape confers a sense of bliss, and quiet contemplation with one can tune you in to the heavenly realm. Encountering a lemon tree in bloom is an especially auspicious occurrence, and inhaling the scent of the flowers is a surefire method of coming into a pleasant alignment with the senses and uplifting the mood to its highest possible degree.

Cleansing and Clearing

Lemons are cleansing in so many ways, both physical and energetic.

- Add lemon juice to water and drink as a simple detoxifying potion.
- Add lemon slices to bathwater to cleanse the physical and energetic bodies.
- Clean house with water into which you've added lemon juice or add lemon essential oil to your cleaners.
- Add a few drops of lemon essential oil to spring water and mist the space as a clearing mist potion.
- Shine copper with half of a lemon dipped in baking soda.
- Exfoliate your face with half of a lemon dipped in sugar.
- Diffuse lemon essential oil to energetically detoxify the space.
- Wash crystals and magical jewelry in water containing lemon juice to clear and reset their energy.

Vitality

When increased energy, immunity, and health are desired, an effective magical strategy would be to go heavy on the lemons. For example, you might diffuse the scent regularly, add the juice to your water, and even place a bowl of the fruit on your altar. Keep it up for at least a week, and notice your vitality level increase.

Magical Correspondences

Elements: Water and Air

Gender: Feminine

Planet: Moon

Linden

*A*lthough the lithe and stately linden (*Tilia*) is frequently called a "lime," she is in no way related to the citrus fruit. A rare balance of masculine and feminine energies, she is a most wise, mystical, and potentially long-lived tree (some trees and coppices are believed to have lived for one to two thousand years).

Magical Uses

Heart Healing

With her broad, heart-shaped leaves and abundant shade, the linden powerfully soothes grief and broken hearts, shifting and healing old pain at the vibrational level. Attractive to large numbers of bees, linden flowers produce honey, and the linden is therefore associated with sweetness, love, and divine healing. Interestingly, linden's heart-healing action works on the physical level too, as linden flower tea is believed to be beneficial to the heart and blood pressure. To help speed the healing of grief or a broken heart, spend time with a linden tree or drink linden flower tea daily until the worst has passed.

Protection

Traditionally aligned with the Divine Feminine, the linden has been magically employed to invoke the protection of the Goddess. In Germany, the goddesses Freya and Frigga are both associated with the linden, and shrines to Mother Mary are found near lindens in Bulgaria.

For this purpose, visit a linden tree, light a white candle, invoke the Great Goddess in any form you like, and inwardly request the protection you seek. Then feel yourself receiving an infusion of fiercely loving, protective energy.

Place a linden branch over your front door to protect the home (after lovingly gathering it, of course).

Sleep

Combined with dried lavender and a little passionflower, dried linden flowers make perfect stuffing for an eye pillow to promote deep and restful sleep. Additionally, linden flowers mixed with chamomile make an excellent bedtime tea.

Stress Relief

With her neutralizing combination of masculine and feminine energy and her profoundly cooling vibration, the linden is an accomplished magical stress-reliever. Her name originates from a root meaning "flexible" and "yielding," and she can support us as we learn to surrender and move with the flow of things, rather than attempt to fight against the present moment. For stress relief, try spending time with a linden tree, drinking linden flower tea, or taking the flower essence.

Magical Correspondences

Element: Water

Gender: Masculine/feminine balance

Planet: Uranus

Locust

The locust (of the Gleditsia or Robinia family) is aligned with the "dark mother" aspect of the Goddess: the destructive, purifying energy that helps us let go, transform challenges, neutralize negativity, and move on.

When I first encountered a honey locust (*Gleditsia tricanthos*), I heard her message loud and clear: "Stay away!" It turns out that her extremely sharp, vicious-looking, head-to-toe thorns may have evolved to protect her from the oversized animals of the Pleistocene (aka Pleistocene megafauna). Don't you just love stories like that? Now you can imagine your thorn-bedecked neighborhood tree looking pretty much exactly the same back in the days when she effectively warded off mammoths and giant armadillos.

Magical Uses

Boundaries

As mentioned, the locust is pretty much an expert at boundary setting. While she often provides nutrition to neighboring animals in the form of her flowers or pods (depending on the species), she can also be really spiky and toxic. So this is good news for magical practitioners who also happen to need help transforming into something other than a pushover or a yes-man, or those of us who have had codependency issues in the past. Simply visit a locust tree, sit in quiet contemplation, and allow yourself to receive an infusion of her wisdom and potent, boundary-setting energy. As you relax into her vibe, let yourself clearly sort out what feels good to you and what doesn't, and resolve to tune in to your heart, gut, and intuition before responding to requests for your time, money, effort, or attention.

Neutralizing Negativity

Burying items with heavy or undesirable energy, or symbols of unwanted conditions, near black locust trees helps neutralize the negative energy they hold. This mirror's the tree's proclivity for growing in poor soil and "disturbed" areas, and improving the quality of the soil in the process. The tree herself is also a metaphor for neutralizing negativity, as her thorns and toxicity give way to her beautiful, abundant, sweet-smelling blossoms. (They are even sometimes edible, depending on the species.)

If you feel that you've picked up or are carrying a lot of negativity, try the following:

Locust Negativity Purge

During a waning moon, light a black candle and roll an organic potato all over your body, consciously sending any and all negative, dark, heavy, or stuck energy into the vegetable. Extinguish the candle and approach a locust tree. Dig a small hole near her base and bury the potato in it, knowing and sensing that the tree will naturally compost the negativity into positivity and nourishment, and that she therefore will see the potato (negativity and all) as an offering. (If you find this hard to believe, consider the way plants thrive when fertilized with rot and manure.) Inwardly express gratitude to the tree for taking care of this negativity for you. Know in your heart that she has instantly, efficiently, and completely neutralized it. For good measure, thank her once more.

Return home. Shower or bathe. Then light a white candle to symbolize your newly purified state.

Sweetness

For a tree aligned with toxins, sharp points, and the dark goddess, sweetness is an unexpected magical use…or is it? Consider Halloween: it's associated with death, darkness, fear, and…candy! Similarly, in Día de los Muertos (day of the dead) celebrations in South America, the traditional ornamental skulls are made pure, unadulterated (but sometimes colored) sugar. So the locust is one more participant in this age-old tradition of interweaving sweetness with the beautiful dark. It's a tradition that points to an underrated truth: in many ways, embracing the darkness and shadows might not be so terrible after all, and it may even be the secret to living the sweet life.

Locust honey (called acacia honey in Europe) is world famous for its light sweetness, and acacia fritters (made with sweet-smelling black locust blossoms) are a European delicacy served with powdered sugar. Consume either of these (or just spend time with a blossoming locust) to bring more sweetness into your life and to find delectable sweetness not just in the brightness and sunshine, but also in the full spectrum of the human experience.

Magical Correspondences

Element: Air
Gender: Feminine
Planet: Saturn

Madrone

*A*ligned with the fire element, the madrone's papery, peeling, multicolored bark appears like a reddish brown and pale green blaze, and his trunk and branches twist and turn toward the sun like sinewy flames. Additionally, he is one of those special trees—like the aspen—who in many ways rely on forest fires to thrive. Also like aspen, his numbers are tragically dwindling due to modern fire control measures.

In the limited area of the west coast of North America where the madrone—also known as the arbutus—thrives, Native Americans have loved and revered him since ancient times. Likewise, to this day he is regarded as sacred by many of his magical human neighbors, including the well-known author and activist Starhawk, who named a main character after him in her excellent novel *The Fifth Sacred Thing*.

Magical Uses

Integrity and Sustainability

The poet Richard Olafsen, in his book *In Arbutus Light*, alludes to an ancient American myth that states that the madrone is a beacon of stability and that the tree's presence on earth provides a sort of etheric fabric that holds everything together.

Indeed, the madrone's vibration is one of deep holistic balance, and each tree sends anchoring and healing cords of light throughout the physical earth beneath his roots. As such, spending time in quiet contemplation with one can be a valuable source of energetic replenishment for those who feel called to take action on behalf of the planet. Additionally, spending time with a madrone can be helpful when you desire to fortify your own integrity and powerfully align your actions with your ideals.

Wisdom

From a magical perspective, madrone is unique: while his native fire element is rapid and dynamic, his energetic pattern is as deep, grounded, and solid as they come. This makes him extremely suited to support us in quickly and effectively aligning with precisely the wisdom that is most needed, particularly wisdom that instructs us to take instant action related to healing, balancing, fortifying, and restructuring. That's why a madrone tree is an ideal companion when planning how to move forward wisely in these areas.

Magical Correspondences

Element: Fire

Gender: Masculine and feminine

Planet: Mars

Magnolia

With grounded wisdom that stretches into the ancient past, a lush femininity that is anything but dainty, *and* the mysterious depths of the watery moon, we might think of the magnolia (the family Magnolioceae) as an arboreal wise woman and botanical high priestess. While her leaves are sometimes evergreen and sometimes deciduous, and her flowers appear in a number of colors, each of the many species of magnolia is visually stunning and magically intense.

Magical Uses

Ancient Wisdom

In *The Magic of Flowers* I wrote, "Deep within us, in our genetic memory and in our buried memories of old lifetimes, we hold ancient wisdom. Magnolia can help us remember this wisdom and allow it to be reborn into our present incarnation." Indeed, not just the flower but the very tree herself is literally a repository of unthinkably ancient genetic coding. So ancient, in fact, that she actually predates bees, which is why she is pollinated by beetles instead.

Spend time in quiet contemplation with a magnolia tree to access the deep inner knowing that is your spiritual heritage and birthright, including ancient genetic memories and wisdom intrinsic to the earth and moon.

Feminine Power

A magnolia blossom is a most beautiful and precious thing to behold, and so fragrant! Still, gaze at a hearty magnolia tree and you'll get the distinct sense that she's invincible. In fact, genetically the magnolia *has* been invincible for hundreds of thousands of years, thriving from *more than 100 million years ago* until the present day. Talk about destroying the myth that feminine beauty is synonymous with tender youth! On the contrary, magnolia demonstrates the immense power and beauty that can accompany mature feminine energy.

....

MAGNOLIA RITUAL FOR FEMININE POWER AND GODDESS ENERGY

Perhaps you feel drawn to get more into your feminine energy: your receptive, open-hearted radiance. And if you feel drawn to work with magnolia for this purpose, chances are good that you also want to access your most invincible power and vast magical strength. If this is the case, visit a magnolia under a full moon and offer her a moonstone by placing it at her base. Then touch her trunk and say:

> *Radiant, receptive, beautiful, free*
> *My Goddess identity now defines me.*
> *Magical, mighty, luminous, bright*
> *I step into my power this night.*

Lunar Magic

Aligned with both the earth and the moon, the magnolia can help us work with lunar energy in the physical realm for the purpose of manifestation. In other words, she can help us work moon magic, and to align with the moon's energy more fully. For this purpose, try meditating near a magnolia for at least five minutes a day for one full moon cycle, starting at the new moon and continuing until the dark moon. As you sit, gaze at the magnolia and let yourself contemplate and attune with the unseen energies of the moon.

Stress Relief

When stress is related to feeling disempowered and/or separated from the energy of the earth, magnolia can help. Simply sitting in quiet contemplation with a tree can be ideal for this purpose, and extracts from a particular type of magnolia—*magnolia officinalis*—have been shown to relax the muscles. (Though only take internally under the supervision of an expert.) Similarly, Hou Po bark (as it's called when used in Chinese Medicine), according to author and herbalist Andrew Chevallier in *Encyclopedia of Herbal Medicine*, "relieves cramping pain and flatulence, and is taken for abdominal distension, indigestion, loss of appetite, vomiting, and diarrhea." (Notice that these are all symptoms that have been known to result from stress.)

Magical Correspondences

Element: Earth
Gender: Feminine
Planet: Moon

Manzanita

*N*o matter how challenged one may be by the prospect of tree identification, once one is familiar with the pint-sized manzanita (*Arctostaphylos*), identifying her is never a problem. The first giveaway is her super smooth, vibrant, red wood that wonderfully twists and crinkles, contrasting gorgeously with her silvery green leaves. Indeed, since the moment I was introduced to this unique little firecracker of a tree, she's felt like a dear and familiar friend.

Her name—as I learned at sixth grade camp—means "little apple," probably in reference to her berries, but also her littleness. She is a fixture in natural California landscapes, and thrives in the western United States, reaching as far north as British Columbia and as far south as Mexico.

Magical Uses

Healing

While it's notable that Native Americans have employed manzanita bark to heal gastrointestinal and genitourinary complaints for centuries, I'm not going to provide a guide to this type of usage here, as I am not an expert and large amounts can be toxic. I will say, however, that magically speaking, manzanita has a vibration that is fiery, vitalizing, and uplifting.

Fire Magic

It's fitting that manzanita is a staple in chaparral landscapes: natural areas that coevolved with fire and literally rely on forest fires to thrive. Additionally, when her bright red wood is dried, it becomes an extremely potent fuel and high-quality firewood. Naturally, if you feel particularly aligned with the fire element in your magic—or if you'd like to improve your alignment with the fire element—spending time with the manzanita will be beneficial.

Magical Wisdom

Finally, manzanita is a magical expert. Visit and spend time in quiet with her if you'd like to quicken your intuition, activate your power, and fuel your magical potency. For example, for this purpose you might try the following:

MANZANITA MOJO RITUAL

Visit a manzanita and spend time in quiet contemplation, silently admiring her magical energy and requesting that she share some of it with you. When it feels right, lovingly collect naturally one or more naturally shed branches or sticks. Take them home and dry them thoroughly in sunlight for a month or more. Build a fire in your fireplace or fire pit. Gaze at the flames and let your mind relax. When you feel centered, place the sticks or branches in the fire. As they burn, feel their magic being released and flying directly into your energy field, augmenting your power and infusing you with great wisdom and magical prowess.

Magical Correspondences

Element: Fire
Gender: Feminine
Planet: Mercury

Maple

$\mathcal{L}$ast October, after three days of travel with all our earthly belongings in tow, my partner, cat, and I arrived at a new rural residence. We beheld the most beautiful sight in our front yard: a lofty sugar maple with the brightest red leaves elegantly dancing in the sunset. Truly, is there a sight sweeter or more glorious than a maple tree (*Acer*) in all her fall glory? If so, it might just be too much to take.

Magical Uses
Appreciation of Beauty

In a very real sense, our capacity to appreciate the beauty within every moment and every *thing* is directly correlated with our capacity to enjoy life. In Japan, there's a custom called momijigari, which entails seeking out and viewing the reddened maple leaves in fall. Similarly, visiting a maple tree at anytime of year, and tuning in to her vast consciousness and graceful presence, can bring with it the great blessing of aligning you with the beauty within you, around you, and in all things.

Directing Energy

If you'd like a magic wand that is flexible, strong, and powerfully resonant, and that will color your magic with harmony, sweetness, beauty, and positivity, maple wood would be an excellent material to choose.

Fun

What would life be without play? Playing reduces stress, builds social relationships, and activates joy. And many of the games we play rely on maple wood: this munificent tree lends her wood to pool cues, bowling pins, baseball bats, basketball courts, and archery bows. As for people who prefer to play with musical instruments, she generously provides for those too. And you know what else is fun? Tennessee whisky (which is filtered through maple charcoal). Also, delicious breakfasts topped with…you guessed it! Maple syrup. Speaking of which…

··

BREAKFAST RITUAL TO ACTIVATE FUN

To magically increase the fun quotient in your life (and perhaps that of your partner or household) or to kick the day off with an extra helping of fun, whip up some pancakes. Say a quick blessing over pure and organic maple syrup, such as:

Fun is magic and magic is sweet
We're feeling playful from our head to our feet.

Put on some silly or joyful music and eat. Be sure to encourage at least a drop or two of syrup for everyone. (Alternate ideas: For nonbreakfast eaters, perhaps put a bit in your coffee or tea. For extra spontaneity, make pancakes for dinner instead of breakfast.)

Harmonious Sweetness

In *The Botany of Desire* Michael Pollan describes the historical definition of the word *sweet* as transcending taste and having been "a metaphor for a certain kind of perfection." He goes on to say that "the best land was said to be sweet; so were the most pleasing sounds, the most persuasive talk, the loveliest views, the most refined people, and the choicest part of any whole…" *This* is the kind of sweetness magically embodied by the maple.

Of course, sugar and black maples are employed to make that sweetest of sweet confections we pour over our pancakes and waffles and use to sweeten our hot beverages and baked goods: maple syrup. Another archetypal sweetness symbol, the honeybee, often relies on maples for pollen and nectar. Additionally, maple wood is the most popular material with which to make many different types of sweet-sounding musical instruments, including violas, violins, guitars, and cellos.

All of that aside, maple emanates a tangible spiritual sweetness. No matter what time of year, her graceful otherworldliness, like a mellifluous symphony, soothes the soul, lifts the spirits, and reminds you of the sweetness of life and the perfect interconnection of all. (In fact, I was particularly struck by this last week when the spring breeze caught the maple tree in our front yard, sending her spiraling, winged seeds continually through the air. For some time I honestly thought they were a giant swarm of tiny butterflies.)

Positivity

A beautiful Salteaux Indian story tells of a grove of bright red and orange maple trees rescuing the grandmother of the creator god. When evil spirits that wished her harm saw the fiery maple grove in which she stood, they believed it to be literally ablaze, and thus felt it unsafe to pass through and left her unharmed. Certainly, consciously appreciating a bright red maple in fall can dissolve negativity, banish negative energy attachments, and remind you of all the most positive and beautiful things life has to offer.

Magical Correspondences

Element: Spirit
Gender: Feminine
Planet: Neptune

Mesquite

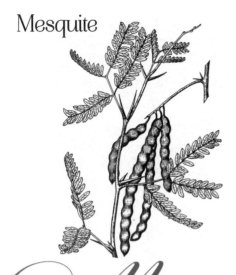

*M*agical, mysterious mesquite (*Prosopis*) thrives in hot, dry climates by sending a taproot deep into the earth to find the buried water within. If you're brave enough to connect with his deep, dark wisdom, you'll be rewarded with awe, inspiration, and healing.

Various species of mesquite trees are native to Mexico and the southwestern United States.

Magical Uses

Creativity

Mesquite plays a central role in a Yaqui myth about a boy who slays a large bird that has been terrorizing his village. The bird alights on a mesquite tree, and the boy shoots the bird with an arrow, killing it. Still standing under the tree, the boy then creates many smaller animals, including coyotes and various types of owls, by throwing handfuls of the bird's body into the air. Later, at this same location under the tree, he teaches the people of the village how to interact with the animals he created and how they can be useful for humans as food, clothing, and decoration.

This story is an accurate depiction of the power of creativity. Through courage, one can look at what one fears, and effectively overcome it. One can then tap into its power and transform it into something that will populate the world with inspiration and sustenance for many generations to come.

Healing

Mesquite has a long medicinal history in the Americas. According to authors Eliseo Torres and Timothy Leighton Sawyer in *Healing with Herbs and Rituals*, in traditional Mexican medicine mesquite sap was employed as a cure for dysentery, and "a tea infused from the seeds and bark can be consumed to combat irritations of the digestive tract." Energetically, spending time in quiet contemplation with a mesquite can support emotional healing by providing a purifying release.

Visions

In much the same way dreams can provide a road map to our true selves, mesquite can support us in waking visions that shed much-needed light on our spiritual and personal path. For this purpose, try:

- Meditating under a mesquite tree when the sun is high in the sky and allowing your mind to show you pictures.
- Burning mesquite incense on your altar as you go on a vision quest.
- Safely creating an outdoor fire with dried mesquite wood and gazing into the flames.
- Making an eye lotion from mesquite, as the Aztecs did. Did it help them have healing visions? We may never know.

Magical Correspondences

Element: Air

Gender: Masculine

Planet: Neptune

Mulberry

*H*ave you ever been walking through the woods and spied a tiny green worm seemingly hovering in midair? That's likely a silk worm. Look up and you'll often see a mulberry tree (*Morus*), which is the silk worm's exclusive food source. The mulberry is also known for her berries, which vary in color depending on the species and can be red, white, or almost black. The red and black varieties have a sweet and tart taste, while the white mulberries are mild and reminiscent of vanilla.

Magical Uses

Comfort amid Challenges

While in a mental hospital, Vincent Van Gogh painted his famous golden-leafed mulberry tree, which grew and thrived outside the window of the hospital despite its rocky surroundings. In a surprisingly positive letter to his brother included with the piece, he wrote, "I'll tell you that we're having some superb autumn days, and that I'm taking advantage of them."

In a much less dramatic past scenario, during childhood summers, I spent hours climbing around in the mulberry tree in my front yard. Regardless of what family challenges may have been going on at the time, I never failed to find sublime comfort in the shade of her spreading branches and emerald green leaves.

Cosmic Oneness

According to author Fred Hageneder, in ancient China some considered the mulberry to be the "World Tree" or "Tree of Renewal" at the center of the universe. He goes on to say that "it dates back to before the separation of yin and yang, male and female, and it represents the Tao, or the all-encompassing cosmic order."

Spend time in quiet contemplation with a mulberry to find the origin, gain perspective, and free yourself of the sorrow that comes from the illusion of separation.

Wholeness and Healing

In addition to being delicious, mulberries are shockingly nutritious. They're high in lots of good stuff, including iron, antioxidants, protein, vitamin C, magnesium, potassium, and resveratrol. As if all that weren't enough, they can be eaten as a remedy for constipation. In the past, mulberries have also been employed to heal the eyes and throat, and the white mulberry is used in Traditional Chinese Medicine to this day to clear heat, hydrate the system, enhance yin energy, and get energy moving in a healthy way throughout the body. Magically, simply spending time with a mulberry can balance the body and awaken the inherent instincts that guide us in healing ourselves effectively.

Magical Correspondences

Element: Water
Gender: Feminine
Planet: Mercury

Myrrh

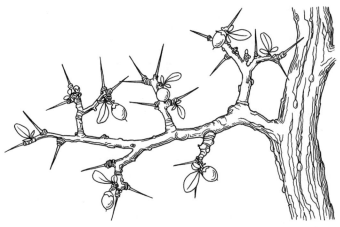

*S*mall and gnarled, the wise myrrh tree features prominently in Judaism, Christianity, and Islam and is native to arid regions of Africa, Asia, and the Middle East. The resin was employed in Egypt for embalming purposes, and it has even been found in ancient Celtic tombs. Please note that in this entry, we'll use "myrrh" to discuss the closely related trees in the myrrh family (or *Commiphora* genus) that produce the famous resin.

Magical Uses

Healing

Myrrh resin is considered extremely useful in Traditional Chinese Medicine, Ayurveda, and Western healing traditions. This should not be surprising, as the tree exudes milk (which eventually congeals into resin) as a means to support his own healing by protecting against insects and bacteria. Employed to heal and support the kidney, stomach, uterus, skin, mouth, teeth, and blood, myrrh resin is also included in herbal healing mixtures for arthritis, excessive bleeding, laryngitis, bronchitis, and menopause, and modern research has indicated that it may be an effective therapy against cancer.

Myrrh is aligned with the Great Mother Goddess and all her many healing abilities. The incense was burned in the temple of Isis and is also aligned with the powerful mother goddess Astarte. Myrrh incense and resin are highly appropriate for any magical work involving physical or emotional healing.

Smoothing Transitions

With a scent that is peculiar in its simultaneous strength and sweetness, myrrh helps smooth the harshness associated with all forms of transitions, including birth, death, changing residence, changing jobs, ending or beginning a relationship, and any form of rebirth or painful loss. Myrrh was employed in Egypt for embalming and for incense honoring the dead, and it is referred to in the gospels surrounding transitions no less pivotal than Jesus's birth, crucifixion, and death. Clearly, myrrh softens the jagged edges of even the most challenging of transitions by lending his pleasant fragrance as well as his heart-healing and grief-soothing properties.

Another aspect of myrrh's expertise at smoothing transitions stems from the fact that the scent is extremely calming and brings one into the present moment so that we can be steady and strong even in the midst of enormous change. For support with any challenging transition, try burning the incense or anointing yourself with a scent blend containing essential oil (oleoresin) of myrrh. If possible, spending quality contemplative time with a myrrh tree would also be an excellent idea.

Magical Correspondences

Element: Spirit
Gender: Masculine
Planet: Neptune

Myrtle

$\mathscr{J}$ust the thought of some plants can transport me to another world: one of magic, mystery, and all possibility. The otherworldly, fragrant-leaved little myrtle (Myrtaceae family)—so beloved and revered by the ancient world—is undoubtedly one of them.

Magical Uses

Love

Myrtle's love magic is uniquely potent and enduring. Strongly associated with such archetypal love goddesses as Venus, Aphrodite, and Hathor, her simultaneously dainty and hearty leaves, as well as her vigorous yet ethereal blooms, mirror her alignment with romantic love (a condition that is at once delicate and robust). Also like myrtle, romantic love possesses some qualities that are fleeting and others that can remain (and even grow stronger) through the ages. That's why wearing a sprig or a crown of flowering myrtle for a wedding or a handfasting would be an excellent idea. So would the following ritual.

Love Goddess Altar Ritual for Lasting Love

To manifest a lasting romantic relationship, create an altar with a framed image or statue of Venus, Aphrodite, or Hathor as a focal point. Add a large pink pillar candle, an incense holder with a stick of rose or violet incense, and at least two vases of flowering myrtle. Light the candle and incense, place your hands over your heart, and conjure up the types of feelings you'd like to have in your forthcoming relationship. When this feels very real and specific, open your heart and emotions to the Goddess and release your wishes like an offering. Open your palms and imagine your desires rising up to the divine realm like incense. Fully release your desires with trust and love, knowing that they will not possibly fail to manifest in the perfect time and the perfect way. Thank the Goddess from your heart. Allow the incense to burn all the way down. You can also allow the candle to burn all the way down or extinguish it and light it again at intervals until it naturally extinguishes.

Passage Between the Worlds

It's said that the location of the Greek city Sida was chosen at the site where the goddess Artemis was seen in the form of a rabbit disappearing into a myrtle tree. This story points to the myrtle's ability to act as a portal from this everyday world to the supernatural worlds of wildness and power. This can come in handy for magical intentions related to visiting other realms, such as the realm of the fae, the realm of the dead, or the realm of eternity.

Speaking of which, during the Eleusinian Mysteries, initiates were crowned with a wreath of myrtle. In *Laws*, Cicero writes of these Mysteries, saying: "In very truth we have learned from them the beginnings of life, and have gained the power not only to live happily, but also to die with a better hope." While to this day no one knows the entirety of what happened during these popular rites in ancient Greece, many who undertook them reportedly expressed that as a result of their experience, they no longer feared death. It's postulated that participants had a sort of induced hallucination of some kind (in some ways like a present-day ayahuasca ceremony) during which they transcended the everyday, illusory world and entered the truer world of the eternal, in order to return with greater perspective and insight into the nature of reality.

Peace

Nothing confers a sense of abiding peace quite like a myrtle tree dancing in a gentle breeze. Spend time in quiet contemplation with a myrtle tree or plant one near your space to discover inner peace or to help establish peace in a household, group, or any type of relationship. Bringing the flowers inside, wearing a myrtle crown, taking the flower essence, or just visualizing the tree during meditation can also help with these aims.

Wealth

Myrtle's alignment with the element of water (not to mention her alignment with sensuous, luxury-loving goddesses) speaks to her ability to help us manifest wealth and prosperity. Plant a myrtle in your yard to increase your abundance or lovingly approach her and request her assistance with this aim. Then, with great reverence, place a shiny silver dollar at her base and pour a bottle of blessed water around her roots.

Magical Correspondences

Element: Water
Gender: Feminine
Planet: Venus

Oak

*I*s there an arboreal superstar of the Western world? As a matter of fact, *yes*, and it's the oak (*Quercus*). All but synonymous with the Druids, the tree is sacred to such heavy mythological hitters as the well-known thunder gods Thor and Zeus, as well as the Celtic thunder god Taranis, the Slavic thunder god Perun, and the Baltic thunder god Perkons. Worshipped by many ancient people, in modern times the oak has been chosen as a national tree by a vast number of countries, including England, Ireland, Italy, Poland, Portugal, Romania, Wales, and—as of 2004—the United States.

Magical Uses

Divination

Dodona—the oldest Greek oracle, originally sacred to the primordial Mother Goddess Gaia and later usurped by Zeus—relied on the sound of wind in oak trees to relay divine messages to the priestesses and priests. Try this yourself by visiting an oak tree in a serene natural setting. Place your hands on the tree's trunk. Relax, ground, and vitalize your energy by feeling that you are drawing energy up from the earth and down from the sky. As a form of offering, place your hands on the oak's trunk and feel the earth and sky energy coming together at your heart and then flowing out through your palms into the tree. Then sit or stand comfortably and bring your question or challenge to mind. Relax deeply and cultivate inner stillness as you simply listen to the sound of the rustling leaves. Continue to do this until an answer presents itself to your consciousness.

Additionally, runes (small pieces of wood on which ancient letters or characters are written or carved for divination purposes) are sometimes made from oak.

Healing

In modern paganism the Green Man is a beloved deity in many circles. Often representing masculine divinity, he is depicted in art and iconography as a man's face made of oak leaves. Generally speaking, he represents rebirth and the wild spirit of the woods and growing things. The herbs and plants that are in his domain are, of course, physically healing in the form of food and medicine, but green natural settings are also profoundly emotionally and psychologically healing. What's more, the symbol of a thriving forest or woodland feels particularly healing to our souls at this moment in history, considering our frighteningly tenuous relationship with our environment.

Call on the Green Man, visit an oak, spend time among oak trees, or incorporate oak leaves or acorns in your magic for any sort of physical, mental, emotional, spiritual, environmental, or existential healing intention.

Manifestation

We are all familiar with the perennial symbol of manifestation: the tiny acorn becoming a vast oak tree. It's also been noted that the oak is hit by lightning frequently, which has been attributed to its deep taproot and proclivity for growing near underground water sources. In addition to explaining the oak's sacredness to thunder deities, this is reminiscent of the Magician in the tarot, who points one finger up to heaven to receive divine energy and one finger down to earth to project that energy toward affecting change in the physical world according to his will.

Prosperity

For many magical practitioners, oak is one of the most obvious magical botanicals to choose when working magic related to wealth and prosperity. Perhaps this partly because in earlier centuries, acorns were a very popular and nourishing food source. While survivalists still keep the acorn in mind for this purpose, most of us are dissuaded by the hassle of cooking away the excess of tannins that make the nut inedible.

Despite our modern lack of enthusiasm for acorns as a food source, the oak emits a very potent wealthy vibration and can be employed for wealth magic of all varieties.

OAK PROSPERITY BATH

On a Thursday when the moon is between new and full, lovingly gather nine acorns and nine oak leaves and wash them in cool water. Draw a bath and float the leaves and acorns in the water. Place your palms over the water and direct vibrant green light with gold sparkles into the water. Soak for at least thirty minutes.

Strength

Oak is one of the original thirty-eight flower essences recognized by the homeopathic pioneer Edward Bach and is recommended for people who feel exhausted and overworked. As opposed to coffee, which would give the patient an artificial boost of energy to continue on with their imbalance, oak gently supports the cultivation of a more sustainable relationship with one's everyday responsibilities and tasks. Similarly, oak flower essence is recommended for those recovering from long-term health challenges, as it promotes a steady, sustained quality of energy that enhances immunity and healing.

Traditionally, the oak tree is associated with the energy of strength in the form of thunder, lightning, masculinity, victory, divinity, and power.

Victory

Oak leaves figure prominently in armed forces imagery in both Germany and the United States, the highest-ranking Viking ships were made of oak, and the tree has been popularly associated with war since ancient times. The Greeks associated the tree with Mars, the god of war. And as mentioned, authoritative thunder gods from many countries were associated with the tree. Certainly, considering all of oak's other magical uses and energetic properties, the fact that he helps one achieve victory should not be surprising.

....

SIMPLE AND POWERFUL VICTORY CHARM

Respectfully gather a single acorn from beneath an oak tree and empower it in bright sunlight. Then visualize and sense exactly the type of victory you desire, exactly as if you're already experiencing it. Send the energy of this victory into the acorn. Carry it with you as you traverse your challenge or trial. When your victory is realized, visit the tree where you gathered it and feel gratitude, sending that feeling toward the tree. Then return the acorn to the tree's base.

Magical Correspondences

Element: Earth
Gender: Masculine
Planet: Sun

Olive

*M*y maternal grandfather, Papa Harry, was an olive farmer. While I didn't get to spend a lot of time with him in the physical world, in the nonphysical he is a beloved ally and friend. A lover of all things green and growing throughout his life, he also worked as a landscaper, and he passed much of his botanical wisdom to my mom, who passed some of it on to me. Now I think of him whenever I see the distinctive silvery green of an olive tree.

Over and above my own personal plant mythology, the olive (Oleaceae family) has been revered as sacred since ancient times and provides an abundance of benefits to humans: magical, medicinal, and nutritional.

Magical Uses

Beauty

Olive trees drip with the energy of pure beauty, and gazing at one can transport a person to the realm of aesthetic bliss. Spend time in quiet contemplation with an olive tree to align with the frequency of beauty and embody and emanate beauty as a matter of course. In a more physical sense, used alone or with other herbs or oils, olive oil is an excellent moisturizer, scalp rub, and conditioning hair treatment.

SHINY HAIR AND HEALTHY SCALP MASK

If you're not overly sensitive to essential oils, add nine drops of rosemary essential oil to a quarter cup olive oil. Warm it slightly, then rub it into your scalp and dry hair. Cover your head with a knit cap and leave it for fifteen to twenty minutes. Wash thoroughly with a mild shampoo and condition as usual.

Diligence

Olives contain the energy of the planet Saturn: the planet of diligence, stamina, focus, and hard work. (Perhaps that's why I crave large amounts of them while I'm editing my books.) Work olives or olive pits into your magic when your intention involves committing to the long haul for lasting, well-deserved success. For example, intentions related to long-term projects—such as completing a book, building a business from scratch, or obtaining a degree—can benefit from the energy of olives.

OLIVE BLESSING FOR COMPLETING LONG-TERM GOALS

When the waxing moon is in Capricorn, make a rice or pasta dish for yourself. Light an olive-green candle. Hold three Greek olives in your right hand and say:

From the present until the end to my goal I shall attend.
I'll weave success into each hour, imbued with olive's focused power.

Remove the pits and slice the olives, adding them to your dish. Eat mindfully, enjoying each bite and internalizing the magic. Wash each pit thoroughly, and dry them on a cloth on a sunny windowpane. When they're thoroughly dried, tie them into a red flannel pouch, along with a hematite. Keep this charm in your pocket or pinned to the inside of your clothes every day until your goal is reached.

Healing

Olive is a master healer of the arboreal world. The 1992 movie *Lorenzo's Oil* tells the true story of parents who look far and wide for a cure to their son's severe and "incurable" neurological disease, and finally find it by adding a blend of oil to his diet, derived in large part from olive oil.

According to Andrew Chevallier's *Encyclopedia of Herbal Medicine*, "[Olive] oil is nourishing and improves the balance of fats within the blood…[It] has a generally protective action on the digestive tract and is useful for dry skin." In *The Way of Herbs* Michael Tierra states, "Internally, 1 tablespoon of the oil once or twice daily is a mild laxative."

The leaves are also medicinal, and have been used since ancient times to disinfect wounds. Olive leaf extract can be taken in supplement form to support the circulatory system, lower blood sugar, and improve blood pressure.

The Greek goddess Athena is associated with both healing and olive trees, and ancient Greeks believed that her spirit inhabited them. *Cunningham's Encyclopedia of Magical Herbs* states: "On an olive leaf write Athena's name. Press this against the head or wear on the body and it will cure a headache."

Peace

Symbolically, the olive is perhaps best known as a physical representation of peace, as demonstrated by the phrase "Extending the olive branch." Athena was chosen as the namesake of Athens in large part because she offered the city an olive branch, which symbolized peace. Once chosen as the city's divine beneficiary, Athena's olive trees were revered as sacred, and a holy lamp—fueled with olive oil from the city's trees—burned around the clock.

PEACE PICK-ME-UP

To create a powder that will help establish peace in any area, mindfully collect forty olive leaves and then dry them on a sunny windowsill. When they are thoroughly brittle, grind into a powder and place in a jar. (It's good to have a coffee grinder on hand specifically for such magical purposes.) Whenever you desire to establish peace, surreptitiously scatter one pinch of the powder around the space.

Wealth

While olive trees thrive in drier climates such as California and the Mediterranean, olives themselves are quite moist, and the tree is energetically attuned to the element of water. Indeed, simply eating olives or olive oil is a sumptuous, luxurious, and nourishing experience that noticeably aligns one with the energy of wealth. The olive may have gained further association with wealth by serving as one of the primary commodities of ancient Athens. Additionally, olives have been magically aligned with fertility and luck, both of which correspond directly with the olive's ability to bestow wealth.

QUICK AND POTENT (AND DELICIOUS) WEALTH BLESSING

To quickly tune your frequency to the energy of lavish wealth and abundance, mindfully eat eight olives on a Thursday while the moon is waxing. All the while, be sure to feel luxurious and even decadent.

Magical Correspondences

Element: Water
Gender: Masculine
Planet: Saturn

Orange

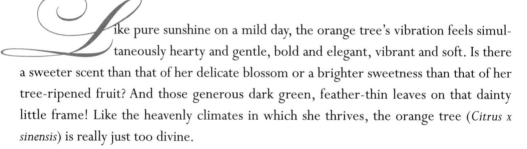

*L*ike pure sunshine on a mild day, the orange tree's vibration feels simultaneously hearty and gentle, bold and elegant, vibrant and soft. Is there a sweeter scent than that of her delicate blossom or a brighter sweetness than that of her tree-ripened fruit? And those generous dark green, feather-thin leaves on that dainty little frame! Like the heavenly climates in which she thrives, the orange tree (*Citrus x sinensis*) is really just too divine.

Magical Uses

Happiness and Joy

Simply bringing an orange to mind—conjuring up its scent, for example, or its tangy sweetness or its bright, textured peel—can palpably lift the mood in an instant. So can inhaling the always surprisingly exquisite scent of a creamy white orange blossom. Indeed, oranges abound at Chinese New Year celebrations to bless the forthcoming year with happiness, joy, and all good things. A classic feng shui recommendation involves bringing in a bowl of oranges for a happy home.

....

HAPPINESS BATH

On a Sunday when the moon is waxing, draw a warm bath. Add a tablespoon of sea salt, the peel from one organic orange, and three drops of essential oil of neroli (aka orange blossom). Using your right hand, stir in a clockwise direction for nine full rotations (or three sets of three if it helps you keep count). During each rotation, chant "Om ma ni pad me hum." In Taoist magic, this chant is known as the "six true words" and activates positive blessings of all varieties by aligning you deeply with All That Is. As you chant, visualize blindingly bright sunlight and the energy of sweetness filling the water. Then soak for at least forty minutes, feeling all heaviness and darkness dissolve completely in the bright light of joy.

Masculine/Feminine Balance

With a nuanced blend of the most fabulous qualities both yang and yin (for example, she's aligned with both the feminine earth element and the masculine sun), the orange tree is adept at bringing the archetypal poles into a most melodious balance. This can be helpful, for example, if you love expressing your feminine gifts of nurturing and beautification, and you'd like to aspect these qualities harmoniously with the masculine gifts of directionality and single-minded focus. Or, conversely, orange can also be helpful if you're constantly focused and directional, and you'd like to balance these qualities with a little more relaxation, play, and feminine enjoyment. If you're in a relationship with someone with an essence that leans toward an opposing pole (i.e., masculine to your feminine or vice versa), orange can be employed to clear away any tension or discord related to your differences and help establish a harmonious dance of opposites in its place.

Spend time with an orange tree to receive these benefits, or diffuse or wear essential oil blends containing petitgrain essential oil (made from leaves and twigs of the bitter orange tree).

Partnership

Speaking of harmonious dances, orange is an excellent magical ally when it comes to partnerships of all varieties. Orange blossoms and neroli essential oil (made from orange blossoms) are employed for rituals related to marriage and long-term romantic partnerships (bringing about new ones or harmonizing existing ones). Planting one or more orange trees in your yard can be an excellent way to bring about or fortify a blissful partnership—romantic, business, or otherwise.

New Business Partner Blessing

To bless a relationship with a new business partner (who happens to be open to doing a magical ritual with you), hand them an orange and instruct them to hold it in both hands. With another orange, do the same. Now, both of you should mentally charge the oranges in your hands with bright, golden-white light filled with general positivity and well-wishes. Conjure up all the feelings you'd like to have in your new venture and envision/sense/feel the two of you laughing together and experiencing all the most wonderful kinds of success. When this feels complete, exchange oranges. Peel and eat.

Sweetness

While skin may not technically have taste buds, on a perfectly temperate spring or fall day, the sunlight on your skin almost *tastes* sweet. Sure, it's sharply, blindingly bright, but it's sweet also. And this is like a fresh, tree-ripened orange or fresh-squeezed orange juice: delightfully, deliciously sweet, but also tangy and with a punch. The orange blossom, also, is energetically sweet, although more gently so, like the first light of morning before the rays begin to glare. And so, when you'd like to bring more sweetness into your life or home, employ the orange. Bring in some blossoms, diffuse or wear essential oil of neroli, add a bowl or oranges, plant an orange tree, and so on. Orange blossom honey is also a great option for sweetness rituals. Try adding some to a bath or creating a sweetness potion by stirring some into some hot tea.

Magical Correspondences

Element: Earth
Gender: Feminine
Planet: Sun

Pagoda Tree

*A*lso called the Chinese scholar tree, the pagoda tree (*Styphnolobium japonicum*) is a native to China and Korea, though he's also lived in Japan for some time and is widely planted as an ornamental. With plenty of year-round leaves that cast a luxuriant shade, the tree's fragrant, pealike white flowers appear in late summer and early fall.

Magical Uses

Earth Alignment

The Chinese character for this tree is a combination of the characters for "wood" and "demon." And in fact, stories from both China and Japan indicate that the tree was suspected of harboring maleficent spirits. On the other hand, the tree has been popularly cultivated around Buddhist temples and has even been employed as a grave marker for Buddhist monks.

In truth, the pagoda tree is like a litmus test: if you are deeply in alignment with the earth—in other words, if the elements are balanced within you—he supports you spiritually and energetically. If you are not—for example, if you recklessly exploit the planet and behave in other ways that take you out of your natural harmony with your environment—he precipitates karma that will give you the opportunity and message to mend your ways. Of course, like being whacked on the head by a Zen master, experiencing this karma may leave a mark.

However, there is no need to fear the pagoda tree. As long as you approach and spend time with him with the sincere desire and willingness to be in the most harmonious possible alignment with the planet, he will not punish you cruelly but will rather nudge you gently toward acting with a respectful, grounded awareness of the interconnection of All That Is.

Healing

In Traditional Chinese Medicine the pagoda tree (called Sophora Japonica or Huai Ha Mi) is considered one of the fifty fundamental herbs. Because of the astringent action of the flowers, the pagoda tree is employed to stop bleeding, treat blood clots and hemorrhages, promote circulatory and vein health, and regulate energy flow. Circulatory health and regulation of energy flow support all varieties of healing (emotional, spiritual, and physical). Considering the pagoda tree's penchant for balancing and activating energy in precisely the way that is most needed, just spending quality time with a pagoda tree can be a wonderful way to supplement any and all healing efforts. Planting a pagoda tree in your yard is an excellent way to have a healer on staff around the clock.

Magical Correspondences

Element: Earth
Gender: Masculine
Planet: Ceres

Palm

*T*he palm's diverse and geographically widespread family has a history that is inextricably intertwined with virtually every aspect of human civilization. Mentioned frequently in the Bible and in Christian iconography, the palm (family Arecaceae) generously provided our tropical and desert dwelling ancestors with food, shelter, paper for sacred texts, and a wide variety of medicines and tools.

As opposed to most trees, which are dicots (plants which branch and spread), palms are monocots (plants with a straighter and more singular growth pattern). This means that they are in a lot of ways more similar to a blade of grass or a stalk of corn than, say, an oak or an elm.

Magical Uses
Cleansing, Transforming, and Transitioning
It's no coincidence that the most archetypal symbol of fiery transformation, the phoenix, is aligned with the palm. Like a scorching desert and the unrelenting sun, palms

are not sentimental or sympathetic, although they will be there for you when you want to clear away old stagnant emotions, purge what you no longer need, and purify your inner landscape, and generally move out of one phase and into another. This quality can be helpful for times when you're ready to really let go of the old and make room for the new.

Palm Sunday in the Christian tradition also demonstrates this magical quality of the palm, as it marks the moment when Christ chose to return victoriously to Jerusalem, symbolically overriding the pattern of oppression and setting in motion the events that led to his transformational resurrection. Additionally, in traditional stories about St. Christopher, the saint's staff flowered like a palm tree after he carried the baby Jesus across the river, serving as another rite of passage and transition symbol. Even the way that palms are included in Catholic images of martyred saints hints at this most intense (to put it mildly) transformational quality of the tree.

As a more modern example, many people move to palm-punctuated Los Angeles when they want to reset their inner compass, let go of limiting beliefs (particularly related to their past and family patterns), and invent a brand-new life for themselves. Many people even change their names and then undergo a rigorous regimen of yoga and energy healing in order to propel themselves into a whole new place. While the city's natural ability to help with this process may lend to the energetically unstable feeling that causes outsiders to label its residents as "flaky" or "shallow," it can in some cases be quite useful: for example, when one would like to cleanse away old expectations, propel oneself out of a rut, and expand one's consciousness beyond the confines of what one has been taught.

But you need not move to Los Angeles to receive these benefits: try working with palm tree energy to cleanse stuck energy, reinvent yourself, and step more fully into your power. (Perhaps not coincidentally, palms and angels—as in the City of Angels—go way back. Historically, the cherubs of Solomon's temple almost always appeared with palm trees.)

Indeed, palms can be an excellent addition to rituals designed for personal cleansing of old patterns or to mark rites of passage into beautiful new phases of life. For this purpose, you might try simply sweeping your aura with a palm frond, decorating your altar with palm leaves, or preparing a feast featuring dates, coconuts, or hearts of palm.

Divine Masculine

The palm tree is not just masculine: it is sacred masculine energy in tree form. With their bladelike growth pattern (i.e., their classification as a monocot), heat (they generally prefer bright sun and tropical locales), and activity (palms are hardworking trees!)— not to mention the undeniably testicular appearance of coconuts and dates while they are still hanging in the tree—Taoist cosmology would definitely classify them as falling under the category of *yang*.

Consequently—as the sole biblical prophetess Deborah may have known when she chose to speak her prophecies near a palm tree—the palm might be a good ally to work with when you'd like to embody or relate more positively to the masculine side of things (i.e., directness, projection, action, aggression, and single-minded focus). While masculinity often gets a bad rap in metaphysical spiritual circles, the truth is that when it is ideally balanced with femininity (i.e., nurturance, beauty, stillness, receptivity, and peace), it is quite useful and positive.

To activate, balance, or harmonize with masculine energy, try spending time in quiet contemplation with a palm tree, bringing one or more palms into your yard, placing palm fronds on your altar, incorporating palm leaves into your rituals, or blessing and then consuming food from palm trees (such as coconuts, dates, or hearts of palm).

Fertility

While this might not be the most appropriate period in history to promote fertility in the usual literal sense (our beloved Mother Earth is grievously overextended as it is), fertility can be a desirable magical intention when it comes to things like our career, vegetable garden, and creative projects. Consider incorporating especially fertile palm ingredients (i.e., dates, coconuts—see "Divine Masculine" section) into rituals designed for this purpose.

Nourishment

Have you ever really considered the coconut palm? It not only provides food (coconut meat and oil are each healthy diet additions, hearts of coconut palm are a gourmet salad ingredient, and coconut milk is a delicious and hearty dairy substitute), it also provides superior hydration to the body and skin (baby coconut water is one of the best hydration drinks, and coconut oil is an amazing moisturizer). As if all that weren't enough, coconut oil is antibacterial and can be used as a mouthwash to pull toxins from the mouth and body. Clearly, when it comes to nourishment and vitality—inside and out—the coconut palm is a one-stop shop! One need look no further than a single tree for evidence that we have coevolved with these botanical neighbors in a most miraculously supportive way.

As such, rituals aimed at increasing personal nourishment—or fostering a sense that one is totally supported by the earth and universe—can be enhanced by coconut palm ingredients, such as any of those listed above. For example, try simply charging a baby coconut full of coconut water (or even a glass of coconut water from a can) with the intention of nourishment. Visualize and affirm that you are completely supported by the universe in every way, and that everything you need is instantly available to you, then reverently drink.

What's more, dates are a densely caloric—and deliciously candylike—nutrition source. Branches of the date palm are incorporated in the Jewish festival of Sukkot, which is, in one sense, a harvest festival and a time of gathering food.

Peace and Relaxation

In our modern times palms are often associated with idyllic settings of luxurious relaxation. The gentle sway of a palm-lined hula skirt certainly evokes a hypnotically soothing sort of stress relief. Interestingly, they also feature into the Islamic vision of paradise. Because they symbolized victory in the ancient world, they came to be associated with the end of conflict, also known as peace.

When relaxing under palm trees or enjoying a mesmerizing hula performance is not an option, the luxurious satisfaction of consuming sweets or sweet drinks made with dates or coconut ingredients can also have quite a peaceful and relaxing effect, as can pampering yourself with a body lotion made with coconut oil.

Victory

While vacations may be the most obvious modern association with palms, victory was perhaps the quality most obviously associated with these trees—particularly palm fronds—in Roman and biblical times. If you're involved in a legal battle in which you are morally in the right, you might gather a small piece of a palm frond and empower it in bright sunlight for one minute. Then, with a black pen, draw a *V* for victory on it. Hold it in both hands and visualize that you have already won. Really conjure up images and feelings associated with the precise form of victory you desire, and know in your heart that in the realm beyond time it is already so. Carry the charm with you to court or to the place where your case will be decided.

Magical Correspondences

Element: Fire

Gender: Masculine

Planet: Pluto

Palo Santo

*Q*uite appropriately, *palo santo* translates to "sacred wood." This South American cousin of frankincense and myrrh has been traditionally employed in folk medicine and ceremony for thousands of years, perhaps beginning with the Incas.

The scent of palo santo (*Bursera graveolens*) is unique. If you haven't smelled it, imagine a combination of cedar, smoky maple syrup, sweet lemon iced tea, and a verdant forest as the day begins to dawn. Although I've never met an actual palo santo tree, I'm well acquainted with the wood because of its popularity in metaphysical and magical supply shops. It's burned like incense, and its smoke is used to smudge (or energetically clear) places, objects, and people.

Magical Uses

Aligning with the Divine

As his name implies, palo santo's wood, incense, and oil are employed to align one with the realm of the sacred. Simply diffusing the oil, misting with water into which you've added the oil, burning the incense, or smudging with a palo santo stick can burn away the illusion of separation and dissolve everything that is not real, true, and from love. It does this in much the same way the rising sun burns away morning dew and bathes everything in blinding illumination. However, while palo santo is aligned with the sun, he is also aligned with the moon, so he possesses a gentleness and a balance that can help one balance out, open the heart, and find the Divine within.

Clearing

As described above, palo santo possesses a clearing action that dissolves away all undesirable energies and attunes areas, people, animals, and objects to the frequency of divine power and love. In fact, many people who dislike the smell of white sage turn to palo santo as a more agreeable alternative.

Interestingly, palo santo oil is also antiviral and antiseptic. This may signify that the smoke also has disinfecting properties, as some studies on smudging have indicated.

Creating Sacred Space

The two uses described above—aligning with the Divine and clearing—place palo santo on the A-list of magical botanicals that create sacred space. Creating sacred space is an intention shared by all magical practitioners as they prepare for spells and rituals. But creating sacred space is also our intention when we dedicate any area to a divine purpose: this could be a yoga or ritual space, or even a home or a business we choose to regularly dwell in. For this purpose, simply diffuse the oil, mist with water containing the oil, or use a stick to smudge.

Healing

Palo santo is burned to create sacred space for healing, and the oil and wood aromatherapeutically support the immune system and relax the mind and emotions. Additionally, the essential oil can be combined in equal parts with a carrier oil and applied topically to disinfect and reduce inflammation.

Meditation

Are you noticing a theme? As you might guess from the previous uses, palo santo is an excellent ally for meditation, as the scent clears the mind, soothes the spirit, and lifts one's consciousness into the realm of the Divine. If you're in South America and palo santo trees are in the neighborhood, lucky you! You can sit in quiet contemplation with a tree and soak in some mighty meditation mojo and super sacred sensations.

Magical Correspondences

Element: Spirit
Gender: Masculine
Planet: Sun and Moon

Paradise Tree

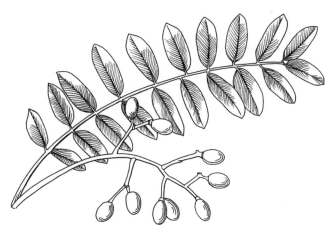

*A*ptly named, the stunning paradise tree (*Simarouba glauca*) is a bringer of great blessings. Her fruit is edible, her leaves and bark are medicinal, and her environmental benefits hint at a whole, healthy, and abundant world to come.

While this lush and multitalented tree is native to Florida as well as Central and South America, activists in India have somewhat recently adopted her as a potential remedy for the climate crisis. The well-known guru Sri Sri Ravi Shankar, in particular, is championing her propagation in India, and even dubbed the tree *Lakshmi taru*, after Lakshmi, the Hindu goddess of abundant prosperity. (*Taru* means "tree.")

Magical Uses

Environmental Healing

As mentioned above, the paradise tree is currently being propagated in India for a number of environmental purposes, which include sustainable sources of biofuel and timber. The tree is also being employed to improve groundwater, heal wastelands, support soil, and reduce the negative effects of carbon on our atmosphere. The fact that the paradise tree is aligned with Pluto—the planet of regeneration and transformation—sheds further light on her status as an arboreal messiah for our current environmental predicament.

If you happen to be in one of the tropical locales in which the paradise tree thrives, sitting in quiet contemplation with her can help attune your frequency to that of environmental healing. Relax, gaze at the tree, silently request guidance, and allow her to bestow a message of how you can best support our beautiful planet at this time. After relaxing deeply for a few moments, you may receive her response as an image, a feeling, or a sense. It may or may not make sense to your linear thinking mind at first. Whatever happens, rest assured that on some level, in some way, you have received the message and it will help to shape your future actions in life-affirming ways.

Making a flower essence with some of her blossoms and taking two to three drops per day in water over a prolonged period of time can also help attune you to the frequency that will allow you to best support the earth and her inhabitants with regard to climate change. (You can find instructions on how to make a flower essence in a number of reputable books about flower essences, including my book *The Magic of Flowers*.)

Physical Healing

What supports the earth supports us, and vice versa. In the case of the beautiful paradise tree, this is quite literal. In addition to healing the planet, she is considered—particularly in India—to be very useful for healing our physical bodies. According to the website LakshmiTaru.com, a decoction of the paradise tree's leaves, barks, and sticks has been used traditionally in its native areas for treating a whole host of challenges, including dysentery, diarrhea, malaria, colitis, gastritis, anemia, gynecological disorders, wounds, sores, ulcers, arthritis, and even cancer.

In the Western world there is not currently a lot of information on how to work with the paradise tree safely. So if you feel drawn to work with her medicinally, first consult with a trusted expert.

Wealth

A tree named after not just the heavenly realm but also the goddess Lakshmi absolutely *must* specialize in the magical quality of wealth. Certainly her glossy leaves and virtual fountain of fruits lend themselves to a sense of luxurious abundance. The fact that she heals environments, nourishes groundwater, and transforms wastelands demonstrates that she brings a verdant sense of affluence wherever she goes. Not to mention her seeds yield oil that is exceptionally useful as biofuel! In a world where oil for fuel is a synonym for money, she is an almost literal example of money growing on trees.

Spend time in quiet contemplation with a paradise tree to receive energy healing and an attunement to the frequency of wealth.

Magical Correspondences

Element: Air
Gender: Feminine
Planet: Pluto

Parasol Tree

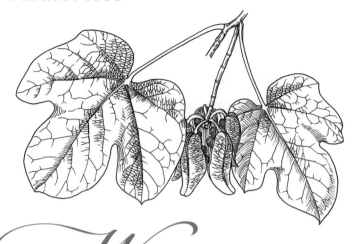

With round clusters of branches that display their broad, three-pointed leaves in mushroom-shaped tufts, the parasol tree (*Firmiana simplex*)—also known as the wutong—lends a luxurious vibration to each of the many warm landscapes he happens to adorn. His delicious extravagance should not be surprising, as he's recently been named a member of the cacao (chocolate) family.

Magical Uses

Good Fortune

It's said that the Chinese phoenix, or fenghuang, loves the parasol tree and will alight on no other tree. It's also said that this mythical bird will only be found in places possessing the utmost harmony and positivity. A lush representative of prosperous and temperate conditions, the very presence of a parasol tree confers a sense of affluence, comfort, and luck. Spend time with one, bring one into your yard, or conjure one up in your visioning mind to reap fortunate blessings of all varieties.

Harmony

In a story recorded during the Ming Dynasty, "the essence of the five planets" descends upon a wutong (parasol) tree. The master craftsman who observed this knew that this would make the tree's wood perfect for creating a Chinese zither (a traditional musical instrument), as it contained the "cosmic essences." Next comes a description of the alchemical creation of a most magical Chinese zither, possessing the eight superior qualities of "delicacy, uniqueness, serenity, elegance, dolefulness, grandeur, sweetness, and lingering vibrations." To this day the parasol tree's wood is used to make Chinese zithers due to its excellent sonic resonance.

Additionally, the Chinese phoenix, which is said to roost in parasol trees, is associated with yin/yang balance as well as cosmic harmony.

Magical Correspondences

Element: Fire
Gender: Masculine
Planets: Sun and Moon

Peach

The peach tree is a magical celebrity in his native land of China, as well as in the other Asian countries where he grows. Powerfully protective against all things negative, and strongly symbolic of all things good and right in the world, the peach (*Prunus persica*) tree is a wonderful magical ally to have. Not to mention, his flowers are breathtaking and his fruit the very pinnacle of palatability.

Magical Uses

Health

Shou Hsing—the white-bearded Chinese god of health and longevity—is sometimes depicted holding a peach. Indeed, peach kernel is used in Chinese medicine to reduce inflammation and activate blood flow, and a ripe peach is a potent symbol of robust physical health.

A Peach a Day Keeps the Doctor Away

To bolster immunity and physical health, bless a single peach every morning. Do this by washing it and then holding it up in both hands in the direction of the morning sun. As you do so, envision a vibrant, peach-colored light filling and surrounding it. Then mindfully eat it, feeling yourself internalizing the light of health as you do so. Begin at the new moon and continue until the moon is full.

Immortality

While I can't guarantee that peaches (or anything else) will bestow literal immortality upon you, the idea of immortality *as a symbol* can certainly enhance one's magical and spiritual work. Chinese tradition states that certain deities ate peaches to prolong their immortal status every three thousand years. Similar to the Greek pantheon's fondness for ambrosia, these special "peaches of immortality" grew in the garden of the Queen Mother of the West, also known as the Taoist goddess Hsi Wang Mu. Peaches can be blessed and eaten in magical work as a way to honor and acknowledge the immortality of the soul.

Protection

Peach wood and peach pits are extremely effective magical protectors. Freshly dried pits can be placed around the home and near entrances to ward off wayward spirits and negativity in general. In China, blossoming branches are traditionally placed around the home as cheerful decorations that also happen to shield against all forms of negativity. In ancient times, peach wood arrows and wands were used to ward off untoward influences and protect against evil spirits.

I have personally found peach pits to be an excellent magical ingredient to have on hand regularly, for anytime you need to protect against anything at all. I have even used one as a ward against parking tickets (mind you, I used to live in Los Angeles, where parking tickets are virtually hiding around every corner).

Extra Strength Protection Ward

Let's say you need serious energetic protection from any form of intensely negative vibes. Empower a dried peach pit and a clove of garlic by holding them in bright sunlight for thirty seconds to one minute. Tie them into red flannel using a small length of hemp twine. Hold it in both hands and say, "Archangel Michael, bless this ward with your fire and light. May it repel negativity all day and all night. With abiding love and thanks to thee, as I will it, so mote it be." Keep it in your pocket or pin it to the inside of your clothes—and of course take every possible precaution in the physical world to stay safe.

Positive Energy

Wherever the peach tree grows in the Asian world, it seems the peach is associated with all good things: happiness, joy, sweetness, victory, health, wealth, protection, longevity, and even immortality. In the Western world we obviously sense this as well, as proven by our popular slang term meaning generally positive and happy: "peachy."

Just Peachy Charm for All-Purpose Positivity

To bless a space with general positivity of all varieties, charm a peach and simply place it in the area. Do this by empowering it in sunlight and invoking a deity of your choice to bless it with the energy of all good things. Afterward, give it back to the earth by placing it at the base of a tree. (Incidentally, don't encourage this, but if someone happens to inadvertently eat the charmed peach, it should be quite interesting to note how they behave.)

Magical Correspondences

Element: Fire
Gender: Masculine
Planet: Venus

Pear

Cultivated since the most ancient of times, the pear tree (*Pyrus*) is sacred to Hera, the divine Queen of Greece herself and quite possibly the reigning indigenous goddess of the region before the patriarchy prevailed. Indeed, the pear is a most magical specimen and transports one's consciousness to the realm of beauty, sweetness, and pure potentiality.

Magical Uses

Cooling the Emotions

In Chinese medicine, pears are considered cooling, and they are used to treat health challenges related to excess heat. On the emotional level, this property of pears can be employed to instantly cool down a hot head and generally help one to "chill." For this purpose, simply empower a clean pear in moonlight (or envision a cool, receptive, lunar light filling the fruit) and then mindfully eat. Simply spending time in quiet contemplation with a pear tree possesses similar benefits.

Good Spirits

While aligned with the receptive, feminine moon, the pear tree simultaneously possesses a masculine energetic charge. This combo, along with his correspondence with the air element, gives him a uniquely mystical vibration, somewhat like that of the poet William Blake. Blake's line "Traveller repose & dream among my leaves" is reminiscent of pear's energetic specialty of holding open a gate to divine perception and being an arboreal channel of divinity.

In Vainakh mythology (of Chechnya), pear trees were worshipped as sacred, because it was believed that divine spirits resided in them. Pear trees indeed possess an otherworldly sweetness, and if a spirit or divinity were in the market for a purely positive physical home, they could certainly do worse than a pear tree. Furthermore, pear wood is used for high quality woodwind instruments and as firewood for smoking tobacco and meats: and this ability to channel the invisible, ethereal air element in tangible ways mirrors the tree's ability to be a physical home for the elusive realm of spirit.

Paradise

In Homer's *The Odyssey*, abundant pears (among other fruit trees) appear in a beautiful, magical orchard outside the idyllic palace of the semidivine King Alcinous:

> Therein grow trees, tall and luxuriant, pears and pomegranates and apple-trees with their bright fruit, and sweet figs, and luxuriant olives. Of these the fruit perishes not nor fails in winter or in summer, but lasts throughout the year; and ever does the west wind, as it blows, quicken to life some fruits, and ripen others; pear upon pear waxes ripe, apple upon apple, cluster upon cluster, and fig upon fig.

Plant and lovingly care for one or more pear trees in your yard to bless your "kingdom" with a verdant, otherworldly, and paradisiacal presence.

Wands

Pear wood makes excellent wands for a number of reasons. First, it's highly positive, and its masculine resonance makes for an excellent tool for projecting energy. Second, it's aligned powerfully with the Divine, so all uses will be blessed with the highest and truest good. Third, its lunar receptivity makes it extremely conducive to energy—upon holding a pear wand, many magical practitioners and energy workers will immediately sense its swift effectiveness.

Magical Correspondences

Element: Air
Gender: Masculine
Planet: Moon

Pecan

*T*he lush pecan is the only major nut tree indigenous to North America. And his leaves are the most vibrant, magical shade of green! Though pecan trees haven't been cultivated until relatively recently, the Native American tribes who coexisted with an abundance of them considered their nuts to be vital nutritional staples.

Please note that while pecans are technically a variety of hickory, pecan species (of the genus *Carya*) have their own unique vibration and magical properties. For non-pecan hickories, see "Hickory."

Magical Uses

Abundance

Some Native American tribes planted pecan trees along trade routes, so that they would have plenty to offer to trade when they came across what they were looking for. For them, you might say that money actually *did* grow on trees, albeit in the form of pecans. Nowadays, in addition to working magic to support sustenance (see "Sustenance"), the modern magical practitioner can employ pecans as a magical wealth and abundance booster. For example, simply placing a bowl of unshelled pecans on your altar as an offering to the Divine can be a wonderful way to enhance your wealth. This works with the magical law of returns, which states that what we send out returns to us multiplied. Or you might try the following:

Quick and Delicious Wealth Boost

On a Thursday when the moon is waxing, empower nine pecans in bright sunlight. (Do this by simply holding them in your open palm and letting them absorb the light for ten to thirty seconds.) Then mindfully eat them, feeling yourself internalizing the energies of wealth and abundance.

Immunity

Used as a carrier oil, pecan oil is excellent for moisturizing and massage blends, particularly when immunity boosting is a goal. Inhaling the oil's scent and rubbing it into the skin can also be great for speeding recovery when getting over an illness or an injury.

Sustenance

The Spanish explorer Álvar Núñez Cabeza de Vaca reported that the buttery and delicious pecan was a main food staple of the Mariame Indian tribe. For this tribe and other Native Americans who lived in areas where pecans grew, the pecan's abundant harvest of nutrient-dense food aligned the tree with the abundant blessings of the Great Spirit. And while it's a relatively new custom, serving pecan pie at Thanksgiving is an echo of this ancient symbolism. Indeed, the nut—which literally grows on trees and requires no preparation at all, other than cracking—is rich in protein, vitamins, minerals, and healthy fats.

BLESSED PECAN PIE FOR CONTINUED SUSTENANCE

Light an orange candle and prepare your favorite recipe of pecan pie. After arranging pecans across the top but before baking, hold your palms over the pie. Visualize golden-orange light filling and radiating from the pie as you say:

Plenty to eat and plenty to share
May those who enjoy have blessings to spare.
Fill our pantries, fuel our cheer
And keep us blessed throughout the year.
With thanks and love to the sacred pecan tree
As I will it, so mote it be.

Bake, cool, serve, and enjoy as usual.

Magical Correspondences

Element: Water
Gender: Masculine
Planet: Sun

Persimmon

While it's important to note that not all persimmon trees (of the genus *Diospyros*) bear edible fruit, persimmons have been called "fruit of the gods" and taste like pumpkin pie–flavored marshmallows. Speaking of pumpkins, the ripe fruit looks like a tiny, particularly bright and robust pumpkin, and (also like pumpkins) is an excellent addition to celebratory autumn desserts.

Magical Uses
Banishing Chills

According to author Scott Cunningham in *Cunningham's Encyclopedia of Magical Herbs*, "If you are plagued with chills, tie a knot in a piece of string (one for each chill you've had) and tie the string to a persimmon tree. This should halt them." While I can't vouch for the effectiveness of this, the persimmon tree is certainly warm, healing, and grounding in nature. It's definitely worth a try.

Wealth

An elegantly petite tree that yields a beautiful little flower and later a showy orange fruit that basically tastes like heaven, the persimmon tree most certainly vibrates to the frequency of wealth. In Korea a delicious dessert beverage (something like a spicy iced cider or fruit punch) is made from persimmons. Its other traditional ingredients make it an excellent wealth potion, particularly when your desire is for activating the finances and getting financial energy moving. I suggest enjoying it at Thanksgiving or during a harvest celebration.

PERSIMMON WEALTH POTION (AKA SUJEONGGWA)
Ingredients:

- The equivalent of 9 thinly sliced, quarter-sized pieces of fresh ginger
- 1 cinnamon stick
- 3 black peppercorns
- 3 red dates (dried)
- 6 cups water
- 4 tablespoons maple syrup (more can be added if desired)
- 9 dried persimmons, first soaked for 40 minutes, drained, and quartered
- Small handful of toasted pine nuts (See "Kernels of Divine Harmony" on page 266 to empower with the energy of divine harmony)

Assemble all ingredients in one spot in your kitchen. Hold your palms above them, visualize them as filled with glowing golden or orange light, and say a blessing over them, such as:

Ingredients of wondrous wealth
Bless us with financial health.

Place all ingredients except the persimmons, maple syrup, and pine nuts in a large pot. Bring to a boil, reduce heat to low, and allow to simmer for fifty minutes. Remove from heat and add the maple syrup, stirring to dissolve. Place the persimmons in a bowl and strain mixture over the top. Refrigerate until ice cold. Divide into four glasses (all at once or one at a time, depending on how many you're serving), with some of the persimmon in each. Sprinkle some pine nuts over the top.

Just before serving, hold your hands over the glasses once more, visualize more glowing golden or orange light filling and surrounding them, and say:

As Earth's great bounty we partake
To our wealth we now awake.

Magical Correspondences

Element: Fire
Gender: Feminine
Planet: Jupiter

Pine

I have spent many precious hours among the pines in the Sierra Nevada mountains, inhaling their delicious scent and absorbing their wisdom of eternal serenity. A veritable synonym of refreshment and comfort, the very word *pine* invokes a sense that all is right with the world.

Please note that there are many different types of pines in the pine family (genus *Pinus*) that thrive in many different regions. For individual pine species, you may want to do your own fieldwork to discover the unique energetic properties they possess. Please also note that this section excludes the pines in the pinyon family, which may be found in the "Pinyon" section.

Magical Uses

Clarity

When clarity is desired—particularly around the topic of finances—the scent of pine can be a great boon. Retreat to a cabin among the pines, take a walk in a pine forest, or simply inhale or diffuse pine needle essential oil. You might also anoint your wallet, bank statement, or other financial documents with essential oil of pine in order to bring clarity about what to do or how to proceed.

Essentially, pine clears away what doesn't serve you, both mentally and physically. In addition to promoting mental clarity, pine is employed in aromatherapy to help clear congestion and to improve respiration and circulation. Diffuse the essential oil in your space or waft a bottle under your nose to receive these benefits.

PINE CANDLE SPELL FOR FINANCIAL CLARITY

If you desire clear insight into the topic of finances, mix a few drops of pine needle essential oil into a small amount of olive oil on a Thursday or a Sunday when the moon is between new and full. Carve the words "Clarity, Energy, Abundance" into a green pillar candle and anoint it with the oil blend. Light it, and safely burn it at intervals until it's burned all the way down. Once it's cooled, dispose of any remaining wax.

Divine Harmony

According to author Joy N. Hulme in *Wild Fibonacci: Nature's Secret Code Revealed*, the number of pine needles in a bundle and the number of spirals in a pinecone—like so many naturally occurring patterns—are arranged according to the famed Fibonacci sequence (i.e., a sequence of numbers in which each number is the sum of the two preceding it). A prominent feature of sacred geometry, the Fibonacci sequence is related to the golden ratio and has been considered since time immemorial to be an important key to the harmony and structure of the universe.

Additionally, pines can live extremely long lives. In the presence of a very old pine, one feels closer to eternity. In fact, a small number of Great Basin bristlecone pines in California (in the Methuselah Grove of the Ancient Bristlecone Pine Forest) are the world's oldest living trees at around 5,000 years old.

Simply spending time in the presence of a pine or spending time in an area where pines grow in abundance can confer a sense of harmony, wholeness, eternity, and loving divine presence. One can also magically bring in the energy of divine harmony by lovingly gathering pinecones in a basket or a bowl and placing them on an altar or elsewhere in the home. Add a dash of divine harmony to any dish by performing the following.

Kernels of Divine Harmony

Toast pine nuts in a dry skillet over low heat until golden brown. As you do so, call on the Divine in a way that feels powerful for you. Visualize the pine nuts glowing and pulsating with golden white light of divine harmony and balance. Cool to room temperature and sprinkle over any dish, sweet or savory, to bless the diners with the energy of divine harmony and the added benefit of deliciousness!

Healing

As ancient cultures all over the world were well aware, the scent of pine supports physical healing. Bring in a bowl of lightly crushed pine needles or diffuse the essential oil to support yourself or others while healing from any illness or injury. According to authors PJ Pierson and Mary Shipley in *Aromatherapy for Everyone*, pine needle essential oil can specifically help with a wide range of issues, including asthma, bronchitis, colds, flu, coughs, digestive problems, hangovers, nervous exhaustion, rheumatism, and sore throats.

Purification

Employ the scent of pine to energetically purify any room or area. Do this by diffusing the essential oil, misting with spring water into which you've added ten to twenty drops of the essential oil, or lightly crushing fresh pine needles and placing them around the space.

Releasing Guilt

Pine flower essence (one of the original thirty-eight Bach Flower Remedies) is employed to alleviate constant thoughts and feelings of guilt and self-blame, as well as the tendency to over-apologize. For this purpose, try two to three drops under the tongue or in water, three times per day for at least one month. As reinforcement, or if you prefer to employ the essence in one fell swoop, add forty drops of the flower essence to your bathwater.

And, if you're plagued by guilt about a specific action or situation, you might try the following:

··

PINE TREE CONFESSIONAL (FOR GUILT BANISHMENT)

Visit a pine tree in a remote location or somewhere you're sure you won't be disturbed. Hold a glass or an open bottle of water in both hands, relax, and center yourself while gazing at the tree. When you feel ready, confess the whole thing to the tree. Speak aloud and wring it all out: everything that you've been holding on to and feeling guilty about. Cry if you need to, and allow yourself to move through any feelings that come up. When this feels thoroughly complete, pour the water around the base of the tree. Feel your load lightening as the tree takes your burden and transforms it into nourishing compost. Notice how forgiving the tree is, and how much lighter you feel. As a gesture of thanks, give the tree a big hug. Then walk away without looking back.

Magical Correspondences

Element: Spirit
Gender: Feminine
Planet: Neptune

Pink Silk Tree

*M*y earliest childhood home had a pink silk tree in the backyard. (They're native to Asia but have made themselves at home in the United States and are cultivated as ornamentals in California.) While my stepmother often cursed the fuzzy mess created by her fallen flowers, it was my view that the tree blessed the space with exotic whimsy, lightness, and joy.

Sometimes called a mimosa (not to be confused with acacia, which is also sometimes called mimosa), you might avoid confusion at the health food store, botanical garden, or nursery by looking for the pink silk tree's official name *Albizia julibrissin*.

Magical Uses

Happiness

In Traditional Chinese Medicine the pink silk tree is employed as a stress-reliever and a mood-booster. In fact, simply gazing at a pink silk tree in sunlight—or even just visualizing one—infuses the spirit with a distinctive brightness and calm. If you know of one growing in your area, it's an excellent idea to visit her often during times of depression or stress. Otherwise, you might seek out a picture of her online and bring her into your mind's eye during meditation.

Sensitivity

The pink silk tree's ornate little bipinnate leaves and soft, brushlike blooms are potent visual and tactile symbols of sensitivity. Additionally, the leaves fold closed at night and when it rains, again conferring the distinct sense that the tree is exquisitely sensitive to every nuance in the world around her. Spending time in quiet contemplation with a pink silk tree can sensitize you to the world around you in a way that increases the pleasure and fullness of each moment, as well as your ability to receive intuitive information and guidance.

Interestingly, children who grow up with a silk tree in their yard (like I did) may find that they become particularly open, intuitive adults who cry easily and are naturally able to feel compassion for virtually everyone and everything.

Conversely, if you are already extremely sensitive and/or empathic, it won't hurt to be near a pink silk tree. But perhaps choose not to work with her in a magical way (unless you are going through a period when you feel deadened or shut off), as this might open you up (spiritually and emotionally) to an uncomfortable degree.

Magical Correspondences

Element: Air
Gender: Feminine
Planet: Venus

Pinyon

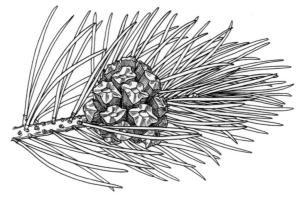

*L*ike the southwestern high desert landscapes in which he's thrived for millennia, there's something exceptionally, undeniably sacred about the pinyon (*Pinus cembroides*). A variety of pine with fragrant resin and nuts that have been an important food source for humans for thousands of years, the pinyon is truly a treasure.

Magical Uses

Communing with Spirit

At times, spirituality can be like a subtle thread weaving under and behind our life experience. At other times, it can be like searing sunlight and vibrant blue, merging everything instantly and powerfully into a single luminous whole. Pinyon's brand of spirituality falls under the latter category.

In incense or firewood, pinyon resin makes for some of the most sacred-smelling smoke you'll ever inhale. Employ it to be powerfully transported to the realm of the

Divine. Or enter into the sacred realm by simply spending time in quiet contemplation with a pinyon tree.

In the inspired words of author Ronald M. Lanner in *The Piñon Pine: A Natural and Cultural History*:

> Nobody who has sat before a roaring, pitch-boiling, bubbling, scented fire of piñon can think of it as the mere consumption of wood. It is the spirited release of centuries of brilliant sunlight absorbed under a cloudless Southwestern sky, the sudden and instant flow of energy patiently accumulated.

The Divine Masculine

In *The Piñon Pine* Lanner also documents a legend from the San Juan Pueblo Indians about the deity and cultural hero Montezuma (as opposed to the historical Montezuma). In this story, during a pinyon nut harvesting expedition, a beautiful girl hears clear direction to empty two rooms of her house and to leave them that way for four days, which she does. On the fourth day, in fulfillment of the prophecy, the first room is constantly stocked with corn, and she comes into her true divine identity as "the Queen of the White Corn." The second room is stuffed with pinyon trees. Upon opening the second door, the largest of the trees rolls out, and she is directed to eat it, which she does. Nine months later, she gives birth to Montezuma, "whom she named Son of the Sun."

In countless cultures, the sun and Divine Masculine energy are synonymous. In this story, the pinyon tree clearly takes on the role of both, first appointing an earthly goddess, and then bringing a divine male human into the world through her womb.

Magical Correspondences

Element: Spirit
Gender: Masculine
Planet: Sun

Pistachio

A resident of the Hanging Gardens of Babylon, the pistachio tree (*Pistachia vera*) and humans have a long history. A popular crop to this very day, the pistachio is mentioned as a food source in the Bible and has been cultivated for somewhere in the vicinity of three thousand years. Although he's originally from Asia and the Middle East, he's been a resident of Italy and the Mediterranean for quite some time and has more recently made a home for himself in my native state of California.

Magical Uses

Breaking Love Spells

If you're concerned that you or another person has been placed under a love spell, head to your nearest grocery store or farmer's market and purchase some pistachios with the shells still on them. Then simply take a small handful and eat it (or direct your friend to do the same), shelling each one just before you pop it in your mouth. Like salt or sage, pistachios possess such primal magical power that they require no pomp or ceremony: as a love spell dismantler, they are ready to go.

Of course, they must be eaten with the simple intention to break the love spell. Either the one eating them must possess this intention or the friend who has offered the pistachios to the one under the spell. In other words, *someone* must be aware that the pistachios are being eaten to break the spell. Otherwise, they are just a snack.

Immunity to Love Spells

Similarly, as a preventative measure, eating a small handful of pistachios daily can keep love spells from entering your energy field and exerting the slightest bit of control over you. Again, they must be eaten with the intention to make yourself immune to love spells. Simply eating pistachios with no awareness or intention will not have the same effect.

Influence

The same magical quality that allows pistachio to break the magnetic/attractive influence of a love spell can allow him to establish an active/projective influence over others.

If you've read *The Lion, the Witch, and the Wardrobe* by C. S. Lewis, you might remember that the White Witch offers Edmund enchanted candy called Turkish delight, which he becomes obsessed with and therefore falls under her spell. But what you may not know is that the real Turkish delight is often made with pistachios. Did the White Witch add them to her enchanted sweets? While it's not mentioned in the story, considering the fact that pistachios can be magically employed to enhance your influence over another person (particularly when that person is induced to eat them), we can only surmise that she did.

Now, of course, as ethical magical practitioners we must be careful about how we wield the influential power of the pistachio. We don't, after all, want to step on anyone else's free will, as—in addition to being morally bankrupt—this will certainly place unfavorable karmic repercussions in our path. (Just ask the White Witch.)

A practice like the following, however, stays just this side of the ethical line. Practice with caution. Use only when necessary and exclusively when you are morally in the right.

Pistachio Treat for Righteous Domination and Influence

When the action (or nonaction) of a person or a group is unfairly holding you or a loved one back from experiencing success, well-being, or happiness in any life area, bring them one or more homemade treats containing pistachios (such as cookies, muffins, baklava, or mini pies, or Turkish delight), and hope that they partake.

Before you assemble the treat, place the pistachios in a white ceramic bowl. (It's ideal if you do this ritual on a Tuesday or when the moon is in Aries, but if it's not practical to wait, anytime will do.) Conjure up all the most positive feelings you can toward the person or group that you'd like to influence, connecting with their true divine essence and the part of them that is wholly good and beneficent. With love in your heart, direct your palms toward the nuts and envision the person or group feeling genuinely inspired to help you in exactly the way you need. See them, in your mind's eye, being benefited by their own actions as they realize how wonderful it feels to do the right thing. Consciously send the energy of your visualization through your hands into the pistachios. Say:

With wishes well and wishes true
I send good energy to you.
For the sake of one and sake of all
You now heed this righteous call.
For the highest good of me and thee
As I will it, so mote it be.

When this is complete, bake or create your treat as you normally would. Then try your best to see that they eat at least a bite within two days of the ritual, but the sooner the better.

Magical Correspondences

Elements: Fire and Earth
Gender: Masculine
Planet: Mars

Plum

A petite yet vital tree that yields sweet and juicy drupes ranging from a misty purple to a deep and sumptuous red, the plum (*Prunus*) is one of the most potent reminders of the obvious magic of the everyday world. Cultivated and widespread since very ancient times, plums have been an important historical food and moisture source for humans in both Asia and North America.

Magical Uses
Abundance and Holiday Magic

In Tchaikovsky's *Nutcracker Suite* the Sugar Plum Fairy escorts the Nutcracker Prince and Clara to the opulent Land of Sweets, where they are honored at a magical ball. Certainly in popular culture there are few more potent invocations of the sweetness, abundance, and magic at the heart of the holiday season. Serving plum pudding or other treats featuring plum at the holidays is an excellent way to honor the Sugar Plum Fairy while invoking her lavish and whimsical spirit.

Boundaries

Flower essence therapy practitioners suggest cherry plum essence for releasing the stranglehold on one's feelings and senses in order to open up and experience the world in its fullness. Perhaps counterintuitively, this actually supports positive boundary setting by allowing one to release fear-based boundaries in favor of allowing an innate connection with the earth, sky, and natural world, which in turn nourishes an abiding sense of confidence and strength. For this purpose, take two to three drops of the flower essence under the tongue or in water two to three times per day. As an alternative or reinforcement, spend time in quiet contemplation with a blossoming plum tree (cherry plum is the tree from which the traditional flower essence remedy is made, but any plum tree will do).

Getting Stuck Energy Moving

Just as the flower essence moves stuck emotions and opens blocked senses, the plum tree helps activate energy and get stagnant energy moving. For example, if something feels like it's at an impasse in your life—a job search that's seemingly in limbo or an iffy relationship that just keeps you hanging on—the plum tree can help. Interestingly, this is mirrored in the physical body in the way that prunes and plums are eaten to help get the bowels moving, and to remove old toxins in the process.

If any life area feels stuck and you're ready to get things moving forward, lovingly gather a plum from a tree or a market and empower it with your intention to get things flowing in a positive way. Then simply place it on your altar. You should see a positive shift within a week. (Do be aware that it might not feel positive at first, but that's just because old toxins and undesirable conditions are rising to the surface so that they can move out of your life.)

Strength

The vibrant nature of the little plum tree, along with her gorgeous blossoms and striking purple or deep red fruit, lend an air of strength and fortitude. Anytime you need to bolster your energy or emotions, or even your physical body, spending time in quiet contemplation with a plum tree would be a good idea. Taking the flower essence or eating the fruit is also an excellent way to fortify your emotional, energetic, or physical strength.

Magical Correspondences

Elements: Water and Fire
Gender: Feminine
Planet: Venus

Poplar

$\mathcal{A}$nne of Green Gables fans will recall the heroine's love of the tall, wistful poplars of her native Prince Edward Island, Canada. Additionally, the poplar is a tree sacred to the Celts, the Greeks, and the Sioux. Indeed, there is something most transcendent about poplars. Magically, they are about movement and change of all varieties, especially the expansion and elevation of the soul.

Please note that while the poplar (*Populus*) genus includes trees commonly called poplars, cottonwoods, and aspens, aspens have their own section in this book. This section will include poplars and cottonwoods.

Magical Uses

Activation

Poplars are aligned with the water element, appearing on riverbanks and thriving even in recently flooded areas. Like a clear mountain stream, they constantly sparkle and effervesce due to their leaf shape, which promotes continuous movement in the breeze.

Magically, spending time in quiet contemplation with a poplar can quickly clear, open, and energize your chakras and invigorate your energy field in a gentle but highly effective way.

Expansion

In addition to being some of the fastest-growing trees, poplars reproduce easily from broken branches and can spread and regenerate quickly through the root system of a single tree. Also aligned with Jupiter (the planet of expansion), poplars can be magically employed for support with expansion in any life area.

For this purpose, visit a poplar and sit in quiet contemplation. When you feel aligned with both the tree and the Divine, express the type of expansion you'd like to experience in your life. Do so by conjuring up the feeling that this expansion has already occurred, and give thanks for this eventuality. Next, lovingly approach the tree and gently gather a small branch, using strong clippers or gardening shears. Thank the tree. Upon returning home, place the branch upon your altar.

Portals

The fact that poplars often appear on the borderlands between earth and water is just one indication of the poplar's alignment with portals and doorways between the worlds. In some landscapes, their golden color is the most prominent herald of autumn and the transition of seasons. The tree is also aligned with both Persephone and Hecate, goddesses who represent spring and fall respectively—the doorways between the seasons—and also goddesses who traverse easily between this world and the otherworld. Perhaps unsurprisingly, they are traditional cemetery trees and trees linked in the Greek mind with the entrance to the underworld.

When a portal appears in your life—when you feel called to make a transition from one realm to another in any life area—visiting a poplar can be helpful in easing your way and clarifying your path. For example, this might be appropriate if:

- You're feeling drawn to let old challenging patterns go and to step into a positive new phase.
- You're transitioning in or out of a career or major life relationship.
- You're exploring deeper realms of your magical or psychic abilities.
- You're stepping into a significantly greater level of responsibility or power.

Prayer

In much the same way the constant waving of prayer flags in the breeze is believed to carry prayers to the realm of heaven, the undulating flutters of poplar leaves are prayers in and of themselves. Send your wishes and divine communications to a poplar, and feel certain that your message is delivered straight to the heart and mind of the Divine. Then, through placing your awareness on the sound of the leaves in the breeze, allow yourself to receive divine messages in return.

Magical Correspondences

Element: Water
Gender: Masculine and feminine
Planet: Jupiter

Privet

The small and elegant privet tree (*Ligustrum*) is often featured in manicured hedges and topiaries like the ones in the film *Edward Scissorhands*. A native of Asia and a member of the same family as olive, lilac, and jasmine, she possesses tiny, radiant, and sweetly fragrant white blossoms.

Magical Uses

Facilitating Communication

With a distinctively airy and clarifying energy, the privet tree can magically facilitate any and all kinds of verbal communication. She can therefore be an excellent addition to yards of businesses that specialize in the written or spoken word, such as publishing houses, newspapers, postal centers, and law offices. Writers and speakers of all varieties can also benefit from the proximity of privet trees. Additionally, a privet tree near the home can support harmonious communication between residents.

Resolving Arguments

To gain insight into and prepare for magical work related to resolving an argument, consider spending time in quiet contemplation with a privet tree. If she's in bloom, inhale the sweet scent of her blossoms, and perhaps incorporate them into charms or spells designed for the purpose.

PRIVET 24-HOUR RESOLUTION CHARM

Charge a privet leaf with the intention for harmonious and ideal resolution; then place it in the shoe or somewhere within the belongings of the other party. Your argument should be resolved within twenty-four hours.

Soothing and Smoothing

In herbal medicine the immune-boosting, inflammation-reducing privet has been employed for a number of conditions, including sore mouths and throats, skin problems, chapped lips, coughs, tumors, and respiratory issues. Similarly, on the energetic and magical side of things, privet has a soothing and smoothing energy that helps with healing old hurts, releasing painful memories from the past, and generally softening harsh energy. For this purpose, try taking the flower essence, putting a few drops of it in with a mister of water and misting yourself or your space, or adding it to your bathwater.

Magical Correspondences

Element: Air

Gender: Feminine

Planet: Venus

Redbud

As I write, the redbud trees (*Cercis*) outside my windows are buzzing with bees. Though they've just barely begun to bloom (it's still early in the spring), they're already a deep, robust red, truly living up to their name. With red wine-colored blossoms in spring and summer and heart-shaped leaves that turn golden in the fall, this mid-sized gem is a giant when it comes to beauty, elegance, and charm.

Magical Uses

Bee Blessing

Our precious friends the bees can use all the help they can get at this particular moment, and redbuds are one of the best trees you can plant to support them, as they provide an abundant source of pollen and nectar. Not coincidentally, bees are sacred to the Great Goddess or feminine aspect of the Divine, with whom the redbud is exquisitely aligned.

Feminine Power and Wisdom

Femininity is multidimensional, with facets that include both soft receptivity and intense strength. With her fine-boned frame, blood-red blooms, and swarthy survival instinct, the redbud quite accurately demonstrates this polarity. Indeed, she is aligned with the Divine Mother in all her many incarnations, and also with Athena, the Greek goddess of wisdom, war, and victory. Visit a redbud during the spring or summer to receive an infusion of intense feminine power and wisdom, or to help heal any old issues you may have about wielding your feminine strength. Redbud flower essence can also help with this intention.

Healing Shame

Although the redbud is native to North America, a (North American) legend states that Judas hung himself from a redbud tree (hence the alternate name, "judas tree"), and that the deep red color of the blossoms reflects the tree's shame at performing this role in history. Personally, I find the spreading of this rumor to be an unacceptable way to treat such a splendid and innocent tree. As we as a culture continue to heal from our famously harsh, prejudiced, and judgmental religious history, it seems appropriate that we redirect this tree's unfair association with shame toward helping us all heal and transmute any lingering effects of religious or cultural shaming.

If you recognize such effects in your consciousness—for example if you notice shame surrounding your sexuality or gender, or if you find yourself feeling guilty simply for being alive—visit a redbud tree in spring or fall and sit near it in quiet contemplation.

Land Healing

The redbud has a healing, stabilizing presence on land and can help bless landscapes with lushness and splendor. In addition to simply bestowing the gift of her beauty and wisdom, she attracts bees, and her roots help enrich the soil. Energetically, she has a stabilizing presence that anchors and interweaves a sense of timeless sacredness.

Love

Ever evolving yet always beautiful, redbud is a direct arboreal translation of an enduring romantic partnership. In early spring, she starts out with small buds of intense, passionate red, which open up to the sweet tenderness of (still hearty) pink buds. In summer, the heart-shaped green leaves speak of verdant love. In autumn (as described by author Charles W. G. Smith in *Fall Foliage*), "the delicate green foliage warms to chromium yellow and gold, like diffuse beacons beaming throughout the woods," reminding us of the enduring warmth and companionship that characterize a relationship's golden years. Plant redbud trees to support a long-term partnership or employ the blossoms or leaves in charms to attract one.

Magical Correspondences

Element: Fire
Gender: Feminine
Planet: Pallas

Redwood (Sequoia)

The truly magical (and closely related) redwoods and sequoias of California have a heartbreaking history: while Native Americans only used wood from them that naturally fell, Europeans literally decimated the trees for all sorts of architectural purposes, although it could take them a full day to bring down a single tree.

While the tallest tree species on earth is the redwood, the largest and most massive tree on earth is a sequoia. We are talking *skyscraper* huge. And sequoias can live for thousands of years. When you spend time in their presence you feel like the smallest and briefest of creatures, and yet at the same time you feel you are a part of something that is infinite and omnipotent. It's a most singular sensation.

Both redwoods and sequoias are in the subfamily Sequoioideae.

Magical Uses

Abundance

The sequoia—the largest tree on earth—comes from the tiniest of seeds. Stumps of redwoods are often miraculously surrounded with a circle of brand-new sprouts, to which they have given birth even in their state of seeming death. Perhaps it should be no surprise, then, that sequoias and redwoods are aligned with the planet of expansion: Jupiter. What's more, the lushness of redwoods and sequoias, the sense that they will live forever and expand forever, their deep green foliage, and their rich red bark all confer a sense of luxurious and deeply rooted wealth. That's why the redwood/sequoia can be especially helpful when you really need to shift your consciousness to one of positive expectation and abiding trust in your divinely designed supply.

Redwood Wealth Petition

To increase your wealth, on a Thursday or when the waxing moon is in Sagittarius, visit a redwood or a sequoia. Take a moment to respectfully tune in to the tree, and then request an infusion of abundance energy and wealth consciousness. Relax and receive. Then, with gratitude, gift the tree with a chrysocolla or carnelian (crystal) by placing it near her base.

Earth Wisdom

Driving into the redwoods confers a feeling reminiscent of being a small child in the presence of grandparents. It's a lovely feeling of continuity, comfort, and the presence of both unconditional love and unfathomable wisdom.

So, when you want to connect with a living, earthly being that is older than Mary Magdalene and wiser than the wisest human guru on the planet, try spending time with sequoias or redwoods, or calling up a vision of them during meditation.

Healing

While removing parts of the tree is no longer prohibited by law, author Fred Hageneder points out in *The Meaning of Trees* that "the Pomo and the Kayasha tribes use poultices of warmed, new redwood foliage for earaches and take the gummy sap with water as a stimulant and a tonic. The Houma drink inner bark infusions to treat jaundice and to purify the blood." As an alternative to working with physical materials from the tree for healing, spending time near redwoods—particularly when consciously tuning in to their energy and wisdom—can provide healing and help prevent health challenges through relieving stress.

Protection

As mentioned above, these ancient trees can give you a sense that you are a small child, protected by wise and loving grandparents. This can be especially useful for those who often feel a lack of safety or a sense of free-floating anxiety. Once you've connected with a redwood or a sequoia in person, you can call on her essence and energy to help surround and fill you with protective energy, perhaps by envisioning yourself energetically encompassed by her trunk. You might do this shielding exercise regularly during meditation or as needed.

Protection from Fire

These trees are able to live so long even in fire-prone California because their wood is actually fire resistant. In fact, you'll often see a thriving redwood or sequoia with a blackened trunk: an indication that the tree has survived a forest fire. Additionally, they are unharmed by lightning and even have something of a symbiotic relationship with it. As such, if you'd like to protect a structure from fire, you could call up the vision of a giant sequoia. Ask her to completely encompass the building with her trunk, and request that she support you in your intention. To keep the energy strong, refresh the visualization at least once a week.

Magical Correspondences

Element: Spirit
Gender: Feminine
Planet: Jupiter

Rowan

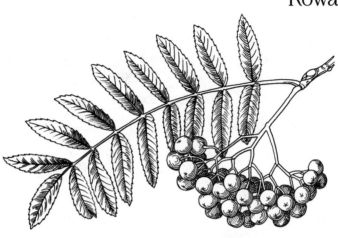

*T*he dainty rowan's brilliant energy and vast power are legendary. Like a full moon in a clear sky or a resonant chime, her magical radiance shines through with a most impressive clarity. Considered in the Norse tradition to be the savior of Thor, the ancient Scots considered the rowan (of the *Sorbus* genus) to be the material from which the first woman was made.

Magical Uses

Divination

Y-shaped rowan branches have been employed as divining rods. An abundantly flowering rowan or a rowan that flowers twice in one year indicates that a prosperous time is about to ensue.

Hearth Goddess Energy

Sacred to the great Irish goddess Brighid, the rowan shares this goddess's bright and fiery spirit, as well as her alignment with inspiration, warmth, and a happy home. When she's heavy with an abundance of her bright red "berries" (they're actually pomes), her radiant, highly auspicious energy is readily apparent. Bring a rowan branch with berries into the home to bless, protect, and summon the many blessings of Brighid.

Love Goddess Energy

The archetypal love goddess goes by many names in many different cultures, but she is always sensual, beautiful, luxury-loving, and attuned to the cycles of nature and the earth. Spending time with a rowan tree aligns us with these qualities, which naturally brings benefits on all levels. A member of the rose family, the rowan's feathery white five-petaled flowers and tiny bright red, orange-centered fruits magically evoke the love goddess's beautiful energy and bountiful blessings.

....

ROWAN FLOWER LOVE CHARM

To protect and bless a romantic relationship by incurring the favor and well-wishes of the love goddess, visit a flowering rowan tree. Send her love and offer her a carafe of iced rose blossom tea by pouring it around her roots. With gratitude, gently clip a single cutting of flowers. Bring them home and place them in water near a photo of you and your beloved.

Protection

Traditionally in England and Scotland, the hardy rowan tree has been associated with warding off or counteracting malevolent witchcraft. Planting a rowan tree by a gate or doorway is allegedly an effective charm against sorcery and evil intentions. Rowan flowers, berries, or wood can be brought inside to protect against lightning. Similarly, the flower essence has been employed to support immunity and general positivity. Indeed, a traditional protection charm can be created by simply tying two rowan sticks together with red yarn to make an equal-armed cross.

Travel

Another traditional belief about rowan trees indicates that she can prevent a traveler from getting lost. Rowan wood has been a traditional charm on boats to protect against storms and getting lost at sea, and her wood has been used for auspicious walking sticks. And in general, her protective and beneficent qualities lend themselves to harmonious travel.

....

ROWAN TREE HARMONIOUS TRAVEL PETITION

Before going on a trip, offer a carafe of iced rose blossom tea to a rowan tree and request that she lend her bright spirit and energy to protect you, guide you, and prevent you from getting lost. Feel yourself receiving this powerful blessing.

Magical Correspondences

Element: Fire
Gender: Feminine
Planet: Venus

Sandalwood

Equal parts heavenly and earthly, the fragrance of sandalwood (*Santalum album*) has been considered sacred for thousands of years. Even today the tree's numerous magical, medicinal, and aromatherapeutic benefits make her extremely popular with modern spiritual people and holistic health practitioners in the form of incense, oil, powder, and beads. Not to mention, inhaling the scent relaxes the body and kindles sensual pleasure.

Unfortunately, the wood of the Indian sandalwood tree has been so beloved for so long that it is now endangered in many of the areas where it once grew abundantly in the wild. Where sustainability is concerned, it's best to seek out sandalwood imported from Australia.

Magical Uses

Blessings

No magical ingredient unites form and spirit, or opens our awareness to the Infinite Oneness of Everything, quite like the scent of sandalwood, which makes it perfect for blessings of all varieties. It's also excellent for prayer and meditation.

To bless anything, anoint the person, place, or object with a small amount of essential oil of sandalwood or smudge with sandalwood incense. If you have the privilege of spending time with an actual sandalwood tree, place your hands on the trunk and feel yourself aligning with the Divine and activating blessings. Anointing a magical object of any sort (such as a wand or a charm) with sandalwood is an excellent way to align it with divine energies and give it a magical boost.

Add sandalwood powder or oil to bathwater to bless, align with the Divine, and cleanse your energy field. To intensely bless yourself and stimulate more blessings to flow in your life, you might work with a sandalwood mala (a specific type of prayer beads with exactly 108 beads, available at many spiritual supply stores). For exactly forty days, sit comfortably and speak or think one positive mantra or affirmation for each of the 108 beads, holding each one briefly in your hands as you do so. After the forty days, wear the mala to align deeply with the blessings you've magically set in motion.

Healing

Herbal healers employ sandalwood for skin issues, colds, respiratory ailments, intestinal and genitourinary conditions, stress and anxiety, and a number of other challenges. (For uses that go beyond aromatherapy, I suggest consulting a professional.)

Love

Sandalwood is extremely sensualizing and gets us right into our bodies by activating our lower chakras while simultaneously opening us up to the realm of Spirit. And since roses open and activate the upper chakras and are the energy of pure and potent love, sandalwood and rose are an irresistible one-two punch when it comes to love magic.

Simple Sandalwood and Rose Love Spell

On a Friday when the moon is waxing, wake up before sunrise and go outside. As the sun rises, anoint your heart, belly, third eye, and both palms with a mixture of rose absolute and sandalwood essential oil in a little bit of sweet almond oil. Stand facing east with your arms at your sides and your palms open to the sun. Relax as the sun continues to rise, and say:

I now draw beautiful love into my life.

I am irresistible to this love

And it nourishes my heart, mind, body, and spirit in every way.

Love, come to me now.

Love, come to me now.

Love, come to me now.

Thank you.

Past Life Healing

When doing past life work, the scent of sandalwood can facilitate memory of prior lives while simultaneously supporting a deep healing and release.

Protection

Sandalwood's extreme positivity and divine alignment helps banish and dissuade anything or anyone with negative energy or ill intent. Try sprinkling sandalwood powder over thresholds or smudging around the perimeter of the space (inside, outside, or both) with incense.

Sensuality

The scent of sandalwood is amazing for releasing excess thought, activating our senses, and helping us feel comfortably luxurious in our bodies and in the world. Try inhaling it and see why sandalwood has been employed as an aphrodisiac for centuries (if not millennia).

And for those times when you feel flighty, anxious, frenetic, or generally ungrounded, sandalwood can dial you right back in to the pleasure and comforts of the earth and physical world. Try diffusing the essential oil, wearing the perfume, or burning the incense for this purpose.

Magical Correspondences

Element: Spirit
Gender: Feminine
Planet: Ceres

Sassafras

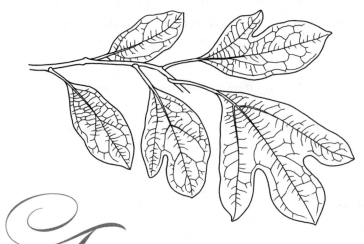

The lush and fragrant sassafras is a fabulous combination of unbounded whimsy and grounded physicality. A native to North America and Asia, the largest sassafras tree—more than 100 feet tall and 21 feet in circumference—dwells in Owensboro, Kentucky.

While sassafras oil that is extracted from the tree's roots and bark was an original ingredient in root beer, it was banned by the FDA in 1960 for use as a flavoring or food additive due to purported health concerns, so now its flavor is approximated with other ingredients. Still, ground sassafras leaves (which do not contain the supposedly cancer-causing constituent found in the roots and bark) are prominently featured in Creole cuisine, most famously in gumbo.

Magical Uses

Creativity

Sassafras is a very creative tree, as he features three distinct leaf shapes, instead of the usual one—single-lobed (diamond-shaped), bilobed (mitten-shaped), and trilobed (like a fig or a maple leaf). Tuning in to this variation, one is reminded of a leafy jigsaw puzzle or the unrestrained aesthetic of a child's artwork.

Additionally, sassafras's unique combination of whimsy and grounding allows us to channel our emotions, imagination, and divine inspiration into concrete form in the physical world—in other words, to create art!

....

Sassafras Creativity Petition

To activate your creativity, bless a creative project, or propel yourself out of a creative funk, visit a sassafras tree with two ice-cold root beers. ("Hard" root beer is an option now—did you know? Although either type—alcoholic or non—will do.) Relax, breathe deeply, and come into the moment as you gaze at the tree and tune in to his energy.

When you feel centered, hold both root beers and feel all the feelings associated with the type of creativity you'd like to activate. Really feel and sense that you're in the middle of a creative renaissance where beautiful ideas and projects flow through you, and you execute them with the assistance of the Divine. Feel deep gratitude for this, knowing that as you see and feel it in your mind's eye and emotions, it shall be. And, because time is an illusion, as you see and feel it, *it already is.*

Approach the tree and pour one of the root beers around his base as an offering. Return to your spot and drink your root beer with relish, attuning further to the frequency of your ideal, divine, creative momentum and flow.

Health

According to Michael Tierra in *The Way of Herbs*, herbal medicine made from sassafras root bark and root "is very effective as a blood-purifying alternative for a wide variety of skin diseases including acne. It is also commonly used by the rural folk of Appalachia and the Ozarks as a diuretic and treatment for arthritic and rheumatic complaints, pains, ulcers, colds, and flus." As for the toxicity of safrole (the constituent the FDA believes to be cancer-causing), when consumed in sassafras-based herbal medicine, Michael Tierra expresses serious and convincing doubts of its veracity. Luckily for herbalists and herbal healing enthusiasts, while sassafras oil is banned as a food and flavoring additive, the herb can still be found in tincture, oil, and herb form online and at many health food stores.

Additionally, any part of the tree can be employed in spells, rituals, and sachets performed or created for the intention of physical healing. For example, the following charm can be assembled to support rapid physical healing of things like colds, flus, aches, pains, and injuries.

HIGH-POTENCY HEALING SACHET

Empower a single garlic clove, a pinch of sassafras bark, and a clear quartz point in bright sunlight for one minute. Then tie them into a red flannel pouch or a scrap of red flannel, and anoint with essential oil of rosemary. Hold it in both hands and feel golden-white healing light flowing into the crown of your head, down to your heart, and out through your hands into the sachet. Know that this charm will emit a strong aura of health and divine healing, and that whoever is within its circle will be bathed in this powerful energy. Keep it close to you, or give it to the person you'd like to help heal. Empower in sunlight and refresh the rosemary oil to recharge the magic.

Prosperity

Simply keeping sassafrass in your handbag or wallet is a traditional wealth-drawing charm.

In kitchen witchery, adding filé powder (a powder made from ground sassafras leaves) to your food can infuse your food with the energy of prosperity, so that as you eat it, you internalize the magic and activate your prosperity magnetizing powers. Just be sure to add it to your food with the intention to draw abundance.

Magical Correspondences

Elements: Water and Earth
Gender: Masculine
Planet: Jupiter

Silk Floss Tree

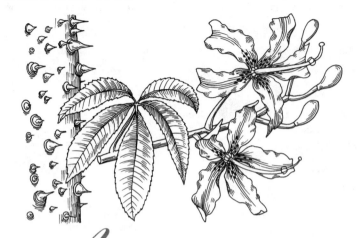

Although she's related to the kapok and the baobab, this gorgeous, spiky, green-trunked, pink-flowered South American tree has an intoxicating, otherworldly vibration all her own. Most commonly cultivated as an ornamental plant, she gets her name from the soft fiber of seedpods. In addition to her scientific name of *Ceiba speciosa*, she's known by a number of additional names, including bottle tree, palo borracho, yuchán, and toborochi.

Magical Uses

Attraction

Like all flowers with five petals, the silk floss tree is sacred to the archetypal goddess of love. Her pink blossom is particularly enticing, not just to humans but also to hummingbirds. In fact, in Santa Cruz, Bolivia, there is a very ancient legend about a goddess named Araverá who was married to the hummingbird god, Colibri. When evil spirits wanted to kill her because of a prophecy that her unborn son would one day slay them, she was only able to find refuge by hiding inside the trunk of a silk floss tree. Although she successfully gave birth to a son who eventually did grow up to slay the evil spirits as prophesied, she was trapped in the trunk for all eternity. But her marriage lives on: she attracts her hummingbird husband with her entrancing pink flowers to this day.

To irresistibly attract a partner or to open your heart more fully to an existing partner, visit a silk floss tree on a Friday during a waxing moon and request Araverá's assistance with your intention. Then gather a flower. Carry it, wear it, or place one on your altar with a pink candle and a stick of sweet-smelling incense. To increase your charm and sexual attractiveness (particularly if you identify as feminine), take two drops of the flower essence under the tongue or in a small amount of pink grapefruit juice twice a day for one month.

Femininity

As described, legend has it that a goddess lives in the trunk of the silk floss tree. In addition to expressing her femininity through using the power of receptivity to attract her mate with her beautiful flowers and nectar, she also expresses her femininity through her (often) curvy, very pregnant-looking trunk. As a matter of fact, in addition to the pregnant goddess story, a legend from the Matacos Indians of northeast Argentina states that the original fish were birthed from the womblike trunk of a primordial silk floss tree.

As such, the silk floss tree can provide support with connecting to the energy center just below the navel. This is the womb area, which is aligned with the water element and the ability to express femininity (i.e., receptivity and radiance) and birth all number of things (such as projects, ideas, and conditions).

Flight

The silk floss tree's pollination by butterflies and hummingbirds—in addition to her fluffy, parachuting seedpod that flies through the air like something out of fairyland—makes the silk floss tree naturally aligned with the magical quality of flight. This is why she can help with things like flying in dreams, astral travel, and connecting with galactic energies and wisdom.

....

NIGHT FLIGHT CHARM

If you'd like to fly in your dreams, when the moon is in Pisces, place one of the silk floss tree's fluffy seedpods in a small muslin bag, tie it closed with lavender ribbon, and then place it under your bed.

Spiritual Awakening

While I'm not an expert on this and absolutely recommend that you *not* try it at home, some recipes for ayahuasca (the potent hallucinogenic mixture prepared by South American shamans) call for this tree. Apparently, she's not one of the active ingredients, but she plays a part nonetheless. Try meditating near a silk floss tree or invoking her presence and visualizing her in your mind's eye for the purpose of awakening to a deeper level of reality.

Magical Correspondences

Element: Fire
Gender: Feminine
Planet: Pallene (a moon of Saturn)

Smoketree

This tiny tree (sometimes a shrub) thrives in dry climates and poor soil. The European variety (*Cotinus coggygria*) hails from the Mediterranean hills, while the American variety (*Cotinus obovatus*) is native to the southeastern United States. With striking pink, cream, or grayish fluffy flowers that appear at the top of the tree, it's no secret how this unique little ornamental beauty got her name.

Magical Use

Cleansing

Like the blinding, relentless sunlight in which she thrives, as well as the fragrant smoke that she visually resembles, smoketree is a potent spiritual and emotional detoxifier. Plant her in your yard to facilitate intentions related to powerful cleansing, such as to remove residual energy from previous residents, or to clear away apparent patterns of unhappiness, misfortune, or discord. For personal cleansing, spend some sacred quiet time with her on a bright, sunny day.

Magical Correspondences

Element: Air

Gender: Feminine

Planet: Saturn

Spruce

A gorgeous tree with a fresh scent and uplifting vibration, it's apt that her name is a synonym for "enliven and refresh." Used in healing balms for muscle aches, spruce (*Picea*) is also a popular choice for Christmas trees, paper, may-poles, and musical instruments.

Magical Uses

Ancient Wisdom

The oldest known living tree in the world is a spruce in Sweden that is believed to be 9,550 years old. (Flanking her are other trees of similar—but not quite so extensive—longevity.) When these *still living* trees were saplings, Rome hadn't yet risen, let alone fallen. Egypt was still lush and green. And the Buddha's great, great, *great* grandparents were not even a twinkle in anyone's eye. Certainly these ancient spruces—but also spruces in general—are powerhouses of ancient wisdom. Spend time with a spruce and inhale her sweet and steadying fragrance to become aligned with this strong current of deep inner knowing.

Goddess Energy

In many ways, the spruce is the primordial Earth Goddess in tree form. To embody your own goddess energy—or if you could use the comfort and guiding hand of a steadfast, beatific foremother and sage—spend time with a spruce. Sitting with your spine against her trunk and allowing her energy to flow up and down your spine can be especially healing and supportive.

Healing

By powerfully uniting earth and sky, and being a repository of the most ancient possible wisdom and knowledge, the spruce's energy is intensely healing in all ways: physical, emotional, psychological, and spiritual. Spend time with her if possible, or bring boughs into a healing room (provided the patient is not in any danger of allergies). Brushing the aura with a branch or a sprig can also be an excellent healing practice.

Protection

The spruce's highly positive and grounded vibration dissuades negative influences of all varieties. A spruce on your property can be enlisted to protect your home: simply offer a libation and request that she lend her magical protective abilities. Using a sprig of spruce to sprinkle pure water across a threshold can prevent negativity from entering. (Of course, also be sure to lock your doors.)

Purification

Spruce possesses a potently purifying vibration. Sprinkling water using a sprig of spruce is a useful magical method of purifying a person, object, or place.

Spiritual Refreshment

To indigenous tribes hailing from the Altai mountains of Siberia as well as southern Canada, the spruce is a cosmological cornerstone, and represents the interweaving of heaven, earth, and all that lives. Indeed, the simple presence of spruce is a great spirit-refresher, and spruce boughs, sprigs, or bundles can be placed on an altar or brought into a space to lift and reset the spirits in winter or any other time spiritual refreshment is desired. For the same purpose, make or seek out soft drinks or beer made from the leaves, buds, or essential oil of spruce, such as spruce beer.

Magical Correspondences

Element: Spirit
Gender: Feminine
Planet: Ceres

Sumac

This fast-growing African and North American native is quite the magical powerhouse. With a personality like a beloved shamanic superhero, the sumac (of the genus *Rhus*) is handsome, fiery, and wise.

Interestingly, some species of sumac leaves have been drunk as tea and added to Native American smoke mixtures, and sumac stems have been used to make sacred pipes. It's also reported that some kinds of dried sumac wood glow under ultraviolet lights.

Beware: This tree was once considered a close relative of poison ivy, poison oak, and poison sumac, so be very sure you know what you're dealing with before making physical contact.

Magical Uses

Activation

Deep purplish red sumac or rhus powder—from sumac berries (actually drupes)—is a Middle Eastern spice that adds a warm, lemony kick to foods…and a fiery, immediate kick to magic. After empowering a bit of the powder in bright sunlight sprinkle it over any magical object or charm to make the magic work extra-quick, or to activate finances add a pinch to cash registers, wallets, or money boxes. Actually, if *anything* in your life feels stuck or in a holding pattern, you can sprinkle sumac powder over a symbol to get it moving.

Grounding

When I was a teenager, my dad planted a bunch of African sumacs around our newly built central California home. Miraculously fast growing, they almost instantly lent a sense of lushness and permanency that was conspicuously lacking in the other newish homes in our cul-de-sac. Similarly, from a magical perspective, these handsome trees can help us to reach our roots down into any soil, no matter how parched or how far removed from the place we once considered home. For this purpose, spend time in quiet contemplation with a sumac or plant one or more in your yard.

Additionally, if feeling grounded in the physical realm is a challenge (i.e., if you feel unsettled, anxious, or uncomfortably cerebral) sumac can help. For this purpose, prepare a delicious Mediterranean or Middle Eastern dish to which you've added a sprinkling of sumac or rhus powder. Then light a deep red candle and enjoy.

Protection

Similar to the way cinnabar is sometimes used in feng shui rituals to bless and protect the space, rhus or sumac powder can be sprinkled around a property to create a protective boundary through which only positivity may enter, and in which only positivity remains. Simply sprinkling the powder across thresholds and windowpanes can seal the entrances from negativity in all forms. Just be sure to empower the powder in bright sunlight first, to clearly and specifically set an intention for what is and is not allowed in your space, and to do all sprinkling while moving in a clockwise direction. (Also, lock your doors!)

Sumac powder can also be added to protection charms and mixtures or sprinkled around a magical circle to protect from challenging energies as you work your magic.

Magical Correspondences

Element: Fire

Gender: Masculine

Planet: Ceres

Sweet Gum

*P*raised since ancient times for the aromatherapeutic and medicinal benefits of his oil and resin, sweet gum (*Liquidambar styraciflua*)
ingredients are employed in perfumery and the tobacco industry to this day. While the
tree originally hails from areas in Mexico, Central America, the Mediterranean, and the
southeastern United States, he thrives in a broad range of areas and is widely planted as
an ornamental plant.

Magical Uses

Creativity

In some climates the sweet gum's vibrant green leaves transform in the fall into a fiery
spectrum of the richest and most varied imaginable hues. Magically, this array of color
and light mirrors the universal creative palette from which we all are free to draw. What's
more, the tree's spiky little "gum balls" draw squirrels, chipmunks, and finches who feed

upon the wealth of seeds they contain. This also magically translates to creativity, as we spread seeds of aesthetic and spiritual nourishment when we disseminate and nurture our creative projects and ideas. To support creativity of all varieties, plant a sweet gum tree or spend time in quiet contemplation with one.

Father/Daughter Relationships

While the sweet gum possesses a distinctly masculine essence, he is also very in tune with the realm of the sensuous and radiant feminine. Truly, the wisdom of the sweet gum teaches honor and balance between the polarities, as he knows the deep and abiding power within both, as well as within the entire spectrum. That's why his energy can be magically channeled toward improving father/daughter relationships.

If you are a daughter or a father and you'd like to magically support your relationship with your father or daughter (respectively), visit a sweet gum tree and tune in lovingly. Request support with honoring and accepting your family member, as well as support with helping him or her honor and accept you. When you feel sufficiently aligned with the tree, offer him your father's or daughter's favorite beverage by pouring it around his roots. Then intuitively gather a gumball or one of his leaves (if possible, it's best if you collect one that's already fallen). Thank him from your heart. Next time you spend time with or speak with your family member, carry the gumball or leaf in a pocket or pouch.

Personal Power

The sweet gum's leaves resemble a five-pointed star or hands with fingers outstretched, visually indicating the tree's ability to activate and fuel our personal power. You might think of him like a coach who sees our potential and won't let us off the hook until we fully embrace and express it. While he may not be gentle in his wisdom, he certainly means well in his unflagging energetic nudges to remember our responsibility to be at our very best.

Tarot

Interestingly, sweet gum is an expert in uniting images with messages and illuminating the patterns and symbols through which universal wisdom regularly communicates. Specifically, he's aligned with the wisdom of the tarot, and can enhance our abilities to receive clear messages through our tarot studies and practice.

Try studying and reading tarot under the shade of a sweet gum tree, being aware of the tree's ancient energy and expertise as you do so. Without overthinking it, simply allow his powerful vibration and wisdom to fuel your insights and elevate your understanding.

Magical Correspondences

Element: Fire

Gender: Masculine

Planet: Pallas (Asteroid)

Sycamore

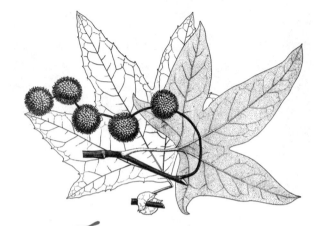

*I*n her beautiful book *American Spirits,* author Judith Robbins recounts the legendary history of a giant sycamore called the "teepee tree" that spread exposed roots on the edge of a creek in Indiana, creating a cavelike structure beneath the trunk. This tree was sacred to a Lenape tribe who chose to settle nearby after Europeans had displaced them. Robbins writes, "Inside the tree, which was lighted by fox fire and fireflies, the children often sat on ermine skins and listened to the tales of an ethereal, old white owl whose name, they learned, was Watcher."

Please note that this section discusses the various sycamore species native to North America (of the *Platanus* genus), which are distinct from the sycamore fig of Egypt and the Middle East (*Ficus sycomorus*), as well as the European variety of maple (*Acer pseudopla-tanus*) often referred to by the same name.

Magical Uses

Ancestral and Earth Wisdom

The owl that lived in the teepee tree was a sacred keeper of ancestral and earth wisdom. Similarly, the sycamore can help us align with the knowledge that we are one with all that lives, and all that has come before. This gives our lives richness and meaning, and fortifies us with support from our spiritual and genetic ancestors, as well as the entire natural world. Spend time in quiet contemplation with a sycamore to receive these benefits, or try the following:

DRINK DEEPLY OF WISDOM AND ALE

Choose or brew a fine organic ale and place two bottles in a small basket, along with a bottle opener. Visit a sycamore in the late spring, summer, or early fall. Connect with the tree with love, silently communing your wish to align with ancient earth wisdom and the wisdom of your spiritual ancestry. Open the ale and lovingly pour an entire bottle as a libation around the roots. As the ale sinks into the earth, enjoy your bottle, feeling as if you are having a drink with an old friend—which, in truth, you are.

Land Alignment

Just as the teepee tree served as a sign to the tribe in *American Spirits* to settle, and as it served as a spiritual and social hub for their community, sycamore can help us feel aligned with the land on which we live, even if—and perhaps *particularly* if—it isn't the land from which we originally hail. Indeed, the tall sycamore in the corner of our backyard welcomed my partner and I when we moved to Missouri from California, and his shade, majestic beauty, and whispering leaves faithfully provided us with grounding comfort as we acclimated to our new environment. This is mirrored by the way that the sycamore makes *himself* at home so swiftly, spreading his roots and branches expansively even before he's been in the neighborhood for a decade.

Magical Correspondences

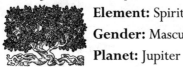

Element: Spirit
Gender: Masculine
Planet: Jupiter

Sycamore Fig

*H*istorically one of the most revered trees of Africa and the Middle East, the sycamore fig (*Ficus sycomorus*) has been cultivated since ancient times. An exceptionally tall member of the fig family, he is quite majestic and lush, and is well loved for the much-needed shade he generously casts over parched desert landscapes.

Magical Uses

Divine Alignment

The sycamore fig was considered the Tree of Life in ancient Egypt: the symbolic uniting of earth with heaven, and humans with the Divine. Various individual trees were aligned with emanations of the Great Goddess, such as Isis, Hathor, Nut, and Neith. It was customary for these trees to be presented with fruit and water offerings, particularly as petitions for prayers. Additionally, as a symbol of life after death, sycamore fig leaves, fruit, and wood were included in Egyptian tombs throughout the centuries.

For the Kikuyu people of Kenya, the tree is aligned with their creator god, Ngai. Offerings to this deity were made beneath the tree, and *Kikuyu* even translates to something like "children of the giant sycamore fig."

To effectively align your mind, body, and affairs with the organizing and activating power of the Divine and heavenly realm, visit a sycamore fig and sit with your back against the trunk. Feel, imagine, and sense wise and healing cosmic energy coming down from the tree's branches and through the crown of your head and spine, as you simultaneously feel the earth's grounding energy coming up from the tree's roots and rushing up through your tailbone. Feel these two energies becoming one within you as they each clear, calibrate, and fuel you in all the most ideal possible ways.

Magical Authority

Experienced practitioners know that when it comes to successful spells and visualizations, magical authority is the one ingredient you can't do without. If you don't believe in your own authority to create positive change, the universe won't either (because when it comes down to it, there is no separation: you and the universe are *one*). If your magical mojo seems to be temporarily missing or misplaced, sycamore fig can help. For this purpose, make an offering of water and grapes to a sycamore fig, either in the physical world or in your mind's eye. Then spend some relaxing and rejuvenating time in quiet contemplation, soaking in the tree's ancient wisdom and power.

Magical Correspondences

Element: Spirit
Gender: Masculine
Planet: Uranus

Tamarisk

The desert-loving tamarisk, native to Africa and the Middle East, is presently a common sight in the dryer areas of the western United States. Every time I see one, I am reminded of the brief months I spent working off the grid at an all-but-forgotten hot springs in a desolate area of California's vast central valley. The water in the hot springs was salty, which is why the tamarisks (Latin name *Tamarix*, also known as salt cedar) thrive there while very few other trees do. As I recharged and recalibrated after a particularly challenging time in my life, the tamarisks played a role in my much-needed emotional detoxification.

Magical Uses

Connection Between Heaven and Earth

The Egyptian god Osiris was at one time hidden in a chest inside the trunk of a tamarisk tree, which was later cut down and transformed into a pillar that was hypothesized by many to be an archetypal "tree of life" or "axis mundi"—in other words, a connection between the realm of the earth and the divine, heavenly realm of the sky. Along similar lines, there's a traditional belief that the "manna from heaven" in fact descended upon the Israelites from the branches of a tamarisk tree.

Spiritual and Emotional Purification

In the Epic of Gilgamesh, Ninsun (Gilgamesh's mother and "the great wild cow goddess") purifies herself in a bath containing tamarisk and soapwort before petitioning Shamash, the sun god, to support and watch over her son. Indeed, the purifying properties of the tamarisk cannot be overstated. Like sea salt and searing sunlight on desert sand, tamarisks effectively dry out and disinfect any and all emotional and/or spiritual darkness, heaviness, and toxicity. This is mirrored in the physical realm by the way their long taproots find moisture hidden deep within the earth, as well as by their mechanism of dispersing salt through their leaves to the ground around their base, discouraging other plants from growing nearby.

Magical Correspondences

Element: Spirit
Gender: Masculine
Planet: Neptune

Tree of Heaven

*I*n *A Tree Grows in Brooklyn*, Betty Smith wrote:

> *The one tree in Francie's yard was neither a pine nor a hemlock...Some people call it the Tree of Heaven. No matter where its seed falls, it makes a tree which struggles to reach the sky. It grows in boarded-up lots and out of neglected rubbish heaps. It grows up out of cellar gratings. It is the only tree that grows out of cement. It grew lushly, but only in the tenement districts.*

Despite her ubiquity and her status as an invasive species in many areas, the fast-growing tree of heaven has been treasured in Chinese medicine since ancient times. Interestingly, her alternate Western name, Ailanthus, is derived from an Ambonese word that also means "tree of heaven," while her Chinese name, chouchun, means "foul-smelling tree."

So is she beautiful or commonplace? Invaluable or invasive? Heavenly or foul-smelling? The answer is all at once or either polarity, according to your perspective. Just as what is infinite excludes nothing by its very definition, this tree's personality brings to mind Walt

Whitman's famous lines, "Do I contradict myself? Very well, then I contradict myself. (I am large. I contain multitudes.)"

Magical Uses

Adaptation to Urban Living

As a small-town girl who tried for years to adapt to big-city living, I can attest that it's not the easiest thing to do. In fact, while many seem to feel right at home in booming metropolitan areas, even people who have lived in cities their whole lives don't always feel totally at home in them. But you know who does? The hardy and unflappable tree of heaven. Even in compromised urban areas such as dumps and demolition sites, she's known for not merely surviving, but actually flourishing. So if you feel the need to live in a city right now (for financial, career, or relationship reasons, for example), tree of heaven is just the magical ally for you. Consider her your personal guru when it comes to blossoming in even the smoggiest and most bustling environments.

For this purpose, spend time with a tree of heaven, call her up in a visualization exercise, or sleep with one of her leaves under your pillow for a week. (Refresh the leaf weekly as needed.)

Beauty

When we only see beauty in what is generally believed to be beautiful, we are missing out on true beauty. True beauty encompasses the full spectrum of human life: the tarnish and the gold, the grimace and the smile, the rubble and the rolling hills. In fact, when we can learn to let it all in—every mood, every polarity, every loss or gain, *everything*—we become constantly joyful, whether or not we are technically happy. Tree of heaven's wisdom is about living bravely through it all, and appreciating the intrinsic beauty of the eternal now. (Incidentally, this may be why tree of heaven was employed in ancient times as a remedy for mental illness.)

To perceive true beauty within yourself, others, and any situation, spend time with a tree of heaven or visualize her in your mind's eye. Breathe (even if you're inhaling her infamous odor), relax, tune in, and then say or think this or something like it:

Tree of heaven, help me see
The splendor in everything: A–Z.
Blackness, brightness, blindness, sight
In all I find beauty, joy, and delight.

Survival

If you've read the preceding sections, you're probably getting the picture that tree of heaven is a survival expert. Perhaps the fastest-growing tree in North America, people who manage outdoor areas often feel compelled to come up with elaborate plans to eradicate her, despite the fact that this is widely believed to be impossible.

From a magical perspective, tree of heaven teaches us to survive as well. So if you engage in any sort of activity or lifestyle in which literal survival is an aim (such as mountain climbing or prepping), making tree of heaven into an ally would be an excellent idea. Maybe even stock up on literature about wildcrafting Chinese herbal medicine ingredients—this would come in handy if, for example, you needed to employ tree of heaven to prevent malaria or treat asthma, epilepsy, dysentery, or hemorrhaging during a zombie apocalypse. (But seriously, don't try this if you don't have to: the plant can be toxic if it's not prepared correctly or taken in very small doses.)

Winning

Tree of heaven actually contains toxins in her roots, bark, and leaves that kill surrounding plants so that she may have a better chance of surviving. Is that evil? No! It's simply a nifty survival skill that's conveniently built into her DNA.

The word "winning," more than "victory," implies vanquishing a foe and actually triumphing over someone else. Because, let's face it: there are times when *triumphing over* and *vanquishing* are totally appropriate. Like when you're involved in a court case with someone behaving maliciously. Or when someone is bullying or threatening you or another member of your household. In both these cases, the wisdom of tree of heaven would come in mighty handy.

So, if a foe needs vanquishing (and you really have to be morally in the right here, or rest assured that karma will swiftly retaliate), try this:

....

TREE OF HEAVEN FOE VANQUISHING POTION

On a sunny day during a waning moon, visit a tree of heaven and sit in quiet contemplation. When you feel tuned in, express through your feelings and thoughts what's going on, why you need her help, and exactly the outcome you'd like to experience. (Important caveat: choose a desired outcome that's about you or your loved one's safety or well-being and *not* about bringing about any sort of revenge on other party. So instead of "Billy gets what he deserves," choose "I am totally safe and free from any harassment." Then you would feel feelings and see visions in your mind's eye that involve a life *without* this foe causing harm in it.)

When you have the inner sense that the tree understands and wants to help, approach and gently gather exactly fourteen leaves. On that same day, at home or somewhere where you won't be disturbed, place a glass bowl of water in sunlight, outdoors if possible (if not, a sunny window is fine). Float the leaves on top of it and let the water absorb the light and the energy from the leaves for twenty to forty minutes. Write the foe's name on a small strip of dissolving paper (available online and at illusionist supply stores) and drop it into the water. As it dissolves, feel/imagine/sense the tree's energy completely exterminating this person's power over you. Say:

My mind, my body, and affairs
Are freed from all your former snares.
As I vanquish, I now see
Peace and safety; so mote it be.

Feel victorious and free, and know your ritual to be a success. Thank the powers that be and pour the water and leaves into the earth or around the base of a tree.

Magical Correspondences

Element: Spirit
Gender: Feminine
Planet: Sun

Tulip Tree

*A*uthor Henry W. Shoemaker recounts the Allegheny legend of a wood sprite named Pale Eyes, who lived inside a tulip tree (*Liriodendron*) and appeared as an enchanting Indian girl with pumpkin-colored skin and light-colored eyes. When the tree was cruelly cut down, the maiden was briefly sighted with bleeding ankles before disappearing into sawdust, never to return.

Magical Uses
Attracting Gifts

The universe loves to give, and so do our fellow creatures. That's why it's imperative that we do our best to receive and accept all gifts (even the everyday ones, like the sound of a loved one laughing or the vision of sunlight on water) without guilt and with the utmost pleasure and glee. Plus, the more gratitude we feel, the more gifts we receive—and our gratitude is also a gift to whomever it is directed toward. So it's an infinite win for all involved; this is the wisdom of the tulip tree.

TULIP TREE GIFT ATTRACTION RITUAL

Visit a tulip tree on a beautiful day. Relax and have an emotional heart to heart, inwardly sharing why you'd like to attract more gifts, and how you'd like to feel when you receive them. Also share how much joy you'd like to bring to others and the universe by accepting these gifts with gratitude and love. Then feel yourself receiving an infusion of the tulip tree's sparkling essence. When this feels complete, thank her and vow to find the most possible delight in every single thing you experience for the remainder of the day. Within one week, you will notice a marked increase in the number of gifts you receive. Remember to be grateful in order to keep the momentum going!

Dazzling Charm

Aligned with the archetypal love goddess, as well as the shimmering and radiant element of fire, the tulip tree can be a most excellent magical ally when it's your intention to dazzle and charm. With her exotic blossoms, and radiant leaves that dance in even in the most imperceptible breeze, she ensnares admiring attention like a mesmerizing dancer with a costume that glitters in the sun. For this purpose, visit a tulip tree in sunlight. Pour an entire bottle of champagne around her roots, and request that she infuse you with her abundant energy of attraction and charm.

Magical Correspondences

Element: Fire
Gender: Feminine
Planet: Venus

Tupelo

*T*he name *tupelo* is derived from Muscogee words for "swamp" and "tree." In culture after culture (and even in modern times) swamps have been unmistakably aligned with negativity and danger while simultaneously being considered places of great magic and power. Indeed, the tupelo (*Nyssa*) is a most magical tree, completely unphased by the perceived perils of swamp living.

Magical Uses

Endurance

Among foodies and honey enthusiasts, tupelo honey is a highly prized delicacy. In addition to possessing an exceptional taste, it never crystallizes because of its fructose (fruit sugar) to glucose ratio, and it's easier on the blood sugar. Heavier on the fructose content than other honeys, it promotes a more enduring variety of energy, which can be helpful for exercise, sports, and everyday life.

Magically, this enduring quality can be employed to lend stamina and staying power. For example, for enduring love, add a dollop of tupelo honey to a small pot of rose tea and share with your partner. For a day that requires sustained focus and energy, add a spoonful to a cup of black tea. For enduring wealth, add a quarter cup of tupelo honey to a bath and soak. For enduring beauty, spread tupelo honey all over your face as a mask and rinse off after ten to twenty minutes.

Transmutation

The tupelo reaches his roots deep into the swampy, rotting depths, drawing up nourishment and eventually transforming it into blossoms that are absolutely irresistible to our friends the bees. In turn, the bees transform the blossoms into the sweetest, lightest, most beloved honey in the world.

Indeed, the tupelo guides us to fearlessly reach deep into our own thoughts, feelings, memories, and traumas—even the stagnant, festering ones—and to efficiently transmute and refine them into pure beauty, sweetness, and sustenance.

Spend time with or visualize tupelo when you're doing work related to transforming past suffering into success, wisdom, and joy.

Magical Correspondences

Element: Water
Gender: Masculine
Planet: Pluto

Viburnum

The many varieties of viburnum appear as shrubs or small trees with enchanting, delicate, often sweetly fragrant white or pink flowers. Vibrationally supportive of both focus and deep relaxation, this priestess of the garden and wild places can help support us when a calm, clear mind is of the essence, or anytime we want to bring our mind, body, and spirit into greater alignment.

Please note: When gathering bark from a viburnum tree for medicinal and/or magical purposes, be careful to take only a little bit. Taking too much can harm or kill the tree.

Magical Uses

Deep Breathing

If you take a moment to tune in to the wisdom of a viburnum, you're likely to find that your breathing naturally begins to deepen. Considering that *viburnum opulus*—also known as cramp bark—is employed in herbal medicine for support with breathing difficulties such as asthma and shortness of breath, it's particularly interesting that viburnum's berries and blossoms often closely resemble alveoli (microscopic structures within our lungs that are instrumental in receiving oxygen). As such, you might meditate near a viburnum or plant one in your yard for support with breathing deeply on a regular basis. For medicinal support with breathing challenges, consider employing a tincture of cramp bark.

Focus

Walter's viburnum (*Viburnum obovatum*) is also known as small-leaf arrowwood, and archers have employed viburnum to fashion arrows since ancient times. In addition to literally helping archers hit their mark, this symbolism translates to helping us focus on and achieve our goals. Not to mention, viburnum's relaxing vibration can help us to simply calm and focus our minds, and to bring our minds into harmony with our bodies and breath.

Pain Relief

Viburnum prunifolium (also known as black haw) and *Viburnum opulus* (also known as cramp bark) are both employed in herbal medicine as muscle relaxants and to soothe pain related to arthritis, menstrual cramps, and muscle cramps or spasms. Similarly, gazing at the flowers or spending time in quiet contemplation with a viburnum can help soothe the tension that can be the cause of many headaches and digestive discomfort as well as some shoulder and back pain. While our daily, tension-inducing activities might be described as masculine and solar in their orientation, the viburnum is feminine and lunar, which makes her an appropriate medicine for our times.

Passage Between the Worlds

In Ukraine *Viburnum opulus* (cramp bark) is known as kalyna and is honored as the most sacred of plants. In addition to being aligned with all aspects of femininity, this bright, red-berried plant is seen as a doorway between the worlds of form and spirit, known and unknown, and the living and the dead. Plant this species of viburnum to commemorate the life of a loved one who has transitioned; the tree can act as a doorway of communication with this person, providing a portal between this world and the other side.

Relaxation

As you might have gathered from the above entries, viburnum is an excellent ally to enlist for help with relaxation of all varieties. While the bark of the species mentioned above can physically help relax the muscles and deepen the breathing, the vibration of all viburnum species is generally soothing and stress-relieving. Her simple presence can be a priceless medicine for this purpose, as can taking two to three drops of her flower essence three times per day.

Magical Correspondences

Element: Spirit
Gender: Feminine
Planet: Moon

Walnut

*W*alnut (*Juglans*) is steadfast, cheerful, and decidedly affluent. With lush green leaves, gorgeous wood, and preciously nutrient-dense nuts, he's a tree with a decided knack for generosity.

Magical Uses

Expansion

The walnut's genus name, *Juglans*, is derived from the Latin for "tree of Jupiter." As a god (and a planet) associated with expansion, Jupiter and his tree can help us with magical intentions related to any form of expansion, including (but not limited to) expansion of our career, finances, perspective, positivity, or life vision.

Health and Healing

Walnut, and his close relative butternut, has been used traditionally for centuries in both the west and the east to treat a number of health challenges including aches, wounds, liver and kidney challenges, and skin conditions. Magically, simply spending time with a flourishing walnut tree can lend great strength to the immune system and energetic field.

Mother Goddess Alignment

In India walnuts are offered at the shrine of the goddess Vaishno Devi (also known as Mata Rani), an emanation of the Great Mother Goddess who supports us in all ways and bestows all forms of blessings: material, emotional, and spiritual. To align with the Mother Goddess and allow her blessings to flow into your life, create an altar to her and place a bowl of unshelled walnuts on it as an offering. This can also be a good way to heal mother issues and to feel naturally nourished and nurtured by the archetypal Divine Mother (known as Gaia, Mary, Demeter, Durga, Ceres, Isis, Mother Earth, and many other names).

Wealth

As a yearly producer of tasty nutrition and sustenance, the walnut tree is an expert in perennial wealth. According to author Sandra Kynes in *Whispers from the Woods*, "As an offering to the Roman goddess of fruit trees [Pomona], the Romans would bury a coin beneath a walnut tree," thus magically aligning prosperity directly to the abundant fruit-fulness of the tree. Of course, as a tree aligned with Jupiter, the walnut is a natural choice for magic related to expanding wealth and prosperity.

....

Ancient Roman Wealth Charm

Bathe a coin in sunlight, empower it with the intention to irresistibly draw more wealth and abundance into your life, and bury it near the base of a walnut tree.

Magical Correspondences

Element: Spirit
Gender: Masculine
Planet: Jupiter

Weigela

*T*he extraordinarily dainty weigela is a Japanese native in the honeysuckle family. With showy trumpet-shaped summer blooms that magically change from white to pink to red, her versatility makes her a favorite with landscapers of a variety of climates.

Magical Uses
Joy

According to author Henry Mittwer, weigela flowers are employed in chabana, the art of floral arrangement for Japanese tea ceremonies. Certainly, the sense of joy they engender would be an ideal enhancement for a ceremony celebrating present moment awareness.

Love

The blossoms on this tiny ornamental tree move through all three Valentine's Day colors in perfect order: white (symbolizing pure new love), pink (symbolizing friendship and sweetness), and red (symbolizing passion and romance). Plant them in even numbers in your yard or spend time with one to draw more romance into your life.

Goddess Energy

Like all plants whose blooms feature five petals, the weigela is sacred to the Goddess. Place a bouquet on your altar or bring the tree into your yard to bless your space with Divine Feminine energy.

Magical Correspondences

Element: Fire
Gender: Feminine
Planet: Venus

Willow

Even his mellifluous name, *willow*, evokes every twisting nuance of the tree's lunar, watery nighttime vibration. Indeed, wherever willow (*Salix*) appears in literature, folklore, or art—which is quite often, throughout cultures and continents—he seems to be shrouded in mystery and magic.

As willow is masculine, and the moon is generally perceived as feminine, you might think of willow as the moon goddess's devoted ethereal priest, and one who is quite the master of his vocation.

Magical Uses

Divine Masculine Support

In *Under the Willow Tree* by Hans Christian Andersen, a lovesick young man named Knud embarks upon an ill-planned foot journey in winter to revisit his childhood home, in large part because his aching heart feels drawn to a willow tree there, which he and his lost childhood love referred to as "the willow-father." Along the way, he encounters a different willow tree, under which he lies down, has a beautiful dream, and dies. The following passage illustrates the willow-father's energetic likeness to a supportive masculine divinity.

> A willow-tree grew by the roadside; everything reminded him of home. He felt very tired; so he sat down under the tree, and very soon began to nod, then his eyes closed in sleep. Yet still he seemed conscious that the willow-tree was stretching its branches over him; in his dreaming state the tree appeared like a strong, old man—the "willow-father" himself, who had taken his tired son up in his arms to carry him back to the land of home, to the garden of his childhood, on the bleak open shores of Kjøge.

Death

When a loved one dies, it is always painful no matter how much peace one has made with the concept of death. Perhaps this, at least in part, is why willow—a tree long famed for its ability to soothe pain—is associated with death. Additionally, the water element (with which the willow is almost synonymous) is associated with the western compass point, as well as sunset, autumn, and endings. What's more, willows adorned gravesites in ancient Rome and were featured on headstones during the Victorian era.

Deities associated with both death and the willow are many, and include Hecate, Persephone, Orpheus, Loki, Ishtar, Cerridwen, Circe, Belili, and Poseidon. In sabbat fires willow wood represents death.

Directing Energy

Like the water element with which it is so aligned, willow's wood is a strong and flexible conductor of energy. This makes willow—sometimes referred to as the *tree of enchantment*—a natural and popular choice for magic wands, particularly for people who feel a strong connection with nighttime, emotions, and the moon.

Willow can also be employed as a sort of broom to sweep away negative or stagnant energy. In fact, willow is a traditional addition to witch's brooms, and the goddess Quan Yin is often pictured with a willow branch to wave away demons.

Ghosts

Particularly in Japan, willow trees are associated with ghosts. In *Ancient Tales and Folklore of Japan,* author Richard Gordon Smith writes, "In Japanese pictures of ghosts there is nearly always a willow tree." On the other hand, in China, during the spring festival Qingming (or "Tomb Sweeping Day"), willow branches are placed on doors and gates to prevent wandering spirits from entering.

Lunar Alignment

Willow, with his deep, mystical personality and abiding affiliation with the water element, is quite the lunar aligned tree. As you may know, the moon is associated with the qualities of receptivity, intuition, and magic. So, if you'd like to embody these qualities more fully, try the following ritual:

....

LUNAR ALIGNMENT RITUAL

When the moon is full or almost full and is bright in the sky (extra credit if it's on a Monday or when the moon is in Cancer), gather a moonstone or a piece of moonstone jewelry, a glass, a bottle opener, and a bottle of red wine (or grape juice if you don't drink). Visit a willow and sit or stand in reverent contemplation. Pour yourself a glass of wine (just a tiny bit is fine) and then pour the rest of the wine around the base of the willow as a libation. While holding the moonstone in your left hand, drink the wine mindfully, enjoying the moonlight and the tree's company as you do so. Thank the willow and the moon before returning home. (It's best to spend the rest of the evening relaxing at home, as you'll be extremely receptive to all forms of energy after this ritual.)

Pain Relief

Although there are hundreds of species of willow, all of them feature sap rich in salicylic acid, which has been used as a pain and fever reducer since very ancient times. Even today, it's the most conventional medicine for this purpose in the form of the active ingredient in aspirin. Energetically, willow can be employed for help relieving all forms of pain, including grief and emotional pain.

....

WILLOW RITUAL TO RELIEVE THE PAIN OF A BROKEN HEART

If you feel that your heart is broken because of a breakup or loss, visit a willow when the moon is in Cancer. Sit comfortably in his shade and allow him to soothe you. Simply notice your breath as it goes in and out. Let yourself relax deeply and allow yourself to be soothed, coddled, and consoled.

Personal Empowerment

Willow is one of the original thirty-eight flower remedies developed by homeopathic medicine pioneer Dr. Edward Bach. It's employed for support with taking full responsibility for your life and feeling empowered to create positive change. It also helps you to release the belief that other people or situations have power over you, as well as the belief that the success and happiness of others somehow creates a shortage of these qualities. In general, willow helps you to know that there are plenty positive life conditions for everyone, and supports you in becoming the master of your own destiny. If this sounds like something that will support you, try taking two drops under the tongue twice a day for one month. You might also soak in a warm bath into which you've added forty drops of willow flower essence.

Magical Correspondences

Element: Water
Gender: Masculine
Planet: Moon

Witch Hazel

The dangling flowers of this mystical North American and Asian native appear between late fall and early spring. With properties related to bewitchment, divination, intuition, and the moon, while witch hazel is not actually a hazel, it is indeed a witch (if a tree can be a witch, and I think it can).

Since the 1700s, witch hazel (*Hamamelis virginiana*) bark and leaves have been distilled into an astringent that is widely used in skin care products to this day.

Magical Uses

Charm and Attractiveness

Do you desire to bewitch? Dried witch hazel leaves may be just the magical ingredient for you. Empower a small pinch of them in bright moonlight, and place it in a small muslin bag along with a moonstone that has been cleansed in running water. Hold the charm in both hands and feel the magical energies merging and mixing with your own to activate your most irresistible attractiveness and charm. Each month, you may choose *one single day* to carry the charm, and on that day you shall bewitch. (Just be careful not to abuse your power so that you don't set in motion any unwanted karmic effects.)

Finding Water

Many believe that witch hazel was so named when European settlers discovered his usefulness in divining for water—also known as water witchery. Indeed, the tree's alignment with water, the moon, and intuition, combined with his masculine utilitarianism, make his branches an excellent material for making a Y-shaped divining rod specifically for the purpose of finding underground water.

Intuition

Witch hazel has a decidedly lunar energy, as well as an intense alignment with water. These qualities together make him an amazing ally when it comes to getting in tune with, and honing, your intuitive abilities. If you have a burning question, you can call on witch hazel's cool inner knowing to support you in discovering your answer. For example:

WITCH HAZEL DIVINATION SUPERCHARGE

Visit a witch hazel tree by moonlight. After pouring a libation of pure water around the roots, offer a moonstone as a gift, placing it at the base. Spread a white cloth and light a white candle. Ask your question aloud. Be sure to phrase it clearly and carefully, really tuning in to the energy of each word you've chosen. (You might want to already have it written down when you arrive.) Then perform a divination ritual of your choosing. For example, you might do a tarot, oracle card, or I Ching reading. Be sure to take your time and explore your deep intuitive understanding of the answer you receive.

Magical Correspondences

Element: Water

Gender: Masculine

Planet: Moon

The yew's magical resume is impressive and unique. Long known to be sacred to the Celts, many scholars now believe that Yggdrasil—the world tree in Nordic mythology from which the god Odin famously hung—was actually a yew, not an ash as previously believed. William Wordsworth evoked the haunting and eternal character of this long-lived evergreen in his poem "Yew-Trees," which includes the lines:

> ...ghostly Shapes
> May meet at noontide; Fear and trembling Hope,
> Silence and Foresight; Death the Skeleton
> And Time the Shadow; there to celebrate,
> As in a natural temple scattered o'er
> With altars undisturbed of mossy stone...

Please note: Every part of the yew is extremely toxic. (Although the red berrylike aril is not technically toxic, the seed within it *is*.)

Magical Uses

Death, Rebirth, and Eternity

The yew is closely associated with the famed Eleusinian mysteries of ancient Greece, which had to do with death, rebirth, and the divine realm. The Celts had a similar association with the tree, and considered it a guardian of the veil between the worlds. Clearly, the yew has a fundamental alignment not just with the portals of birth and death, but also with the portal between them and even the space beyond time: the realm of eternity.

While the yew (*Taxus*) has a reputation as a "gloomy" tree (Wordsworth's poem "Yew-Trees" includes the lines "of vast Circumference and gloom profound / This solitary Tree!"), it's also associated with incredibly sacred sites and stories. Perhaps this is because a brave gaze into the truth of our physically finite nature may initially be uncomfortable, but it's the only thing that will support an authentic realization of our infinite nature. This is why some Buddhist monks are instructed to meditate on the inevitable death and decay of their physical bodies, and to visualize it in ornate detail. Once the monks get through the frightening feelings and reach the other side, they come into contact with the eternal, indestructible nature of consciousness. Indeed, for many, looking death in the face is the key to really living fully. As Odin perhaps knew, this is wisdom of the yew.

Spend time with a yew to contemplate and to be initiated into the mysteries of death, rebirth, and eternity.

Hallowed Ground

An ancient yew tree sometimes grows in the center of extremely old churchyards in Europe. And quite often, these churchyards were once pagan sacred sites. In some cases, one can find a chapel made from the yew herself, with a door placed at the border of her huge, hollow trunk. To be sure, considering her alignment with eternity and the doorway between the worlds, she is perfectly suited to serve as an anchor for places of worship and divine communion.

Longevity

The yew is an extremely slow-growing, long-living tree with many exceptional survival strategies. While it's difficult to say precisely how old the oldest yew trees are (because of their hollow trunks and consequent lack of rings), some of the oldest ones are definitely into the thousands. With all of this in mind, you might want to spend time with a yew and request an energetic infusion of support when your magical intention involves longevity. This would include not just physical longevity, but also the longevity of other things, such as a business, relationship, or career.

In the realm of modern medicine, the yew has been employed to support longevity in the form of paclitaxel, a yew-derived cancer drug that's been in use since its discovery in 1962.

Shamanic Visions

On warm days yews may emit a gas that has hallucinogenic properties. It's been postulated that this had something to do with the Norse god Odin's vision during his hanging. His experience may have been a sort of shamanic journey to another level of reality, assisted by the yew. Similarly, in the 1881 volume *British Goblins* by Wirt Sikes, there is a tale of two "farm servants" who become enveloped in a mist while in a yew forest, find themselves bathed in an otherworldly light, and subsequently fall asleep under a yew tree. Upon awakening, one of the farm servants finds the other one missing, and after much searching retrieves him from fairyland, where he had been transported during the night.

To work with yew for the purpose of shamanic visioning, try meditating in the shade of a yew tree on a warm day. Ground and center your energy, and call on divine protection in a way that feels powerful for you. Then close your eyes and consciously explore an inner world for the purpose of receiving wisdom, power, and guidance. You might do this on your own or with the help of a guided meditation recording.

Magical Correspondences

Element: Earth

Gender: Feminine

Planet: Ceres

Magical Uses Overview

Abundance/Prosperity/ Wealth

Apple
Avocado
Baobab
Bay
Chestnut
Coffee
Empress Tree
Eucalyptus
Fig
Fir
Fringetree
Ginkgo
Jacaranda
Myrtle
Oak
Olive
Paradise Tree
Peach
Pecan
Persimmon
Pine
Plum
Redwood (Sequoia)

Sassafras
Walnut

Activation/Getting Energy Moving

Buckthorn
Dragon's Blood Tree
Juniper
Plum
Poplar
Sumac

Ancestors/Heritage/ Ancient Wisdom

Aspen
Baobab
Carob
Catalpa
Ginkgo
Magnolia
Redwood (Sequoia)
Sycamore

Angelic/Divine/ Heavenly Assistance or Alignment

Baobab

Bodhi
Boswellia
Catalpa
Cedar
Cherry
Fringetree
Hazel
Kamani
Larch
Lemon
Mulberry
Oak
Orange
Palm
Palo Santo
Paradise Tree
Pear
Pinyon
Poplar
Sandalwood
Spruce
Sycamore
Sycamore Fig
Tamarisk
Tree of Heaven
Yew

Animals, Supporting or Attracting
Aspen
Birch
Chestnut
Elder
Jabuticaba
Larch
Locust

Astral Travel
Silk Floss Tree

Authority and Leadership
Acacia
Almond
Hemlock
Oak
Sycamore Fig

Balance/Harmony
Banana
Beech
Birch
Cedar
Chaste Tree
Elder
Fig
Fringetree
Hazel
Juniper
Katsura
Madrone
Maple
Mulberry
Oak
Olive
Pagoda Tree
Palo Santo
Parasol Tree
Pine
Viburnum

Balance, Masculine/Feminine
Banana
Birch
Chestnut
Hazel
Kapok
Linden
Orange
Palm
Palo Santo
Parasol Tree
Sweet Gum

Beauty, Charm, and Attractiveness
Almond
Apple
Avocado
Cherry
Coral
Elder
Fig
Hazel
Hemlock
Jacaranda
Kamani
Magnolia
Maple
Olive
Pear
Sandalwood
Silk Floss Tree
Tree of Heaven
Tulip Tree
Tupelo
Witch Hazel

Bees, Attracting or Blessing
Chaste Tree
Redbud

Beginnings
Alder
Birch
Buckthorn
Orange

Blessing
Apple
Baobab
Bodhi
Buckthorn
Chestnut
Dragon's Blood Tree
Elder

Hawthorn
Hazel
Lemon
Olive
Palm
Rowan
Sandalwood

Boundaries, Setting/ Maintaining
Hornbeam
Locust
Plum

Broom Making
Ash

Childbirth Support
Hickory

Clarity/Focus/ Diligence
Cedar
Cypress
Hornbeam
Olive
Pine
Viburnum

Cleansing/Clearing/ Purifying
Aspen
Boswellia
Buckthorn
Cinchona (Fever Tree)

Cypress
Dragon's Blood Tree
Eucalyptus
Hemlock
Joshua Tree
Lemon
Locust
Palm
Palo Santo
Pine
Smoketree
Spruce
Tamarisk

Communicating/ Writing/Speaking
Cypress
Fig
Hazel
Privet

Cooling (Passions/ Emotions/Energy)
Aspen
Eucalyptus
Ginkgo
Pear

Creativity/Fun
Catalpa
Maple
Mesquite
Sassafras

Digestion, Aiding
Cinchona (Fever Tree)
Mesquite

Divination/Dowsing
Fig
Hazel
Rowan
Witch Hazel

Enlightenment
Bodhi

Expansion
Empress Tree
Poplar
Walnut

Fairies/Nymphs, Alignment/ Communication with
Apple
Ash
Elder
Elm
Hawthorn
Holly

Fame
Bay Laurel
Coral
Eucalyptus
Katsura

Family/Community
Aspen
Carob

**Feminine Power/
Goddess Energy**
Apple
Birch
Chaste tree
Cherry
Coffee
Dragon's Blood Tree
Elder
Elm
Locust
Magnolia
Myrrh
Myrtle
Redbud
Rowan
Silk Floss
Spruce
Walnut
Weigela

Fertility
Almond
Banana
Bodhi
Fig
Palm

Fidelity
Acacia

Fire, Protection from
Ginkgo
Redwood (Sequoia)

Forgiveness
Kamani

Generosity
Baobab

Gifts, Attracting
Tulip Tree

Grounding
Bodhi
Boswellia
Cedar
Fig
Fir
Pagoda Tree
Sumac

Guilt, Banishing
Pine

Hair Growth
Avocado

**Happiness/Joy/
Positivity**
Avocado
Coffee
Elm
Fig
Ginkgo
Holly

Hornbeam
Lemon
Maple
Orange
Peach
Pink Silk Tree
Weigela

**Harassment, Protection
from**
Bay Laurel

**Healing, Emotional/
Spiritual**
Aspen
Avocado
Beech
Birch
Boswellia
Carob
Cedar
Cinchona (Fever Tree)
Cypress
Elm
Eucalyptus
Fir
Hawthorn
Hemlock
Holly
Jacaranda
Linden
Mesquite
Mulberry

Palo Santo
Pine
Pink Silk Tree
Privet
Sandalwood
Spruce

Healing, Physical
Alder
Aspen
Avocado
Bodhi
Boswellia
Carob
Elder
Eucalyptus
Jacaranda
Juniper
Kamani
Manzanita
Mesquite
Mulberry
Myrrh
Olive
Pagoda Tree
Palo Santo
Paradise Tree
Peach
Pecan
Pine
Privet
Sandalwood

Sassafras
Spruce
Viburnum
Walnut
Willow

Hope
Almond
Ginkgo

Influence
Pistachio

Insects, Repelling
Cedar
Eucalyptus

Integrity
Kapok
Madrone

**Intuition/Psychic
Abilities/Visions**
Acacia
Elder
Kamani
Kapok
Manzanita
Mesquite
Pink Silk Tree
Silk Floss Tree
Yew

**Invisibility/
Concealment**
Alder

Justice/Legal Success
Ash
Hickory

**Land Nourishment/
Healing**
Hickory
Paradise Tree
Redbud

Longevity/Immortality
Acacia
Crepe Myrtle
Cypress
Hazel
Peach
Yew

**Lost Objects and
Hidden Treasures,
Finding**
Almond

Love, Romantic
Apple
Avocado
Cherry
Crepe Myrtle
Dragon's Blood Tree
Empress Tree
Fig
Hawthorn
Myrtle
Orange

Redbud
Rowan
Sandalwood

Love, Self
Apple

Love Spells, Protection from
Pistachio

Luck / Good Fortune
Avocado
Banana
Coral
Fig
Ginkgo
Parasol Tree

Magical / Spiritual Power
Baobab
Cedar
Dragon's Blood Tree
Elder
Fig
Hazel
Magnolia
Manzanita
Maple
Sycamore Fig

Masculine Power / God Energy
Alder

Bay Laurel
Bodhi
Kapok
Palm
Pinyon
Willow

Magical Wisdom and Knowledge
Apple
Ash
Baobab
Catalpa
Cedar
Magnolia
Manzanita

Meditation
Bodhi
Boswellia
Cedar
Mesquite
Myrrh
Palo Santo
Viburnum

Moon Cycle Support
Dragon's Blood Tree

Music
Elder
Jacaranda

Nature Spirits, Alignment with
Bodhi

Otherworld Awareness / Spirit Summoning
Baobab
Catalpa
Myrtle
Pear
Pinyon
Poplar
Viburnum
Willow

Partnership
Orange

Past Lives / Ancient Wisdom
Baobab
Sandalwood

Peace
Myrtle
Olive
Palm
Privet

Petitions / Prayer / Wish Granting
Acacia
Bodhi
Buckthorn

Hawthorn
Poplar

**Power/Strength/
Confidence**
Cherry
Larch
Plum
Willow

Productivity
Coffee

Protection
Acacia
Alder
Ash
Bodhi
Boswellia
Cinchona (Fever Tree)
Dragon's Blood Tree
Elder
Fringetree
Ginkgo
Hawthorn
Holly
Joshua tree
Juniper
Larch
Linden
Peach
Redwood (Sequoia)
Rowan
Sandalwood

Spruce
Sumac
Tree of Heaven

Rainmaking
Bodhi

Rebirth/Renewal
Avocado
Birch
Empress Tree
Fir
Kamani
Yew

Relaxation/Stress Relief
Cinchona (Fever Tree)
Eucalyptus
Jacaranda
Linden
Magnolia
Palm
Privet
Redwood (Sequoia)
Sandalwood
Viburnum

Sacred Space
Boswellia
Cedar
Myrrh
Palo Santo
Yew

Secrets/Mysteries
Hemlock

Sexuality/Sensuality
Avocado
Banana
Fig
Sandalwood

Shame, Healing
Redbud

Shape Shifting
Joshua Tree

Sleep/Dream Magic
Carob
Linden
Silk Floss Tree

Spell/Hex Breaking
Cedar
Dragon's Blood Tree
Pistachio

Success/Victory
Bay Laurel
Holly
Palm
Tree of Heaven

Sustainability
Madrone
Paradise Tree

Sustenance/Nourishment

Banana
Baobab
Carob
Jabuticaba
Palm
Pecan

Sweetness

Apple
Cherry
Jabuticaba
Locust
Maple
Orange

Transformation/Transmutation

Chestnut
Joshua Tree
Locust
Palm
Tupelo

Transitions/Changes

Elder
Elm
Hickory
Kamani
Myrrh
Sycamore
Tree of Heaven

Willow
Yew

Travel

Baobab
Fig
Rowan

Unicorns, Alignment with

Apple

Uniqueness, Embracing

Catalpa

Vampires, Protection from

Hawthorn

Vitality/Energy/Endurance

Avocado
Banana
Fig
Holly
Hornbeam
Lemon
Maple
Pecan
Tupelo
Walnut

Wand Making

Apple
Ash

Avocado
Pear
Willow

Warming (Body/Energy)

Eucalyptus
Hemlock
Manzanita
Persimmon
Rowan

Weddings

Hawthorn
Orange

Wisdom/Knowledge/Learning

Baobab
Bodhi
Cedar
Ginkgo
Hazel
Jacaranda
Madrone
Magnolia
Redwood

Worry and Anxiety Relief

Chestnut

Youthfulness

Apple

Appendix B

Elemental Correspondences

Earth
- Apple
- Banana
- Buckthorn
- Carob
- Cinchona (Fever Tree)
- Fig
- Fir
- Hawthorn
- Hornbeam
- Jabuticaba
- Magnolia
- Oak
- Orange
- Pagoda Tree
- Pistachio
- Sassafras
- Yew

Air
- Alder
- Almond
- Ash
- Aspen
- Bodhi
- Boswellia
- Cedar

- Cypress
- Fringetree
- Hickory
- Juniper
- Lemon
- Locust
- Mesquite
- Paradise Tree
- Pear
- Pink Silk Tree
- Privet
- Smoketree

Fire
- Bay Laurel
- Birch
- Cherry
- Coffee
- Coral
- Empress Tree
- Eucalyptus
- Hemlock
- Holly
- Joshua Tree
- Katsura
- Madrone
- Manzanita

- Palm
- Parasol Tree
- Peach
- Persimmon
- Pistachio
- Plum
- Redbud
- Rowan
- Silk Floss Tree
- Sumac
- Sweet Gum
- Tulip Tree
- Weigela

Water
- Avocado
- Chaste Tree
- Crepe Myrtle
- Elm
- Eucalyptus Tree
- Jabuticaba
- Jacaranda
- Lemon
- Linden
- Mulberry
- Myrtle
- Olive

Pecan
Plum
Poplar
Sassafras
Tupelo
Willow
Witch Hazel

Tree of Heaven
Viburnum
Walnut

Spirit

Acacia
Baobab
Catalpa
Chestnut
Dogwood
Dragon's Blood Tree
Ginkgo
Hazel
Jabuticaba
Kamani
Kapok
Larch
Maple
Myrrh
Palo Santo
Pine
Pinyon
Redwood (Sequoia)
Sandalwood
Spruce
Sycamore
Sycamore Fig
Tamarisk

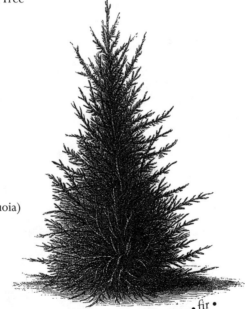

• fir •

Appendix C

Planetary Correspondences

Ceres
- Alder
- Chaste Tree
- Cinchona (Fever Tree)
- Hawthorn
- Jabuticaba
- Joshua Tree
- Pagoda Tree
- Sandalwood
- Spruce
- Sumac
- Yew

Chiron
- Beech

Gliese 667 Ce
- Juniper

Jupiter
- Almond
- Aspen
- Coral
- Fringetree
- Jacaranda
- Kapok
- Persimmon
- Poplar
- Redwood (Sequoia)
- Sassafras
- Sycamore
- Walnut

Mars
- Ash
- Buckthorn
- Coffee
- Dragon's Blood Tree
- Hickory
- Holly
- Madrone
- Pistachio

Mercury
- Chestnut
- Cypress
- Hazel
- Manzanita
- Mulberry

Moon
- Birch
- Elder
- Katsura
- Lemon
- Magnolia
- Palo Santo
- Parasol Tree
- Pear
- Viburnum
- Willow
- Witch Hazel

Neptune
- Baobab
- Bodhi
- Carob
- Maple
- Mesquite
- Myrrh
- Pine
- Tamarisk

Pallas
- Redbud
- Sweet Gum

Pallene
- Silk Floss Tree

Pluto
- Banana
- Fir
- Hemlock
- Kamani

Palm
Paradise Tree
Tupelo

Saturn

Crepe Myrtle
Dogwood
Elm
Eucalyptus
Larch
Locust
Olive
Smoketree

Sun

Acacia
Bay Laurel
Boswellia
Cedar
Fig
Ginkgo
Hornbeam
Oak
Orange
Palo Santo
Parasol Tree
Pecan
Pinyon
Tree of Heaven

Uranus

Catalpa
Linden
Sycamore Fig

Venus

Apple
Avocado
Cherry
Empress Tree
Katsura
Myrtle
Peach
Pink Silk Tree
Plum
Privet
Rowan
Tulip Tree
Weigela

mulberry

Acknowledgments

Thank you, Elysia Gallo, Becky Zins, Stephanie Finne, Bill Krause, Sandra Weschcke, Jonathan Kirsch, and Ted Bruner.

Thank you, Carl Weschcke, for paving the way and holding the space.

Thank you, trees.

Thank you, Mother Earth, Father Sky, Sister Water, Brother Fire, and Grandmother Spirit.

Thank you, angelic and archangelic allies.

Thank you, All That Is.

Thank you, thank you, thank you.

Bibliography

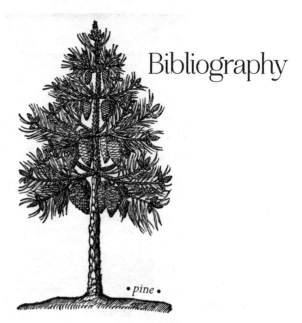

• *pine* •

Achan, Jane, Ambrose O Talisuna, Annette Erhart, et al. "Quinine, an Old Anti-Malarial Drug in a Modern World: Role in the Treatment of Malaria." Malariajournal.com (May 2011). doi: 10.1186/1475-2875-10-144.

Althea Press. *Essential Oils for Beginners: The Guide to Get Started with Essential Oils and Aromatherapy*. Berkeley, CA: Althea Press, 2013.

American Chemical Society. "'Gift of the Magi' Bears Anti-Cancer Agents, Researchers Suggest." Sciencedaily.com (December 2001). www.sciencedaily.com/releases/2001/12/011205070038 .htm.

Andersen, Hans Christian. *Under the Willow Tree and Other Stories*. London: George Routledge and Sons, 1869.

Andrews, William. *Antiquities and Curiosities of the Church*. London: W. Andrews & Company, 1897.

Arbor Day Foundation. "Oak Trees." https://shop.arborday.org/content.aspx?page=tree-oak.

———. "Tree Guide." www.arborday.org/trees/treeguide/.

Arvigo, Rosita, and Nadine Epstein. *Rainforest Home Remedies: The Maya Way to Heal Your Body and Replenish Your Soul*. San Francisco: HarperSanFrancisco, 2001.

Ashkenazi, Michael. *Handbook of Japanese Mythology*. New York: Oxford University Press, 2008.

Assmann, Jan. *Ägypten. Theologie und Frömmigkeit einer frühen Hochkultur*. Germany: Kohlhammer, 1991.

Bane, Theresa. *Encyclopedia of Fairies in World Folklore and Mythology*. Jefferson, NC: McFarland & Company, 2013.

Barber, Paul. *Vampires, Burial, and Death: Folklore and Reality*. Binghampton, NY: Vail-Ballou Press, 1988.

Barnes-Svarney, Patricia, and Thomas Svarney. *The Handy Biology Answer Book, 2nd Ed*. Canton, MI: Visible Ink Press, 2015.

Bazar, Ron. "Sacred Trees: Arbutus (Madrone) Tree." www.arbutusarts.com/sacred-trees.html.

Belanger, Michelle A. *Psychic Vampire Codex: A Manual of Magick and Energy Work*. Boston, MA: Red Wheel/Weiser, 2004.

Berger, Markus. "Taxus Spp.—A Psychoactive Species?" psychotropicon.info. (March 2011). http://psychotropicon.info/taxus-spp-eine-psychoaktive-gattung-2/.

Bishop, Holley. *Robbing the Bees: A Biography of Honey—The Sweet Liquid that Seduced the World*. New York: Free Press, 2005.

Blacker, Carmen. *The Catalpa Bow: A Study of Shamanistic Practices in Japan*. London: Routledge, 2004.

Boliviabella.com. "The Legend of the Toborochi Tree." www.boliviabella.com/legend-of-the-toborochi.html.

Burne, Charlotte Sophia. *The Handbook of Folklore*. London: Sidgwick & Jackson, 1913.

Burrows, George E., and Ronald J. Tyre. *Toxic Plants of North America: Second Edition*. Ames, IA: Wiley-Blackwell, 2013.

Caldecott, Moyra. *Myths of the Sacred Tree*. Rochester, VT: Destiny, 1993.

Chestnut, Victor King. *Plants Used by the Indians of Mendocino County, CA*. Charleston, SC: Nabu Press, 2012.

Chevallier, Andrew. *Encyclopedia of Herbal Medicine*. London: Dorling Kindersley, 1996.

Chiffolo, Anthony F., and Rayner W. Hesse. *Cooking with the Bible: Biblical Food, Feasts & Lore*. Westport, CT: Greenwood Publishing Group, 2006.

Connor, Sheila. *New England Natives: A Celebration of Trees and People*. Cambridge, MA: Harvard University Press, 1994.

Cunningham, Scott. *Cunningham's Encyclopedia of Magical Herbs*. St. Paul, MN: Llewellyn, 1985.

————. *Magical Aromatherapy: The Power of Scent*. St. Paul, MN: Llewellyn, 1989.

Davis, Gerald. *Gilgamesh: The New Translation*. Bridgeport, CT: Insignia, 2014.

Davis, Michael. *William Blake: A New Kind of Man*. New York: HarperCollins, 1977.

Deida, David. *Dear Lover: A Woman's Guide to Men, Sex, and Love's Deepest Bliss*. Boulder, CO: Sounds True, 2005.

Dolina, Alejandro. *Crónicas del Ángel Gris*. Buenos Aires: Colihue, 2006.

Doolittle, Justus. *Social Life of the Chinese*. London: Samson Low, Son & Marston, 1866.

Dowden, Ken. *European Paganism: The Realities of Cult from Antiquity to the Middle Ages*. New York: Routledge, 2000.

Drewes, Gerardus Willebrordus Joannes. *The Romance of King Anlin Darma in Javanese Literature*. Heidelberg: Springer, 1975.

Duke, James A. *Duke's Handbook of Medicinal Plants of Latin America*. Boca Raton, FL: CRC Press, 2009.

Dweck, A. C., and T. Meadows. "Tamanu (*Calophyllum Inophyllum*)—The African, Asian, Polynesian, and Pacific Panacea." *International Journal of Cosmetic Science* 24, 1–8, Article 160 (2002). doi: 10.1046/j.1467-2494.2002.00160.x.

Easton, M. G. *Illustrated Bible Dictionary*. Scotland: T. Nelson and Sons, 1893.

Ensminger, Marion Eugene, and Audrey H. Ensminger. *Foods & Nutrition Encyclopedia,* 2-volume set. Boca Raton, FL: CRC Press, 1993.

Eyers, Jonathan. *Don't Shoot the Albatross! Nautical Myths and Superstitions*. New York: Bloomsbury Academic, 2012.

Feinberg, Miriam P., and Rena Rotenberg. *Lively Legends—Jewish Values: An Early Childhood Teaching Guide*. Denver, CO: A.R.E. Publishing, 1993.

Flood, Nancy Bo. *Marianas Island Legends: Myth and Magic*. Honolulu: Bess Press, 2001.

Flood, Nancy Bo, Beret E. Strong, and William Flood. *Micronesian Legends*. Honolulu: Bess Press, 2002.

Folkard, Richard. *Plant Lore, Legends, and Lyrics: Embracing the Myths, Traditions, Superstitions, and Folklore of the Plant Kingdom*. London: Sampson, Low, Marston, Searle, and Rivington, 1884.

Foster, Steven, and Rebecca L. Johnson. *National Geographic Desk Reference to Nature's Medicine*. Washington, DC: National Geographic Books, 2008.

Frazer, James. *The Golden Bough: A Study in Comparative Religion*. Oxford: Oxford University Press, 1890.

Fred Soll's Resin on a Stick. "About the Incense." www.fredsoll.com.

Gasparro, Giulia Sfameni. *Soteriology and Mystic Aspects in the Cult of Cybele and Attis*. The Netherlands: E.J. Brill, 1985.

Gibson, Ruby. *My Body, My Earth: The Practice of Somatic Archaeology*. New York: iUniverse, 2008.

Giddings, Ruth Warner. *Yaqui Myths and Legends*. Tuscon, AZ: University of Arizona Press, 1959.

Golden Field Guides. *Field Guide to Trees of North America*. New York: Andrew Stewart, 2008.

Graves, Thomas E. "Keeping Ukraine Alive Through Death: Ukrainian-American Gravestones as Cultural Markers." *Ethnicity and the American Cemetery*. Ed. Richard E. Meyer. Bowling Green, OH: Bowling Green State University Popular Press, 1993.

Gulmahamad, Dr. Hanif. *Stories & Poems by a Guyanese Village Boy*. Dr. Hanif Gulmahamad, 2009.

Hageneder, Fred. *The Meaning of Trees: Botany—History—Healing—Lore*. San Francisco: Chronicle Books, 2005.

Halpern, Georges N., with Peter Weverka. *The Healing Trail: Essential Oils of Madagascar*. North Bergen, NJ: Basic Health Publications, 2002.

Hancock, Graham. *The Sign and the Seal: The Quest for the Lost Ark of the Covenant*. New York: Touchstone, 1993.

Hoadley, Bruce R. *Understanding Wood: A Craftsman's Guide to Wood Technology*. Newtown, CT: Taunton Press, 2000.

Hoffman, David. *Medical Herbalism: The Science Principles and Practices of Herbal Medicine*. Rochester, VT: Healing Arts Press, 2003.

Homer. *The Iliad: Penguin Classics Deluxe Edition*. New York: Penguin, 1990.

———. *The Odyssey*, translated by A.T. Murray. Cambridge, MA: Harvard University Press, 1919.

Hoss de la Comte, Mónica. *Argentine Cookery*. Buenos Aires: Maizal Ediciones, 2006.

Huang, Kee C. *Pharmacology of Chinese Herbs: Second Edition*. Boca Raton, FL: CRC Press, 1999.

Hulme, Joy N. *Wild Fibonacci: Nature's Secret Code Revealed*. Berkeley, CA: Tricycle Press, 2010.

I Love Pecans. *History of Pecans: A Pecan Timeline and Fun Facts*. www.ilovepecans.org/pecans-101/history-of-pecans/.

Illes, Judika. *The Element Encyclopedia of 5,000 Spells: The Ultimate Reference Book for the Magical Arts*. London: HarperElement, 2004.

—————. *The Element Encyclopedia of Witchcraft: The Complete A–Z for the Entire Magical World*. London: HarperElement, 2005.

—————. *Encyclopedia of Spirits: The Ultimate Guide to the Magic of Fairies, Genies, Demons, Ghosts, Gods & Goddesses*. New York: HarperOne, 2009.

Jaimoukha, Amjad. *The Chechens: A Handbook*. Oxford: Routledge Curzon, 2005.

Keeler, Harriet L. *Our Native Trees and How to Identify Them: A Popular Study of Their Habits and Their Peculiarities*. New York: Charles Scribner's Sons, 1915.

Kendall, Paul. "Mythology and Folklore of the Alder." http://treesforlife.org.uk/forest /mythology-folklore/alder/.

Kiple, Kenneth F., and Kriemhild Coneé Ornelas, eds. *The Cambridge World History of Food, Volume 2*. Cambridge: Cambridge University Press, 2001.

Kirsch, Jonathan. *The Harlot by the Side of the Road: Forbidden Tales of the Bible*. New York: Ballantine, 1998.

Koepell, Dan. "Can This Fruit Be Saved?" *Popular Science* (June 19, 2005). www.popsci.com /scitech/article/2008-06/can-fruit-be-saved.

Kynes, Sandra. *Whispers from the Woods: The Lore and Magic of Trees*. Woodbury, MN: Llewellyn, 2006.

LakshmiTaru.com. "Decoction Preparation" and "Medicinal Values." http://lakshmitaru.com /index.php/component/content/article/14-general/73-decoction-preparation.

Lanner, Ronald M. *The Piñon Pine: A Natural and Cultural History*. Las Vegas: University of Nevada Press, 1981.

Largo, Michael. *The Big, Bad Book of Botany: The World's Most Fascinating Flora*. New York: HarperCollins, 2014.

Lawless, Julia. *The Encyclopedia of Essential Oils: The Complete Guide to the Use of Aromatic Oils in Aromatherapy, Herbalism, Health, and Well-Being*. San Francisco: Conari Press, 2013.

Layne, Desmond R., and Danielle Bassi. *The Peach: Botany, Production, and Uses*. Wallingford, England: CABI, 2008.

Lewis, C. S. *The Lion, the Witch, and the Wardrobe*. London: Geoffrey Bles, 1950.

Lewis, Thomas H. *The Medicine Men: Ogala Sioux Ceremony and Healing*. Lincoln, NE: University of Nebraska Press, 1990.

Loewer, Peter H. *Solving Weed Problems: How to Identify and Eradicate Them Effectively from Your Garden*. Guildord, CT: Lyons Press, 2001.

Lorenzo's Oil. Film. Directed by George Miller. Universal, 1992.

Loudon, John Claudius. *Arboretum et Fruticetum Britannicum*. London: J.C. Loudon, 1838.

MacKillop, James. *Fionn mac Cumhaill: Celtic Myth in English Literature*. Syracuse, NY: Syracuse University Press, 1986.

Mahanama-Sthavira, Thera, and Douglas Bullis. *Mahavamsa: The Great Chronicle of Sri Lanka*. Asian Humanities Press, 1999. (Original text: 5 CE)

Manniche, Lisa. *Sacred Luxuries: Fragrance, Aromatherapy, and Cosmetics in Ancient Egypt*. Ithaca, NY: Cornell University Press, 1999.

Martin, Paula, and Margaret Read MacDonald. *Pachama Tales: Folklore from Argentina, Bolivia, Chile, Paraguay, Peru, and Uruguay*. Santa Barbara, CA: Libraries Unlimited, 2014.

Mbiti, John S. *African Religions and Philosophy*. Oxford: Oxford University Press, 1990.

McCabe, Melina, Dorothy Gohdes, Frank Morgan et. al. "Herbal Therapies and Diabetes Among Navajo Indians." diabetesjournals.org (June 2005). http://dx.doi.org/10.2337/diacare .28.6.1534-a.

Medici, Marina. *Good Magic*. New York: Fireside, 1988.

Menglong, Feng. *Stories to Caution the World: A Ming Dynasty Collection, Volume II*. Seattle: University of Washington Press, 2005.

Metcalf, Woodbridge. *Native Trees of the San Francisco Bay Region*. Oakland, CA: University of California Press, 1961.

Mitchell, Stephen. *Tao te Ching: A New English Version*. New York: HarperPerennial, 1988.

Mittwer, Henry. *The Art of Chabana: Flowers for the Tea Ceremony*. Tokyo: Charles E. Tuttle, 1974.

Moerman, Daniel E. *Native American Ethnobotany*. Portland, OR: Timber Press, 1998.

Mojay, Gabriel. *Aromatherapy for Healing the Spirit: Restoring Emotional and Mental Balance with Essential Oils*. Rochester, VT: Healing Arts, 1997.

Monaghan, Patricia. *Encyclopedia of Goddesses and Heroines*. Novato, CA: New World Library, 2014.

Monarch, Matt. *Three Reasons to Eat Raw Mulberries*. *Natural News* (February 2009). www
    .naturalnews.com/025649_berries_mulberries_food.html.

Moorey, Teresa. *The Fairy Bible: The Definitive Guide to the World of Fairies*. New York: Sterling Press, 2008.

Murray, Michael T., Joseph Pizzorno, and Laura Pizzorno. *The Encyclopedia of Healing Foods*. New
    York: Atria Books, 2005.

Murthy, B. V. Venkatesha. *Plants of Arogyashram and Their Healing Powers: A Redaction by B. V. Venkatesha
    Murthy*. Nanjangud, India: The Sadvaidyasala Pvt. and Sri Dhanvantari Arogyashram Trust, 2012.

Myung-sub, Chung (ed.). *Encyclopedia of Korean Folk Literature: Encyclopedia of Korean Folklore and
    Traditional Culture Volume III*. Seoul: National Folk Museum of Korea, 2014.

Olafson, Richard. *In Arbutus Light: Saturna Poems*. Vancouver, BC: Ekstasis Editions, 1997.

OneIndia.com. "Lakshmi Taru Tree Answer to Climate Change Problems: Experts." (April 2007).
    www.oneindia.com/2007/04/15/lakshmi-taru-tree-answer-to-climate-change-problems
    -experts-1176620662.html.

Patai, Raphael. *The Hebrew Goddess, 3rd Enlarged Edition*. Detroit: Wayne State University Press, 1990.

Peattie, Donald Culross. *A Natural History of Western Trees*. Boston: Houghton Mifflin, 1950.

Peschel, Lisa. *A Practical Guide to the Runes: Their Uses in Divination and Magic*. St. Paul, MN:
    Llewellyn, 1989.

Phillips, Roger. *Trees of North America and Europe: A Photographic Guide to More than 500 Trees*. New
    York: Random House, 1978.

Pierson, PJ, and Mary Shipley. *Aromatherapy for Everyone: Discover the Scents of Health and Happiness
    with Essential Oils*. Garden City Park, NY: Square One, 2004.

Pollan, Michael. *The Botany of Desire: A Plant's-Eye View of the World*. New York: Random House, 2001.

Raghuram, M. "Bangalore's Art of Living Ashram Now Flush with Paradise Tree." (September 4,
    2011). www.dnaindia.com/bangalore/report-bangalore-s-art-of-living-ashram-now-flush
    -with-paradise-tree-1583151.

Redford, Donald B. *Oxford Encyclopedia of Ancient Egypt, 2-volume set*. New York: Oxford University
    Press, 2001.

Rhoads, Ann Fowler, and Timothy A. Block. *The Trees of Pennsylvania: A Complete Reference Guide*.
    Pennsylvania: University of Pennsylvania Press, 2004.

RoadsideAmerica.com. *Owensboro, Kentucky: World's Largest Sassafras Tree*. www.roadsideamerica .com/tip/7879.

Robbins, Judith Fowler. *American Spirits: The Sugar Creek Anthologies of Jesse Freedom Stories*. Lincoln, NE: Writers Club Press, 2002.

Rocky Mountain Tree-Ring Research. "Old List." (January 2013). www.rmtrr.org/oldlist.htm.

Rodgers, Jane. "Joshua Trees." National Park Service. www.nps.gov/jotr/index.htm.

Rose, Jeanne. *Jeanne Rose's Herbal Body Book: The Herbal Way to Natural Beauty and Health for Men and Women*. New York: Grosset & Dunlap, 1976.

Rushforth, Keith. *Trees of Britain and Europe*. London: HarperCollins, 1999.

Schafer, Peg. *The Chinese Medicinal Herb Farm: A Cultivator's Guide to Small-Scale Organic Herb Production*. White River Junction, VT: Chelsea Green Publishing, 2011.

Scheffer, Mechthild. *The Encyclopedia of Bach Flower Therapy*. Rochester, VT: Healing Arts Press, 2001.

Scoble, Gretchen, and Ann Field. *The Meaning of Flowers: Myth, Language, and Lore*. San Francisco: Chronicle Books, 1998.

Seeto, Lance. "Secret History of Avocado." *Fiji Times* (May 5, 2012). http://emedicalnews .net/?p=33212.

Shafer, Sarah L., Patrick J. Bartlein, and Robert S. Thomson. "Potential Changes in the Distributions of Western North American Tree and Shrub Taxa Under Future Climate Scenarios." *Ecosystems* magazine, 4, Issue 3 (April 2001): 200–215.

Shoemaker, Henry W. *Allegheny Episodes: Folk Lore and Legends Collected in Northern and Western Pennsylvania*. Altoona, PA: A'Toona Tribune Company, 1922.

Shuter, Jane. *Life on a Viking Ship*. Edina, MN: Capstone Classroom, 2005.

Sikes, Wirt. *British Goblins: Welsh Folklore, Fairy Mythology, Legends and Traditions*. Boston: James R. Osgood and Company, 1881.

Simoons, Fredrick J. *Food In China: A Cultural and Historical Perspective*. Boca Raton, FL: CRC Press, 1990.

Skinner, Charles Montgomery. *Myths and Legends of Flowers, Trees, Fruits, and Plants in All Ages and in All Climes*. Philadelphia: J.B. Lippincot, 1911.

Small, Ernest, and Paul M. Catling. *Canadian Medicinal Crops*. Ottawa: NRC Research Press, 1999.

Smith, Betty. *A Tree Grows in Brooklyn*. New York: HarperCollins, 1943.

Smith, Charles W.G. *Fall Foliage: The Mystery, Science, and Folklore of Autumn Leaves*. Guilford, CT: The Globe Pequot Press, 2005.

Smith, Richard Gordon. *Ancient Tales and Folklore of Japan*. London: Forgotten Books, 2008 (originally published 1918).

Starhawk. *The Fifth Sacred Thing*. New York: Bantam, 1994.

Stevenson, Angus, ed. *Oxford Dictionary of English*. Oxford: Oxford University Press, 2010.

Struthers, Jane. *The Book of Christmas: Everything We Once Knew and Loved About Christmastime*. London: Ebury Press, 2012.

Sunset Publishing Corporation. *The Sunset Western Garden Book*. Menlo Park, CA: Sunset Publishing Corporation, 2001.

Teague, Gypsey Elaine. *The Witch's Guide to Wands: A Complete Botanical, Magical, and Elemental Guide to Making, Choosing, and Using the Right Wand*. San Francisco: Weiser Books, 2015.

Te'o, Tuvale. *An Account of Samoan History up to 1918*. New South Wales: Public Library of New South Wales, 1968. nzetc.victoria.ac.nz.

Theocritus. *Idylls: Oxford World Classics*. New York: Oxford University Press, 2002.

Tierra, Michael L.AC., O.M.D. "Albizia: The Tree of Happiness." East West School of Planetary Herbology. www.planetherbs.com/specific-herbs/albizia-the-tree-of-happiness.html.

———. *The Way of Herbs: Complete, Easy-to-Use Information on Simple Herbal Remedies—for Natural Health and Healing*. New York: Pocket Books, 1980.

Torres, Eliseo, and Timothy Leighton Sawyer. *Healing with Herbs and Rituals: A Mexican Tradition*. Albuquerque: UNM Press, 2006.

Turcan, Robert. *The Cults of the Roman Empire*. Oxford: Blackwell Publishers, 1996.

Turner, Patricia, and Charles Russell Coulter. *Dictionary of Ancient Deities*, 3rd Edition. Oxford: Oxford University Press, 2001.

Union of American Republics. *Bulletin of the Pan American Union, Volume 40*. Washington, DC: US Government Printing Office, 1915.

VanGoghGallery.com. Vincent Van Gogh: *The Mulberry Tree*. www.vangoghgallery.com.

Vegetarians in Paradise. "Pecans—The True Blue-Blooded Americans." www.vegparadise.com.

Venefica, Avia. "Symbolic Meaning of Koala Bears." www.whats-your-sign.com/symbolic-meaning -of-koala-bears.html.

Vergano, Dan. "Gold Grows on Eucalyptus Trees." (October 22, 2013). http://news .nationalgeographic.com/news/2013/10/131022-gold-eucalyptus-leaves-mining-geology -science/.

Voigt, Werner. "Erythrina Caffra." PlantZAfrica, South African National Biodiversity Institute (October 2006). www.plantzafrica.com/plantefg/erythrinacaff.htm.

Weaver, William Woys. "Cornelian Cherries." *Mother Earth News,* Ogden Publications, Inc. (December 2005). www.motherearthnews.com/real-food/cornelian-cherries.aspx.

Welch, Patricia Bjaaland. *Chinese Art: A Guide to Motifs and Visual Imagery.* North Clarendon, VT: Tuttle Publishing, 2008.

Whitehurst, Tess. *The Magic of Flowers: A Guide to Their Metaphysical Uses & Properties.* Woodbury, MN: Llewellyn, 2013.

Whitman, Walt. *Leaves of Grass.* Brooklyn, NY: Walt Whitman, 1855.

Wordsworth, William. *The Poetical Works of William Wordsworth.* London: E. Moxon, Son & Co., 1870.

Woudenberg, Rene, Sabine Roeser, and Ron Rood. *Basic Belief and Basic Knowledge: Papers in Epistemology.* Piscataway, NJ: Transaction Books, 2005. (Source of Cicero quote.)

Wright, John. *Hedgerow: River Cottage Handbook No. 7.* London: Bloomsbury, 2010.

Zell-Ravenheart, Oberon. *Grimoire for the Apprentice Wizard.* Franklin Lakes, NJ: Career Press, 2004.

Zohary, Daniel, Maria Hopf, and Ehud Weiss. *Domestication of Plants in the Old World: The Origin and Spread of Domesticated Plants in Southwest Asia, Europe, and the Mediterranean Basin.* Oxford: Oxford University Press, 1988.